A Strategic Analysis of Science and Technology Policy

About the Author

Harvey A. Averch is currently Visiting Professor of Policy
Science and Economics at the University of Maryland,
Baltimore County. He is on leave from the National Science
Foundation, where he has served as assistant director for
Scientific, Technological, and International Affairs and for
Science Education.

Harvey A. Averch

A Strategic Analysis of Science & Technology Policy

The Johns Hopkins University Press
Baltimore and London

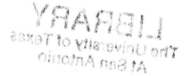

©1985 by The Johns Hopkins University Press
All rights reserved
Printed in the United States of America

The Johns Hopkins University Press,
Baltimore, Maryland 21218
The Johns Hopkins Press Ltd., London

The paper in this book is acid free and meets the
guidelines for permanence and durability of the
Committee on Production Guidelines for Book
Longevity of the Council on Library Resources.

Library of Congress Cataloging in Publication Data

Averch, Harvey A.
   A strategic analysis of science and technology policy.

   Bibliography: p.
   Includes index.
   1. Science and state – United States. 2. Technology
and state – United States. I. Title
Q127.U6A9   1985   338.973   84–47961
ISBN 0–8018–2467–2 (alk. paper)

For Barbara, who had patience.

Contents

Preface and Acknowledgments

I spent the first ten years of my professional life as a practicing policy analyst and economist, and I spent the second ten years as a science administrator. In the practice of policy analysis, I learned that argument and evidence should be valid, clear, timely, and relevant to decisions that someone wanted to make or had to make. Latent assumptions in analysis were supposed to be flushed out and made explicit to explain differences in recommended outcomes. Sensitivity analysis was to be applied to ensure that action recommendations were robust and practical. Methods of analysis and modes of reasoning were to be articulated and documented, giving decisionmakers reasonable, if not perfect, guarantees that the analysis they were going to use was not affected by many possible "pitfalls."

When I became a federal science administrator, I was surprised. Policy analysis for the science and technology enterprise seemed to stand outside the mainstream of the analysis that first developed in the national security area and then spread to civilian areas. There seemed to be no canons or even craft rules giving guidance on what constituted reasonable and legitimate analysis and advice to decisionmakers. In contrast to the doing of science, the doing of science and technology policy was casual. There were no standards for debate or argument. The most bizarre kinds of reasoning and the weakest kinds of evidence were offered in support of action recommendations. Scientists, engineers, and university administrators offered views and made assertions that could not pass minimal standards of rigor, if one accepted the canons of policy analysis developed over the last twenty-five years. Yet action recommendations were seriously offered, passionately defended, and sometimes followed.

Part of the difference between arguments over science and technology policy and policy arguments in other fields may lie in our limited understanding of how the science and technology enterprise works.

Since understanding is limited, any and all arguments and proposals may be entertained seriously. In other domains, theory and empirical knowledge bound what can be considered reasonable arguments, but this cannot be the entire explanation. We understand many fields — welfare, military strategy — very poorly; however, we are able to apply analytical tools and techniques. We can and do make various computations about the benefits and costs of alternatives even when we do not fully understand a field.

In science and technology policy, there are very few benefit/cost calculations but much appeal to the intuitive judgments and assessments of the science and technology community about what would be best policy. The reason for this appeal may lie in the structural character of science and technology policy argument. We are usually asked to act now to forestall some undesirable effect over the long run or to insure a desirable one. The effects with which we have to deal are said to be large, systematic, and irreversible. All we can know with confidence are minor perturbations around present conditions. Such knowledge is usually sufficient for decisionmaking, since our alternatives are not strikingly radical ones. The large-scale, systematic, and irreversible social and economic changes produced by applying science and technology may imply that all we can do is appeal to the informed judgment of scientists and engineers. There are other policy fields that have the same characteristics, yet we try to bolster informed judgment with many kinds of formal analysis and reasoning. Strategic nuclear policy, for example, deals with large-scale, irreversible consequences, but this is a field for which we demand and prize care and rigor. Challenges to assumptions, calculations, and conclusions are common. Such challenges cannot ever guarantee "good" decisions, but they do illuminate why we may differ over policy.

There are no flourishing, competitive schools of thought in science and technology policy. Policy differences do arise, because some actors prefer market mechanisms and incentives as policy instruments and others prefer direct government programs and central planning and resource allocation. Such differences are not derived from the internal logic of science and technology policy but from external preferences and value judgments concerning political economy. The content of science and technology policy analysis itself does not reveal much about the relative merits of markets and planning in making policy.

Given this situation and the opportunity to write this book, I decided that it was very important to obtain some feel for the way scientists, engineers, and decisionmakers argue about science and technology policy. Since little has been written in this field other than the "war stories" of participants, I thought it was important to do so as systematically and completely as possible. Arguments about science and technology policy are always elliptical and implicit. An elaborate negotiation takes place over the resources to be made available for science and technology, the regulatory treatments the government will give them, and the jobs they will be asked to do. However, the language used for this negotiation will be very high-level and abstract and not amenable to the techniques of mainstream policy analysis. The traditional language and rhetoric of the scientific community has to be translated into the language of policy and decisionmaking. For my own understanding, I have attempted to make this translation; thus, the reader of this volume will find in it what I call conceptual strategies. They are the collected and reconstructed propositions used by the various actors and agents engaged in making science and technology policy. To some, the word *strategy* may imply statements with coherent, fully linked relationships along with empirical verifications, but *strategy*, as used in this book, means that statements are stuck together loosely. They come as a package, but there is only some partial logical, or empirical connection between them. Strategies are admixtures of factual assertions, values, and predictions. They are glued to one another by an incomplete logic but a very strong belief. Strategies are what decisionmakers offer us when we ask for the justifications to support action. Alternatively, we could call these strategies, images, paradigms, appreciations, or, possibly, models for dealing with policy questions.

In addition to stating the strategies, I have tried to show, within the available historical record, how the strategies have worked out in actual disputes and debates, what decisions have resulted, and what decision rules have been adopted. What I wanted to observe was the way in which significant policy disputes worked themselves out in history. There are clearly other kinds of things going on in policy debates than the acceptance or rejection of substantive ideas or positions. Every policy dispute carries with it organizational and personal maneuvers and motivations, but, whatever the bureaucratic and personal stakes and motivations, substantive arguments and justifications have to be offered publicly. Arguments and justifications may be weak or strong, persuasive or unpersuasive. Their qualities, in turn, will impinge on bureaucratic and personal outcomes. I believe agencies and individuals that have high-quality intellectual goods tend to be viewed more favorably than those whose goods are shoddy and not well made.

Thus, this book is first about the ways in which we think about science and technology policy and second, about the things we can do to improve our thinking. To judge the worth of my suggested improvements, it is necessary to read strategies carefully and to think hard about their contents as they appear, disappear, and sometimes reappear over time. In science and technology policy, we find some strategies are so comfortable and well established that we rarely reflect on them any more. The facts that the strategies we use today were once only a very few among many competing alternatives and were not inevitably and correctly chosen are often lost in contemporary policy debate. There are, of course, different ways to state strategies, and the reader may be able to construct somewhat different ones with the evidence at hand. But I am betting that their correlation with the ones in this book would be high.

In writing this book, I had to think very hard about what science and technology policy really is. I concluded that, at the federal level, it is limited to a few key issues. At heart, it is about money and priorities and who gets them. The regulation and governance of the science and technology enterprise, we have been convinced, should be left to practitioners. Even though controversies over governance arise periodically, science and technology decisionmakers spend most of their time worrying about getting money and spending it in the "right" directions, once it is obtained. Consequently, much of this book is concerned with disputes over money — money for basic research, for the development and commercialization of technology, for innovation. But awarding public resources to any enterprise raises questions about the effectiveness and absorptive capacity of the recipients. Thus, correlative policy issues arise concerning information flow and the education of practitioners and the public. Each of these issues has to be approached with strategies that complement those concerning resource allocation.

The first six chapters cover policy debates and disputes in each significant area of national science and technology policy. The seventh chapter provides some reasonable criteria for judging the merits of proposed policy models. Here I can offer nothing fancy, but I do try to lay out some rules and procedures that reflect the state of the art in mainstream policy analysis and that may be useful in evaluating competing strategies. The final chapter discusses prospects for the emergence of a critical policy analysis tradition for decisionmaking concerning science and technology.

The National Science Foundation, which gave me a chance, over the years, to be a practitioner of science and technology policy, generously provided leave so that I could write this book. And the University of Maryland, Baltimore County (UMBC), provided not only an opportunity to think seriously about this policy but also to teach it. Many of the themes I discuss here were first raised in my graduate seminar on science and technology policy.

The study could not have been done at all without the active assistance of the staff of the National Archives. One measure of performance in an archives or a presidential library is the rate at which requested information appears on the researcher's desk. I measured this by mean time between request and the time documents appeared. The times of all the libraries were, in my judgment, remarkably small, indicating high efficiency. In Washington, D.C., Lee Johnson and Sharon Gibbs Thibodeau kept the material in Record Group 359 — the records of the Office of Science and Technology — flowing. Since this is a voluminous file containing large masses of classified material, every request I made forced them into a security clearance review. During the time I worked there, the staff of the Archives was reduced, so my requests put additional pressure on tight resources. But they always came through cheerfully.

Four presidential libraries were also involved in the research — the Eisenhower, Kennedy, Johnson, and Ford libraries. The last, of course, also contains substantial material on the Nixon administration. Since the files of many individuals, offices, and agencies are collocated in a presidential library, it is possible to compare and contrast how the actors saw substantive and technical issues, how they saw the bureaucratic issues, and how they decided to handle each other on these issues. It is especially interesting to observe how high-level preferences, rhetoric, and ideas about economics and politics constrain science and technology policy decisions. My principal guide at the Eisenhower Library was Rod Soubers; at the Kennedy, Bill Johnson; at LBJ, Tina Lawson and Linda Hanson; and at Ford, Dennis Dillenback and William McNatt. They all take great care of both their documents and their researchers.

A study of how we think and act with respect to science and technology policy is complex. It has elements of economics, politics, history, and logic. One needs strong critics to keep everything straight. Len Lederman of the National Science Foundation read the manuscript with great care and made many valuable suggestions for improving content and style. Alex Morin of the Foundation and William A. Wells, formerly Director of Public Sector Programs, American Association for the Advancement of Science, also made a number of very useful comments. But the responsibility for all interpretations and errors is mine alone.

During the study I became aware of a university institution called Interlibrary Loan. The multidisciplinary inquiry in which I was engaged required many sources in philosophy, logic, the history of science and technology, and economics. Sara Crest of UMBC's library staff always managed to find the required source somewhere.

Carolyn Ferrigno of UMBC's Ancient and American Studies departments produced the typed version of the manuscript. She is one of the rarest persons I know in that she was able to read my bad typing along with the interpolations I usually make in variously colored inks. Each chapter went through many, many drafts, and she maintained grace and good humor as she did each one.

A Strategic Analysis of Science and Technology Policy

Introduction

1

Strategies for Science and Technology Policy

The United States spends over $85 billion each year on research and development (R&D), employs some 3 million scientists and engineers, and supports an astonishingly diverse array of scientific and technical activities. From the scientific and technical information that its citizens collectively decide to create and distribute, the United States derives new goods, services, and processes, thereby enlarging its range of economic and social choices. Over time, the science and technology (S&T) enterprise has proved to be an important source of rapid growth and increased productivity – perhaps the most important source. Furthermore, U.S. citizens believe that eventually this enterprise can deliver the information needed to attack social and environmental problems and to make enlightened public policy.

In spite of their strong relevance to social choice, the inputs, outputs, and transformation processes of the science and technology enterprise remain mysterious, and there is little likelihood that the mystery will disappear quickly. The enterprise is a "messy," adaptive system whose interconnections are constantly changing. It uses the information it produces reflexively, on itself to change itself. No persuasive theory of its operations has been advanced or may be advanceable.

Even with our lack of knowledge, we still have to determine the resources we will devote to the enterprise and the ways the government will treat it. Substantive discussions and arguments about science and technology policy, however, are not usually explicit or rigorous. Alternative strategies have historically been deployed without too much examination of their premises and conclusions. Strategies are combinations of factual assertions, predictions, prescriptions, and preferences designed to persuade decisionmakers to act in one way or another. In the domain of S&T, strategies contain strong preferences and prescriptions for how the enterprise ought to be run, along with associated predictions of disaster if it is not run in the prescribed way. On the empirical side, strategies commonly present indicators to depict "health" or "illness," international comparisons of indicators, anecdotes about those who produce science and engineering, and, of course, informed judgment of actors in the system. The indicators, preferences, prescriptions, and predictions combine in asserting claims for resources and for assuring the favorable treatment of science and technology in the policy process.

There is no alternative to using such strategies in this domain or in others, but their quality is always at issue. Tests for the validity and soundness of S&T strategies are weak. Many of their assertions are not testable; these assertions are often made to avoid a perceived crisis, or to persuade decisionmakers that not acting would be very costly or harmful. If decisionmakers take action to avoid predicted costs or damage, there is no way of knowing whether the costs and/or damage would actually have occurred without intervention or whether the action was truly effective. If decisionmakers want to wait and see whether the predictions come true, their knowledge will come too late. In the S&T domain, policy intervention must usually be started now to be effective later. For example, if the scientific and technical community predicts or believes that the nation will be short of scientists and engineers a decade from now, prudent decisionmakers cannot afford to wait and see if the predicted shortages actually materialize. The making of competent scientists and engineers has a long lead time. Thus, in the conduct of S&T policy, decisionmakers proceed more often on faith than on validated strategies with robust predictive capabilities.

Even when factual assertions turn out to be wrong and predictions do not work out, the high-order value judgments and beliefs contained in a strategy serve to maintain allegiance. These values and beliefs have extraordinary staying power, because they are connected to our general traditions of open inquiry and educational excellence. They will be changed only with reluctance even when there is strong empirical proof that some beliefs are untenable. Consequently, arguments and policy debate aimed at inducing changes in preferences or procedures have to be unusually persuasive.

If S&T activities are a major source of socially useful information, we should be as clear as possible about the assumptions, logic, and rhetoric we deliberately or unconsciously choose to employ. New scientific and technical information helps us reach our objectives in other domains. Consequently, the level and direction of scientific and technical activity is a public policy issue, but clarity on this issue does not come cheaply. Messy systems are hard to analyze successfully. With very little formal theory about the behavior of an enterprise, one way to proceed is by untangling the claims, predictions, and justifications in the strategies that different actors have used for making public decisions about S&T. At a minimum, we can gather and examine some of the traditional claims and arguments about S&T policy, state them in a systematic way, and examine their relationships.

The operations of the enterprise are highly decentralized. Decision-making at the national level is primarily concerned with the volume of public resources that scientists and engineers will get to do their work and the social terms for providing that volume. Thus, national S&T policy can be reduced to decisions and actions in a few critical areas: resource allocation, technological innovation, science education, information dissemination, and advisory structures. In these critical areas, I propose to examine positions and perceptions put forward by contending parties, particularly the S&T community and national decision-makers. By being explicit and formal about strategies, we can make the grounds for choice clearer and we can point out the beliefs and actions that are logically entailed as policy positions are defended and attacked.

There are no powerful tests for discriminating justified policy positions from unjustified ones or true positions from those that are false — for example, who knows what would have happened if the federal government had not begun to support basic research on a large scale. If we examine the recent history of S&T policy, however, we can see the outcomes of conflict between strategies. By illustrating how contending strategies first develop and then play themselves out, we can better understand claims that have been publicly employed and considered acceptable in the political arena. Further, we can see how strategies change in response to competing models and exogenous events. Based on this analysis, we should then be able to design some reasonable tests or questions that can be applied whenever we encounter an S&T strategy.

Plan of the Book

In Chapter 2 I examine alternative strategies for determining the level of resources for research, particularly basic research. The strategies the scientific community has traditionally used to argue for more public resources are compared with the strategies employed by those who control the resources. In Chapter 3 I examine alternatives concerned with government support for civilian technology and innovation. Because industry, labor, and the public all have much more of a stake in this area, a larger number of strategies and a wider spread of prescriptions are discussed than is the case for resource allocation. In Chapter 4 I look at the federal role in science education and try to distinguish policy for developing the human capital necessary to operate the S&T enterprise from more general policy for promoting the scientific and technical literacy of citizens at large. The quality of human capital flowing into research and engineering, the scientific and technical literacy of average citizens, and national capability to handle social and economic issues with high scientific content are all connected to policies for dissemination and diffusion of the information produced inside the S&T enterprise. Chapter 5 contains a history and analysis of national policy concerning the dissemination and diffusion of scientific and technical information. In Chapter 6 I consider relations between science and technology policy and foreign policy. In Chapter 7 I ask whether the process of argument, debate, and decision over the S&T enterprise can be improved. I discuss possible improvements in the design of the policy process – the ways in which we conduct science policy debate and analysis – and suggest that, with current procedures, the policy wants of scientists and engineers commonly encounter political and economic realities far too late. The initial design of S&T policy work is the most critical part, and I argue that it should not be left to scientists and engineers to do by themselves. The design of public policy is not an area in which scientists and engineers, as such, have any comparative advantage, and I suggest that it is better to have economic and budget issues contained in the initial design of a policy inquiry rather than to encounter them for the first time when the final positions of contending parties arrive on a decisionmaker's desk. The latter has happened so frequently and so consistently over different administrations that it seems to be structural.

The other suggestion I make concerns language and discourse in S&T policy. Scientists, engineers, and decisionmakers need to judge performance and outcomes in broader terms. They need to think in terms of a world of information production, social insurance against missing significant new information, resilience, and adaptation. Science and technology are called an enterprise, and an enterprise is judged not only on its current budget and operating plans but also in terms of its character. Is it quick on its feet? Can it rebound from adversity? Does it contain enough variety to insure innovation and self-renewal? If we measure performance in these terms, policy conflict will not disappear. A common language and pattern of thought will not automatically remove conflict; they may even make conflict more likely because positions become far more transparent. Nor is it easy to measure resilience or willingness to innovate. But at least actors and decisionmakers would be using a "systems" logic to address the character of the enterprise; it would be possible to talk about desired qualities rather than whether S&T did well relative to last year's budget or to the budgets of other sectors this year — which is the way outcomes are casually, but consistently, judged.

Assumptions and Methods

The analysis in this book is not so much about the making of S&T policy as about *how we think* about such policy. Making policy involves more than thinking about it casually or systematically; it also involves calculations of bureaucratic power and personal gain. The premise of this study is that public policy toward science and technology will be better served with the most well-justified and well-grounded strategies that can be produced.

Since alternative strategies most often appear wrapped in the cloak of advocacy, the method I use is to examine important issues and to try inducing latent strategies. This method is analogous to regression analysis in statistics: one collects a large number of numerical observations and finds a suitable statistical model that "best" explains the data. Using qualitative, textual analysis, I try to tease out the strategies that lie behind proposed actions and policies. And like regression analysis, these "fitted" strategies only partially explain proposed actions and actual decisions, but they do explain with some power.

For each issue, I fit the strategies associated with a particular set of interested actors. For example, I speak of the S&T "community" as offering one strategy and of decisionmakers as countering with an alternative. But the S&T community consists of many actors and agents, and there are multiple decisionmakers as well. My presentation of a strategy, therefore, means that I believe it is an expression of central tendency. Although belief by scientists and engineers in, say, a laissez-faire strategy for basic research would show a distribution, scientists and engineers will be much closer to each other in their views than they will be to decisionmakers, who control the resources for basic research. "On the average" is what I mean when I use expressions such as "the scientific community believed x" or "decisionmakers believed y." Similarly, I obtain the average values and beliefs of industry, labor, and public interest groups, with respect to civilian technology policy.

In my statements of the strategies, I construct their constituent parts by using salient texts, documents, and available written and oral histories. The reader, I hope, can make some judgment about the "goodness of fit" of stated propositions, given some of the citations and quotations from original sources. Here, there are two points: the representativeness of a citation, and the logical and empirical strength of the expressed position. With respect to the first, the reader must assume that a quoted illustration or citation does reflect consistently presented beliefs or positions. The illustrations, of course, do not come from a random sample of all policy arguments but from those that have had the most force in policy argument, those considered landmarks of thought about S&T policy, or those that have truly been considered seriously by decisionmakers.

With respect to the second point, many of the relevant texts, histories, and accounts have advocacy as their purpose. The purpose of advocacy is winning, and to win, one may endorse, simultaneously, any and all propositions believed to have persuasive power, irrespective of whether one believes they have substantive merit. The "kitchen sink" mode of argument is highly natural in S&T policy debate, since there is very little validated theory. It is difficult then to exclude any asserted propositions or beliefs as irrelevant. For example, the justifications offered for a policy or a program may include, simultaneously, meeting national needs, preserving technological leadership, compensating for market failure, preserving educational excellence, and so forth. Advocates hope that at least one of these justifications will "score," whether or not they hold it strongly.

The historical approach to policy debates and disputes provides some protection against the "kitchen sink" mode. Over time, some values, judgments, and factual assertions appear over and over again, whereas others appear and disappear according to shifting tastes and general political fashions. For example, the notion that basic research deserves public resources because it leads to unpredictable but assured social payoffs has been constant since World War II. The notion that it deserves resources because it is an adjunct to higher education is much more restricted in time, to periods when decisionmakers and the public have had strong preferences for expanding higher education. The idea that public investments in basic research will provide social benefits many times over is asserted in all eras. Beliefs asserted strongly in times of adversity as well as prosperity can be judged to be part of the necessary core of a strategy. These cores are the subject of this inquiry.

Principles of Resource Allocation 2

At the end of World War II, the scientific community developed and proposed a set of connected arguments, concepts, and beliefs – a strategy or model – that would provide a basis for permanent federal support of the nation's research activities and, specifically, of basic research. The strategy was initially predicated on meeting national needs through assured, but unpredictable, contributions to economic growth and social progress. Such contributions were at first judged sufficient to warrant public funding without any complicated discussions of whether the private sector could or should deliver the required level of resources. The private sector applied the existing stock of knowledge for profit but had little interest in producing additions to the stock.

In a strategy proposed right after World War II, it is understandable that the role of the federal government should be defined as expansive. The federal government clearly had direct interests in defense, health, welfare, commerce, and many other sectors, and the war had demonstrated its capabilities and competence. Consequently, it was felt that public funding could and should be used to create a general information base that would eventually be applicable in furthering the government's extensive interests and in improving overall social welfare.

While the public and politicians might have agreed with this strategy in the abstract, there was initially nothing in it that specified the level of public resources to be provided. Vannevar Bush, the designer of the strategy, saw a relatively low required level, as did other scientists at the time. Bush foresaw a stable, presumably real budget for basic research of about $120 million (Bush [1945] 1980, 40). Writing in 1947, the members of the President's Scientific Research Board (PSRB) argued for a basic research budget of $250 million by 1957 (PSRB 1947, 1:6). But whatever their size, actual claims for resources have always turned out to be politically significant. The level of resources government should provide has always been a subject of dispute between decision-makers and scientific claimants. At various times, decisionmakers have restricted the flow of resources to the scientific and technical community, but the ambiguity about resource levels has permitted politicians and bureaucrats to pay homage to the core concepts of the strategy while meeting their own perceived budget requirements. Even when they have restricted budgets, decisionmakers could argue that they agreed with the concepts and that science has always been treated well, on a relative basis. Ambiguity, however, has permitted a continuous process of resource claims rather than a final resolution of the optimal level of resources. Each year the scientific and technical community could argue that the level of resources provided was too low, threatening the strategy upon which science and government had agreed.

Each party believed it could gain from more precise information in arguments with the other. It was natural for both to search for rules or principles that would more precisely determine the level of resources to be provided for research. The desired or optimal level has been justified at various times, or simultaneously, by comparisons with the efforts of other nations, by relative comparisons of federal investments in important economic sectors, by the need to keep even with inflation, by the standard set by a prior peak year, and, ultimately, by the ever-increasing costs of new discoveries in S&T. New technologies of inquiry provide, on the one hand, more opportunities to address important scientific issues, but at continually increasing costs. These rising costs stake a claim by scientists for increasing real resources. On the other hand, they foster concern about the cost-effectiveness of science (Rescher 1978).

Agreed rules and standards would establish a priori claims on resources. They would prevent disputes and any need to bargain with political authorities. The number of credible claims for science and technology, however, will always outrun any available budget, and fixed claims for one sector result in difficulties in handling other sectors. Continuous tension was to be expected between the scientific and technical community and decisionmakers. And so it has worked out.

In general, resource allocation debates over the last twenty years have produced similar outcomes. From the perspective of the scientific and technical community, decisionmakers have consistently acted to impose budgetary austerity and constraints, relative to scientific needs, expectations, and "legitimate" demands. Within budgets perceived as austere, decisionmakers have frequently mounted efforts to make research more relevant to national needs and problems, but the scientific and technical community has consistently resisted such efforts. The arguments used by both sides have been remarkably constant. Given budget austerity,

Democratic science advisers sound remarkably like Republican science advisers; the advice they give their own scientific and technical colleagues does not vary much from administration to administration.

Nevertheless, the scientific community is continually surprised by questions about its use of resources, let alone by actual restrictions or reductions in federal support. Its resource strategy implies that federal research funds are a necessary and legitimate low-cost investment in the future, relative to public investments designed to influence the present. Consequently, whatever is happening elsewhere, budget priority and protection are justified. Granting such priority and protection, however, does not usually meet political or bureaucratic imperatives. Investments with known returns and results will usually be more attractive than the prospect of high, but uncertain, returns sometime in the future.

If we look at these budgetary decisions as social purchases of new information and as investments that provide new social alternatives, there is something unsatisfying about the conventional strategies of resource allocation and the public postures they induce. Minor changes in budgets are taken as a major crisis within the scientific and technical communities. While such a posture is necessary to mobilize scientists and engineers for political action, the actual debate about resource levels is a bounded one. The range of uncertainty is a few percentage points up or down from previous levels, but any percentage drop is seen as disastrous for scientists and research performers, particularly those at universities. They speak as if they have little capability to adapt, substitute, and compensate. In contrast, for an increase of a few percentage points, they promise truly significant differences in performance or rate of discovery, and yet the new resources will not be used much differently than old resources. Different ways of producing scientific knowledge will not be explored, because "factor proportions" — the relative amounts of labor, equipment, and plant actually used in doing research — are set by traditional ways of delivering training and educational services, and these factor proportions are very hard to change.

This chapter examines how the scientists' initial strategy for resource allocation fared during different administrations, competing against the preferred strategies of decisionmakers and straining against budget austerity. I try to show how some of the substance of the scientists' strategy had to be dropped or modified at the same time its core was tenaciously defended. At the end of the chapter I suggest some improvements in the way public resources for research are set and discussed. Serious argument over resource levels might be more effective if it addressed the desired capabilities of the scientific and technical enterprise and also its efficiency in achieving these capabilities. The usual focus of attention for all parties is the percentage increase or decrease each fiscal year. Argument over percentages is easier, but argument over capabilities would provide a more relevant basis for decisionmaking.

For clarity, compactness, and later reference, I have constructed alternative strategies as sets of numbered propositions which a party strongly believes. For example, a tag of *S.1* below means that scientists, in general, believe and employ a proposition, whereas a proposition tagged *D.1* means that decisionmakers, in general, believe and use it. Beneath some of the propositions, I have provided quotations from the relevant texts so that the reader can obtain some idea of the "degree of fit" of the propositions to actual positions and beliefs.

The Initial Strategy

The initial strategy is summarized in various reports commissioned by the federal government in the late 1940s and the 1950s and is stated below (Bush [1945] 1980; PSRB 1947; PSAC 1958). The strategy contains, respectively, (1) a statement linking positive social outcomes with the use of new knowledge, (2) a statement that we only acquire new knowledge through basic research, (3) a statement that the production function for basic research does not have diminishing returns, (4) an assertion of the government's stake, and (5) a denial of any stake for industry. The strategy is not complete, because it has no rule for determining the level of resources to be allocated to the basic research activity.

S.1 *New knowledge is a necessary condition for economic growth and social progress.*

> Progress in the war against disease depends upon a flow of new scientific knowledge. New products, new industries, and more jobs require continuous additions to knowledge of the laws of nature and the application of that knowledge to practical purpose. (Bush [1945] 1980, 5)

> Only through research and more research can we provide the basis for an expanding economy, and continued high levels of employment. (PSRB 1947, 1:4)

S.2 *New knowledge can only be derived through basic research.*

> **S2.1** *The supply of new knowledge is unlimited, but not predictable, and is not subject to diminishing returns.*

>> There are no known limits to the discovery of knowledge, and boundaries for effective expenditure of research and development funds are fixed only by the availability of men and facilities. (PSRB 1947, 1:4)

An action implication of *S.2* is that any limits imposed by the supply of manpower could be lifted by government programs in science education; limits imposed by shortages of facilities could be removed by supporting capital investment in the universities.

S.3 *The government should provide resources for basic research, because of its direct stakes in national security, general health, and commerce.*

These responsibilities are the proper concern of the government for they vitally affect our health, our jobs, and our national security. (Bush [1945] 1980, 8)

It is difficult to think of any other national activity which more directly benefits all the people or which makes a larger contribution to the national welfare and security. (PSRB 1947, 1:26)

S.4 *Industry will not provide the support necessary for basic research because expected profits are perceived to be too low.*

We cannot expect industry adequately to fill the gap. Industry will fully rise to the challenge of applying new knowledge to new products. The commercial incentive can be relied on for that. But basic research is essentially noncommercial in nature. It will not receive the attention it requires if left to industry. (Bush [1945] 1980, 1)

Basic research is so broad in its application and so indirectly related to any industrial process or, in fact, to any particular industry that it is not profitable for private enterprise to engage in extreme basic research. (PSRB 1947, 1:30)

S.5 *Once a given level of resources has been provided, its distribution should be left to those who will conduct research.*

Support of basic research in the public and private colleges, universities and research institutions must leave the internal control of policy, personnel, and the method and scope of the research to the institutions themselves. This is of the utmost importance. (Bush [1945] 1980, 33)

Direct technical supervision of scientific research and development should be in the hands of scientists. (PSRB 1947, 1:56)

Although this strategy contained no formal rules for determining resource levels, it seemed evident that more was necessary and that more would always be necessary. Writing in 1947, the PSRB argued that the budget for basic research should be doubled by 1957 (PSRB 1947, 1:13). In 1960 the President's Science Advisory Committee (PSAC) argued for exponential growth in the budget (PSAC 1960).

Between 1950 and 1964–65, this strategy provided the base or warrant for federal support of R&D and, in particular, of basic research. The budgets, arguments, and testimony presented by scientific and technical agencies all followed the general outlines above. There were, of course, other arguments and warrants proposed for government support of research. To obtain resources, bureaucracies and their clients will employ any argument they believe others will find halfway credible. The resource allocation strategy described here was accompanied by propositions about the important linkages between science and technology and education and culture. However, neither the scientific community nor decisionmakers ever considered such statements sufficient or even necessary to justify significant flows of resources. Policy argument, as the historical record indicates, consistently centers on science and technology as sound public investments and on whether the social and economic payoffs from such investments can be improved by alternative arrangements, those arrangements being derived from different and conflicting resource allocation models.

How the Strategy Worked—The Eisenhower Administration

As the scientists' strategy came into play in budget arguments, there was initial resistance by decisionmakers. The Eisenhower administration was dedicated to cutting the total federal budget and to curing what it perceived as excessive government activity in all fields. To Eisenhower, the federal government had a limited role in most domains, and one way to control the government was through budgetary stringency. On taking office in 1953, he had announced that he wanted a balanced budget and that he believed in a very limited federal government. His general rule for federal activity was that the central government was to do only what citizens could not do themselves or could not do as well themselves as the government could. Naturally, there were few activities that met this criterion when it was applied narrowly. In the president's view, significant funding for S&T clearly did not meet this criterion. During his entire eight years in office, the scientific community and its representatives in the White House worked very hard to change Eisenhower's mind and his administration's position.

The administration had begun with pronounced skepticism about the government's research efforts. The director of the Bureau of the Budget (BOB) (and later the Office of Management and Budget [OMB]) is almost always the single most crucial decisionmaker in setting the research budget, and Eisenhower's first director, Joseph Dodge, had strong views about efficiency and effectiveness of the federal research effort:

> There is a conviction that the Federal government is currently spending too much money on research and development pro-

grams, that there is considerable unnecessary duplication, that the programs underway need to be revalued, and that these and other circumstances result in an uneconomical use of scientific personnel which is not in the best interests of the Government, of industry, and of science. (Dodge 1953, 1)

Dodge observed that the administration was very interested in a "prompt and aggressive" approach to the problem of waste and inefficiency in research. He was well aware, however, that the government did not have the analytical machinery to attack this problem. Dodge tried to persuade the National Science Foundation (NSF) to assume the policy analysis and evaluation role in its organic legislation, but, after a lengthy effort, he concluded that this was impossible.

In an effort to achieve greater cost-effectiveness and coordination, the president in 1954 issued Executive Order 10521, clarifying the R&D role of NSF and the mission agencies. The administration hoped the executive order would provide the means for the research agencies to coordinate or at least keep track of their research support. Formal coordination, in the administration's view, would reduce duplication and promote efficiency. In a series of meetings between R&D officials and the president, the theme of coordination and cost-effectiveness in science funding was hammered hard. Despite NSF's discomfort with any policy or evaluation role, the president felt that it should help the Bureau of the Budget achieve the best use of limited funds (Minnich 1956). NSF proved too weak and too reluctant as a research coordinator. To its director, coordination was a matter for scientists, not administrators. He felt that those doing science naturally selected the most worthwhile projects because of strong communication linkages inside the scientific community. The Bureau of the Budget concluded that it did not have the power to change the NSF or its attitude and that Executive Order 10521 had failed to produce a central mechanism for formal executive leadership (Hughes 1956).

Despite the philosophical and conceptual discomfort with government support of research and development, Eisenhower's budgets continued to grow, perhaps without his intending that they do so. The government seemed to be satisfying the demands of the scientific and technological community. Between 1953 and 1958, total annual federal support for R&D almost doubled. The basic research component also almost doubled, from $113 million in 1953 to $210 million in 1957. While the latter sum did not quite meet the scientists' 1947 projections for the most desirable level of funding, these amounts represented significant advances in an administration that was inherently suspicious of scientists' claims for resources. Furthermore, these increases were occurring at a time when the scientific and technological community had no formal voice within the White House staff to represent its views and interests. It gained such a voice through technological and educational competition between the United States and the Soviet Union.

Soviet orbiting of the sputnik satellite in 1957 suggested a powerful and open-ended rule for determining the level of federal resources for science and technology and science education – fund at a level to overcome national security problems. In response to sputnik, the administration expanded NSF's budget from $50 million in FY 1958 to $136 million in FY 1959, with a heavy emphasis on science education. It created the National Aeronautics and Space Administration (NASA), passed the National Defense Education Act, and carried out organizational reforms to provide more central oversight of important R&D sectors. Always interested in coordination and oversight, the president created a special assistant for science and technology (hereafter called the science adviser) and an external advisory and policy analysis group, the President's Science Advisory Committee (PSAC). This organizational change allowed the scientific community to promote its research funding strategy from within the White House. The science adviser and PSAC provided channels around the always conservative Bureau of the Budget. Thus, a member of Eisenhower's PSAC could comment to the science adviser that he was concerned about the latter designating PSAC to be the "accelerator" for funding while the Budget Bureau was the "brake" (Weinberg 1960). In fact, PSAC produced a series of philosophical reports laying the basis for even further growth in research and science education.

But no growth rate could be sufficient. In 1958 PSAC defined a continuing and permanent crisis in resource allocation. In research, the nation had to run hard to stay in the same place. It confronted implacable competition from the Soviet Union, and, in PSAC's view, the Soviets knew how to spend research money effectively. PSAC, like other government bureaucracies concerned with the Soviet Union, believed that the Soviets were "ten feet tall" and would run a very hard R&D race, and it told the president so. The race with the Soviet Union required continuously more resources because of the need to cover more bets and opportunities (PSAC 1958). In this race there were increasing returns to investment in research, but each new investment revealed unexplored opportunities that required subsequent additional investments. Because of the race with the Soviet Union, none of these could be left fallow.

To PSAC and the scientific community, the administration's budgetary stringency was the real limit on research output. It prevented the natural dynamics of scientific growth from taking place, interfering with the effectiveness of the enterprise. Budgetary stringency in research funding also implied that the perceived shortage of scientists and engineers could not be relieved. Newly revealed opportunities required more scientists and engineers. They learned their professions by doing research, primarily in universities, and the universities were stifled because of short research funds, lack of capital equipment, and obsolete plants.

Still the president kept asking his science advisers whether or not the research enterprise had been saturated with federal dollars and whether or not the federal government should continue current levels of support for basic research. George Kistiakowsky, the president's second science adviser, noted that this issue still concerned Eisenhower at the end of his second term.

> The President then said he was very anxious for the Science Advisory Committee to explore the basic problem as to whether we are doing too little, too much or just enough research. He felt that there might be some waste of money and manpower; that maybe we have exhausted the available supply of talent and are now putting second rates on problems they are not qualified to undertake and are not getting our money's worth. (Kistiakowsky 1960, 1)

In the last months of his administration, both the science adviser and PSAC kept telling Eisenhower that the government would have to do more for science and education, not less, despite the president's well-known desire to have the private sector do more. PSAC argued that research and education were joint outputs and that both needed more federal support. Sounding a theme that persists today, PSAC argued that research "vitality" required continuous injections of young investigators. If the president wanted a cost-effective research establishment, a necessary condition was more support for education (PSAC 1960a, 1960b).

A nation could never have too large a base of scientific and technical information. More money for both research and education meant an increasing rate of discovery. The only real constraints on scientific and technical output were the numbers of available scientists and engineers and the quality of the facilities and equipment at their disposal. These constraints could be alleviated by increasing federal support for education, particularly science education. Increasing budgets for S&T were justified, whatever fiscal constraints the administration faced. For without an enlarging knowledge base, the United States would not win its race with the Soviet Union or maintain social and economic progress.

At the end of the administration, the president's science adviser summed up the resource allocation debate this way:

> Eisenhower, of course, was not terribly enthusiastic about federal dollars going to support research which was not relevant to the

government objectives, and that meant that it wasn't relevant to national security matters or health. And things outside of it, he felt they should be, as he used to say, private sector. I think we accomplished a major task by convincing him toward the end of that administration that in order to be first in the world, the United States had to have across the board support of basic research by the Federal government. (Kistiakowsky 1976, 12)

However, Eisenhower's commitment did not really rest on the scientists' own strategy. At the end of his second term, the president was implicitly convinced that some uncorrectable market failure affected the private sector when it came to research. The private sector would not fund basic research or else would not provide as well as the government. The president swung philosophically to government support, because there seemed to be no alternative (Kistiakowsky 1976, 13).

The Kennedy and Johnson Administrations
Relative to the inflated expectations induced by the scientists' basic strategy and the perceptions of permanent crisis, whatever Eisenhower did was seen as too little and too late. Nor did he really accept the strategy. Presidential acceptance seemed to come in the Kennedy administration. At least in his rhetoric, President Kennedy argued directly in terms the scientists themselves had put forward. The president did not argue so much in terms of market failure as he did in terms of the expected payoff from letting scientists pursue their own ends. Technological advance was a function of pure basic research, and the more the scientific community worked at stating and solving its own questions, the more vital it would be (Kennedy 1963).

Despite his apparent willingness to fund research in ways the scientific community preferred, President Kennedy began his administration with a perceived need to appear fiscally conservative. He worried about being labeled a reckless spender by adversaries in the Congress and elsewhere. As his first budgetary act, he did not want to unbalance the last Eisenhower budget, and he certainly did not want to do so on the civilian side of the budget. He gave very strong instructions to the director of BOB to hold down expenditures as well as federal employment (CEA 1964, 174).

The advice the president was getting about resources for S&T, of course, ran the other way. The R&D build-up in defense and space in the Eisenhower administration became sufficient reason for more federal funding of basic research. Thus, the outgoing and incoming science advisers could jointly argue that prior increases in R&D had used up the presputnik slack in scientific manpower and that most (87 percent) of federal R&D did not help in the production of technical

Table 2.1.   Scientists' Strategy in 1964

Science Adviser	Statement of Strategy
1. Basic research adds to our reservoir of knowledge about the universe, on which all technology rests.	1. *Statement S.2.* Connection between technology and basic research.
2. Such research is always full of surprises, and, with our recent experience demonstrating the impact of science on our security and world leadership, it is clear that we must preserve and protect this portion of our technical enterprise as a vital hedge against the unknown.	2. *Statement S.1.* Connection between social outcomes and science and technology.
3. In fact, I believe that we must be prepared to allow an increasing level for this purpose. To a very large extent, this level of support is set by the supply of competent scientists.	3. *Statement S.3.* Increasing returns within relevant range of operation; implicit statement on science education.
4. Within this level, priorities must be set largely by the scientific community itself — by factors of curiosity and desire to work on the scientific frontier — in contrast to priority setting for development. (Wiesner 1964, 257)	4. *Statement S.5.* Preferred governance.

manpower but flowed to defense and space contractors who were consumers, not producers, of manpower. Sufficient funds were not flowing to university campuses, where scientists were trained. Increased defense and space R&D required more government funds for basic research and the universities as well as increases in science education at all levels (Wiesner, Kistiakowsky, and Brooks 1960).

Despite the president's concern about appearing to be a reckless spender, and despite early warnings from the BOB about de facto increases in the basic science budget because of the increased costs of remaining on scientific frontiers (Bell 1961), the administration delivered significant increases in R&D. Government expenditures for R&D jumped from $9.3 billion in FY 1961 to $10.3 billion in FY 1961 and from $12.2 billion in FY 1963 to $14.9 billion in FY 1964. Although there were significant increases in defense and space spending, other areas, including basic research, also prospered. But no level of basic research funding would suffice until all scientists were employed doing research. Speaking before Congress, the president's science adviser provided a compact version of the apparently triumphant scientists' strategy that had been presented earlier. As a reminder of its staying power, in table 2.1, the strategy is matched against the science adviser's statements.

Increased basic research carried with it a desired upgrading in the

quality and quantity of scientists and engineers. As the science adviser
put it:

> *Science education statement: Inseparability of research and
> education (see chap. 4).*
>
> Such activities enable teachers to derive fresh ideas and insights on the
> frontier of knowledge and thereby advance the pace and quality of our
> educational programs. Advanced training of students in the science at the
> graduate level is also inseparable from involvement in research. (Wiesner
> 1964, 258)

At its sudden end, the Kennedy administration appeared committed
to continued expansion of basic research funds. Further, it felt it had to
alleviate perceived shortages in scientific and technical manpower. The
jobs the administration expected the scientific community to perform
were so numerous that shortages were to be expected. President Kennedy had been made aware of them even before taking office, and his
science adviser subsequently kept reminding him that demand was out-
stripping supply and that the current supply could not meet the unprece-
dented requirements for both economic progress and national security
(Wiesner 1962, 1963).

In addition, the administration was having difficulty moving its
educational programs through the Congress. But science education programs could be sold in terms of their contribution to economic growth
and could serve as a wedge for the general education programs the
administration desired. The administration seemed ready to realize the
decision rule on funding which scientists preferred — fund basic
research to the point where all who want to do it and are capable of
doing it now or in the future have the resources to do it.

In addition to increasing its support for basic and applied research,
the administration saw S&T as providing solutions for social and
economic problems. Themes that became prominent in the nation's
search for an innovation policy were first sounded at this time. Acceleration of innovation would reduce costs of production, and there
would be an increased supply of new products and processes. These, in
turn, would improve the U.S. position in international trade (Cabinet
Committee on Economic Growth 1962). The president's science and
economic advisers both tried hard to design programs to increase industrial innovation and to encourage industry to do socially useful research
that it would not ordinarily choose to pursue. Industry, in the administration's view, was not pursuing profitable technological opportunities
that would also improve social welfare, but industry's "myopia" could
be corrected by making the opportunities more visible through government programs. At this time, no one doubted the government's compe-

tence to design and operate such programs. The government could help markets work better by insuring that participants had relevant information, by increasing ties between industry and universities, and by support of "generic" basic research, that is, research benefiting a significant number of industries, no one of which had a strong enough interest to do the research itself (Wiesner 1964, 268).

The relatively liberal budgetary prospect for S&T ended in the Johnson administration, although the levels of civilian research and basic research doubled between the end of the Kennedy administration and the end of the Johnson administration. Understandably, S&T budgets could not remain immune to resource pressures generated by the Vietnam War and the needs of the Great Society. As early as the fall of 1965, the director of BOB warned President Johnson that, despite program cuts, his attempts to keep the budget below the then horrendous $100 billion level were not likely to succeed. Uncontrollable increases in spending for Vietnam, space, and veterans' compensation simply pushed the budget up. Although the president's economic advisers wanted tax increases to control the incipient inflation, the president did not permit them. Johnson, who appeared to want both guns and butter, consistently had to cut his budgets well below what he preferred. He thus insured that BOB would exert strong budgetary pressure downward on the nominally controllable items in the budget. Of course, R&D is a prominent item among controllables (Schultze 1965a, 1965b, 1965c).

On the S&T side, Donald Hornig, the science adviser, continued to advance the scientists' demands for permanent real growth in funding. He urged the president to accept, in principle, steady if moderate growth in research funding, and he continued to press for science education programs (Hornig 1964). The "in principle" was important, because the scientists had proposed a rule of thumb that funding increase by 15 percent a year. "In principle" meant some minimum increase above inflation each year.

The warrant for this 15 percent rule did not rest so much on the expected output of basic research investments as on educational grounds. Education was the domestic area with most appeal to the president. Since the country was experiencing annual college enrollment increases of about 10 percent, then a 10 percent increase was required for research in universities. Research was an input into education and vice versa, and input ratios seemed permanently fixed to educators and scientists. The increasing costs of staying at the frontier of knowledge implied an additional 5 percent growth. More sophisticated equipment delivered more knowledge, but it cost more. In fact, 15 percent was not an upper limit but a lower boundary (Brooks 1968b, 201).

If the president did not respond with 15 percent increments, he did respond with instructions to all agencies, telling them to maintain existing research performance and, as was characteristic of him, to increase the number of high-quality research institutions (Johnson 1965). But these objectives ran into the administration's growing lack of resources and its unwillingness to obtain more. As budgetary pressure began to build up, the science adviser reminded the president that he was now politically committed to high-quality research *and* the development of new institutions. Without new resources, however, there was a trade-off between current quality and new capability (Hornig 1965). Two years later, Hornig was still reminding President Johnson of the continuing need to increase basic research funds. He also reminded the president of the latter's commitment to greater geographic distribution of funds and the development of new institutions with research capability. According to the science adviser, suspicion of the administration was growing among scientists. The decline of the growth rate in basic research meant retrenchment for the universities, but the flow of students into the sciences still remained high. Thus, the universities were short of resources to provide the requisite training, which was now a well-defined federal responsibility (Hornig 1967a).

Despite suspicion of the administration by scientists, the flow of real federal resources for basic research continued to increase up to 1968. As noted, civilian research doubled between the end of the Kennedy administration and the end of the Johnson administration. Basic research funding increased by more than 33 percent; it was not so much the absolute level of funding as the falling growth rate that was troublesome to scientists. A falling growth rate and the traditional inability or unwillingness to vary input proportions in higher education meant that high expectations, partly induced by the Great Society, could not be realized.

Crisis in the Nixon Administration

Perhaps more important than the level of funding, perceptions of what S&T was supposed to do were changing. Demands for relevance, payoff, and applications were natural in a Great Society. The scientists' now traditional strategy did maintain, of course, that the research enterprise delivered social payoff and applications but that these did not have to be, could not be, and should not be specified a priori. Now the administration, the Congress, and the public seemed to be asking for just such specifications. To the scientific community, such demands at any time immediately raise a budgetary threat. Given an immediate relevance or utility test, it believes that applied research and applications will always drive out basic research in the competition for funds from federal agencies. A priori relevance tests imply as well that the organization and decision process of the federal S&T establishment needs an overhaul, but that organization and process derives from adherence to the preferred strategy discussed above.

To respond fully to demands for relevance meant abandoning the core of the strategy. The issues could be side-stepped if it could be shown that the one institution truly designed to deliver socially meritorious products, services, and information broke down in the research domain. This institution was the free market. If market failure could be demonstrated and the market, inherently and structurally, could not read future technological possibilities correctly, then it would not produce the socially optimal level of R&D. Consequently, strong government support of R&D was a necessary compensation to reach the optimal level. Arguments about market failure were never in the scientists' original strategy, although there were statements about industry disinterest. Ironically, the social welfare justifications for government support were recast in the language of economists. In the 1960s, economic analysis began to show that R&D had direct and positive connections with important economic magnitudes — national income, productivity, rates of growth, and inflation rates (NSF 1971, 1977a; Nelson 1981).

Most economists argued that private markets, especially strongly competitive ones, by themselves would never allocate sufficient resources to research, although a few held out the possibility of overinvestment. Microeconomic theory implied that entrepreneurs operating in strongly competitive markets would underinvest in basic research, because its results were not usually appropriable and competitors could not be excluded from using them. If so, there would be no direct government interest in general support of S&T; rather, the issue would be whether there is divergence between social and private rates of return and when and whether private markets will work, especially in production of basic research. Consequently, from the theoretical side, federal support of basic research was warranted, not because the federal government had clear needs and interests (except as a direct user of R&D), but because the market for R&D inevitably and inherently possessed characteristics that prevented it from working properly, and furthermore, there was no market correction that the government could use to make it work properly.

On the empirical side, a number of economic studies appeared, investigating the relationship between investments in R&D and economic growth and productivity. These studies usually dealt with aggregate dollar inputs to R&D and their average or marginal contributions to output. The most persuasive ones argued that the marginal social returns from R&D were positive and greater than private returns and that, ex ante, private returns might be seen as too low to justify R&D

investments. Although these studies, by their nature, could not address the specific contributions of basic research to growth and productivity, the case for basic research investments was quickly constructed. Basic research was seen as a necessary condition for new technology, although it was well known that much new technology often resulted from using old technology and improving on it (Rosenberg 1976a, 1976b). Numerous anecdotes about the spillovers between university basic research and the market supply of innovation were produced to bolster this case. Thus, the divergence between social and private returns for aggregate R&D, rather than perceived national need, became the economic justification for government funding of basic research.

A revised and more sophisticated scientists' strategy is stated as follows (this strategy is denoted Revised Scientists [RS]):

RS.1 *Social rates of return from R&D are high and differ significantly from private returns.*

> **RS1.1** *Expectations from private returns are too low to induce current R&D investments that will provide high social returns.*

> **RS1.2** *Basic research is necessary to realize social rates of return because new products, services, and processes are eventually derived from basic research findings.*

RS.2 *The nation underinvests in R&D, and the greatest underinvestment comes in basic research.*

> **RS2.1** *The market for basic research fails because its output, that is, information, is inappropriable and no one can be prevented from using it.*

RS.3 *Failures in the R&D market imply government responsibility and support for R&D.*

> **RS3.1** *The government is competent to make market corrections and cost-effective when doing so.*

S.5, the laissez-faire preference concerning government regulation or supervision of research and governance of research performers is carried over intact. A rule for setting the level of resources completes the revised strategy. As noted, the scientific community proposed a rule of 15 percent per year in the Johnson administration. Such a (minimum) rate came from perceptions of ever-expanding scientific and educational needs and the rising capital intensity required to stay at the scientific frontiers.

Propositions *RS.1, RS.2,* and *RS.3* provided decisionmakers with a basis for intervention and support which satisfied minimum social welfare criteria — as economists define social welfare — but provided no guidance on where and how decisionmakers should intervene. Given budgetary stringency, the RS propositions were consistent with a possible decisionmaker's proposition that:

D.1   *Given limited resources, research designed to improve productivity, innovation, or national needs should have priority.*

Given budgetary pressures and the political demands of the Great Society, decisionmakers could be expected to urge concentration in certain areas they believed to be socially necessary or politically useful. But these were not necessarily the areas with the highest payoff, from a scientific or technological perspective. Although the Eisenhower, Kennedy, and Johnson administrations had all sought methods for ordering priorities among fields in basic research, no credible methods existed then (nor do they now). Within fields, scientists could and did rank the technical merits of alternative projects, but they had (and still have) the utmost difficulty in setting priorities among fields. The latter were set by history, by the political weight of particular scientific constituencies, and by bargaining and lobbying.

It was natural for decisionmakers to want to allocate public research money according to relevance, to some proximate national purpose or need. President Johnson, before Vietnam, wanted to shift spending toward the programs of greatest direct benefit to the American people. To the president, science was an activity that should shift its priorities toward discernible improvements in national problems such as transportation, housing, and health.

S&T was not a primary concern in the last years of the Johnson administration, and pressures for relevance were not as intense as they might have been without the war. Yet, the revealed strategy of the Office of Science and Technology (OST) and the science adviser emphasized research application. Hornig tried hard to involve his office in long-range R&D activities that might contribute to urban development, increased housing output, improved transportation, and decreased pollution. In his view, there were at least some roadblocks that could be overcome by R&D and by applying the talents of universities to non-defense areas, but his efforts drew scant attention. As all science advisers must, he continued to warn the president of suspicion in the scientific community that the administration did not understand the importance of basic research.

Although the Johnson administration could not follow through, the concept of mobilizing R&D for national purposes was an attractive one; it was politically appealing to the public at large and to research performers themselves. Since the basic research growth rate was falling and universities faced demands for relevance from some of their own clients, the universities argued that they were competent to deliver research with some nominally discernible relevance.

The search for social relevance and priority was carried further in the Nixon administration. Not only was the nation shifting priorities from space and defense, but the Nixon decisionmakers and their S&T advisers believed they knew exactly which sectors needed infusions of research funds. In his first State of the Union message, President Nixon identified energy, transportation, health and environment, and protection from natural disasters as deserving of incremental research funds (Nixon 1969). Even though resources were scarce, these national priorities could be met without undue pain to the scientific community because:

D.2   *The basic scientific enterprise is inefficient or contains some slack, which can be allocated to public purposes.*

Suspicions of inefficiency in research operations go back to the Eisenhower administration. In fact, whenever budgets pinch, one would expect decisionmakers to assert *D.2*. If inefficiency is characteristic of the scientific enterprise and actually is induced by an oversufficiency of funds, then budgetary stringency will improve performance. Stringency forces the scientific community to make difficult decisions about scientific priorities, which it can avoid in richly endowed periods. Thus, President Johnson's OST warned of the need to find a way to cut off outdated and mediocre science. President Nixon's second science adviser argued that tight resources implied greater effectiveness in improving the quality of research (David 1972). In a later period of stringency, President Reagan's science adviser has made the same point — moderate budgetary restraint forces decisions that the scientific community would prefer not to make: "the best overall quality of research may not occur in times of accelerating support but in times of moderate restraint that force qualitative decisions" (Keyworth 1981, 9).

Complementary to notions that it was possible to distinguish efficient and inefficient scientific ventures was the notion that the output of research could be measured and evaluated and thus improved. During an upsurge of optimism about benefit-cost and systems analysis in the mid sixties, President Johnson had extended program planning and budgetary (PPB) analysis to the entire federal establishment. Basic to PPB was the notion that an organization's performance should be measured against what it did relative to intended results, rather than to the resources it was receiving for operations. The Nixon administration, while less wedded to PPB, imposed its own management by objectives

(MBO) system, which again assumed that performance could be measured and related to agreed objectives.

Although PPB, MBO, or other resource allocation schemes were difficult to apply to the R&D agencies, the agencies were not immune from them. Decisionmakers knew there were inherent difficulties in applying PPB, MBO, or later, zero-based budgeting (ZBB), but these methods permitted tougher scrutiny of claims for resources and could easily be used to make budget reductions. With respect to R&D, budget examiners can and do routinely hold that the PPB, MBO, ZBB, or other systems analysis that the Office of Management and Budget (OMB) requires and that agencies submit are unpersuasive. So decisionmakers proposed:

D.3 *Proper budget and management structures and procedures reveal the payoff from public investments, including the payoff from R&D investments.*

Statements *D.1, D.2,* and *D.3,* joined to the *RS* statements, provide a decisionmaker's strategy for R&D funding, based on economic criteria. Using the criteria of welfare economics meant that scientists and decisionmakers could agree on the times when government support was needed. They could agree that market failures in the R&D sector were inherent in a capitalist economy or in any market-oriented economy. And they could agree that significant government support of basic research would always be needed. Both sides probably preferred not to address the issues of the extent of market failure, its persistence over time, and whether such failure was socially important. Such an inquiry would have raised the issue of discretionary R&D policies and would not have been consistent with large-scale permanent, untied support. If one knew the extent of market failure and the social costs involved, then one could set a baseline for government support and know when to phase it out.

Decisionmakers and science spokesmen parted company over the operational propositions — the level and direction of support. The Nixon administration had the intent and skill simultaneously to impose tight budgets and to break with the scientists' strategy. The administration decreased the real level of resources overall and tried to redirect the nation's research efforts. Surprisingly, for a conservative administration, the objective of R&D was assisting in the solution of domestic problems (David 1972). There were to be special efforts for energy, transportation, protection from natural disasters, emergency health care, and environmental protection; the administration provided increases for R&D in those areas. Believing that it could cure society's ills with technology, it searched for new technological opportunities believing that it could predict which technologies really could be applied to solve social problems. But the scientists' strategy continued to emphasize that undirected streams of research provided unexpected payoffs or at least deepened the knowledge base so that problems could be attacked at a more fundamental level, if not solved (Nelson 1977).

The administration's severe budget problems were recognized by the science establishment, and it was not expected that R&D would be immune to cuts, but no science adviser, regardless of administration, can avoid making the case for leniency with respect to basic research. Nixon's first science adviser argued that basic research should have stable, predictable funding from year to year and that it should not be oriented toward national needs or cost-benefit calculations (DuBridge 1970). In a by now typical confrontation between directors of OST and directors of OMB over research funding, DuBridge, for example, argued with Caspar Weinberger that increments to the NSF budget over and above a $125 million increment programmed by OMB were necessary, because the quality of the U.S. scientific enterprise was declining and because of the need for stability, that is, a steady, if small real increase. Weinberger believed that stability was desirable, but an overall budget constraint meant that $125 million more for science would have to be sufficient (Weinberger 1970).

Relations between the Nixon administration and the scientific community were bad for a number of reasons unrelated to resource allocation strategies. In the eyes of both Johnson and Nixon, the scientific community had been politicized; it had spoken out against technical systems that the administration preferred, like the ABM and the SST. The president's science advisory mechanism was seen not as a tool or an extension of the president, but as an embodiment of the scientific community. The traditional push for more resources by the OST, and its persistent attempts to gain control of the R&D budget, created suspicion that the science advisory apparatus was more interested in the welfare of the scientific community than the welfare of the White House. The White House believed the OST was becoming more and more of a "special pleader" for its S&T constituencies — advocating positions and ideologies not always consistent with administration policy. The White House staff also believed that, instead of serving to advise the president, the OST had become his critic. It was thus defined as a problem to be overcome (Simmons 1975; Cannon 1975).

In July of 1973 President Nixon disestablished his science advisory apparatus and assigned its residual functions to the director of the National Science Foundation. The nominal reason for this action was the increase in science policy capability in the agencies, particularly the NSF, and the need to streamline the Executive Office of the President. And this was, in fact, partly true. Other units within the White House had acquired technical analysis capabilities, especially in defense, and nearly all major agencies had also expanded their policy analysis capabilities. To the White House, the agencies were better equipped to integrate political, economic, and technical factors than was the highly specialized OST. A specialized office was not well articulated with the overall perspective that presidential decisions require. Since the administration had other analytical resources, there was less of an analytic requirement for the OST, and the office certainly was seen as a political embarrassment.

The Scientists' Strategy Restored: Ford and Carter

The principal federal spokesman left for the science community's *RS* strategy was the director of the National Science Foundation, doubling as the science adviser. There was no way for him to avoid asking for more effort in R&D, and he did. For example, in developing the FY 1976 budget, Guy Stever, then serving in this dual capacity, wrote the president about the low increase for civilian R&D, as compared with defense and space R&D. Stever believed that total civilian R&D could continue to grow for awhile at a rate below the inflation rate because there was a need for stocktaking and evaluation. He argued that real basic research funding had fallen from its 1967 peak under Johnson. This plus a rising inflation rate made prospects for basic research look bleak. Yet technological advance was more and more closely linked with basic research; the number of basic fields on which technology had to draw was increasing, while the ability of the science enterprise to supply new information was declining (Stever 1974).

The science adviser's desire to increase basic research funding conflicted, as usual, with the always present desire of the OMB to hold down spending (and with an accelerating inflation). President Ford, early in his tenure, had declared a moratorium on all new spending initiatives except for energy. Although his FY 1976 budget contained an 11 percent increase for civilian R&D, it contained only a 3.8 percent increase for basic research. But 1977 was to be the year of redress. After a long internal debate, the Ford administration decided that its relations with the scientific community needed improvement and that the decline in real basic research support had, in fact, been harmful. The OMB itself admitted it had not responded sufficiently to the decade-long decline in constant dollar funding (Loweth 1976). While the president's budget restricted total expenditures to a 5.5 percent increase over 1976, it provided an 11 percent increase for basic research. To go along with the increase, the Ford OMB, for the first time, produced a set of criteria for funding R&D. Insofar as basic research was concerned, the problem was market failure. The OMB argued that there was a tendency to underinvest in basic research because of the inappropriable nature of information, a classical reason for market failure (OMB 1978). Because basic research was inherently inappropriable, market output would always be too low. For this reason, the administration wanted to follow a policy of constant real growth of 3 percent in basic research. For the first time, basic research had an a priori budgetary claim, always an objective of the scientific community.

The Carter administration raised Ford's 3 percent to 5 percent and employed the *RS* strategy to justify the increase. President Carter argued that there was a strong connection between investment in R&D and productivity — increasing productivity maintained international competitiveness, but the federal government had been underinvesting in research. Carter sought to redirect agency priorities toward basic research activity.

> One of the substantial changes that I have made in preparing the Federal budget has been to increase the portion of each major agency's budget that goes into basic research and development.... I would say that the countries that have maintained a high commitment to research and development have a tendency to have much higher productivity. . . . So, I'd say research and development is a very fruitful investment. And we're going to have that trend around. (Carter, as quoted in Press 1979, 8)

Consistent with the *RS* strategy, real growth for basic research came at the expense of federal funds for development and demonstration. In the *RS* strategy, a priori economic grounds for general development support by government are weaker than those for basic research. In the development phase of innovation, results are presumably appropriable and excludable. If so, OMB could argue that development was more appropriate for the private sector, although the government has long been active in development work, for example, military and commercial aircraft, nuclear power plants, and agriculture (OMB 1978; Nelson 1982).

In addition to using the *RS* strategy for its justifications of increased research funding, the Carter administration, like its predecessors, began a search for innovation opportunities. After a large-scale search and review of federal policies and programs concerned with technological innovation, the administration proposed a few new actions to make the market for R&D work more smoothly and to correct certain externalities and imperfections. A center to enhance scientific and technological information flow was to be established, as were generic technology centers at universities. Generic technologies are feasible technologies of benefit to many industries but not of sufficiently great benefit to any single industry to induce investments in them. Small business R&D was to be bolstered, and some new venture capital was to be provided, because private sources were seen as drying up (Carter 1979a, 1979b).

The Reagan Administration

Carter's research policies were not carried out following the election of President Reagan; budgetary stringency arrived immediately and predictably with the new administration. The last Carter budget, for FY 1982, provided for 4.3 percent real growth for basic research, with R&D as a whole to increase at a real 10.1 percent. Civilian R&D received a 4 percent real increase. The FY 1982 Reagan revision of the Carter budget provided no real increases anywhere.

The Reagan FY 1982 and FY 1983 budgets portrayed the classical position of decisionmakers under severe budgetary constraints. The stringency stemmed from the nation's inflationary difficulties and from a very strong desire to reduce the role of the federal government in all sectors. Austerity themes common in past administrations were replayed, but with far more rigor. The new administration, however, found propositions *RS.1* and *RS.2* consistent with its philosophical views and laissez-faire economics. Some government activity in the case of bona fide market failure was appropriate, and research and development were good candidates for assertions of market failure. Investment in basic research was a good social investment and a hedge against future contingencies (Keyworth 1981).

But from the time the Reagan administration came into office, it adhered to a stricter version of the decisionmakers' proposition *D.3,* about priorities, relevance, and funding levels. Proposition *D.3* was expanded to include the setting of priorities for all research activity, not just applications. A revised *D.3* can be stated as follows:

RD.3 *Restricted budgets imply that research must meet a test of international comparative advantage in basic research and a test of relevance in applications.*

Undisputed world dominance in all fields of science and technology is not a goal to which U.S. national science and technology can aspire. (OSTP 1982, 6)

There are a number of good reasons why we cannot expect to be preeminent in all scientific fields *nor is it necessarily desirable.* The idea that we can't be first across the spectrum of science and technology is not simply a function of our current economic situation. . . . Japan and Western Europe have achieved technological competitiveness, not parity. . . . It follows that, because of the diversity inherent in industrial democracies, there are certain areas of science and technology that are more pertinent to other countries than to us. . . . In science and technology as in all endeavors, available resources must be identified, comparative advantages assessed, tough choices made and priorities established before resources are allocated. (Keyworth 1981, 7)

As expected, there is also an expanded efficiency proposition in the Reagan strategy. Austere budgets imply that research quality can be upgraded.

RD.4 *The basic scientific enterprise can be made efficient, and scientific output does not need to fall in proportion to budgets.*

> In this time of economic restraint we need to make tough decisions — tougher than were necessary during areas of rapid growth. There is an inevitable tendency when budgets were increasing to hold resources to the best research areas but not to take money away from the production areas, even if they have passed the days of their most important and exciting work. We can no longer afford that luxury. (Keyworth 1981, 9)

Upgrading quality implied that informational payoff between fields of science and technology be assessed a priori. The administration had no doubts that this could be done, although such assessments have always bothered the scientific community. The logic of science does not carry with it propositions allowing for the ordering of priorities among fields and the reshuffling of priorities as information increases. Priorities have to be imposed according to external relevance constraints, and we have already seen that the scientific community holds such constraints to be counterproductive (Brooks 1978). The science adviser seemed to believe that he could establish informational returns per dollar of expenditure. If so, economics tells us that fields should be funded to the point where incremental information per dollar of expenditure is equal for all fields. In fact, the administration made few changes in the way that R&D agencies do business.

The policy implication of the Reagan strategy is clearly that R&D cannot expect automatic real increases in available resources. But increases are not precluded because of the asserted connections between growth, productivity, and research. This strategy is highly similar to that of earlier administrations. When presidents act to constrain budgets, the search for persuasive and credible arguments to convince scientists that pain is endurable probably leads to statements about the inefficient use of resources. Such arguments are certainly not proposed during prosperous times. Then science advisers and administrations hold that more science can always be done effectively and efficiently.

The view that scientists can know the efficiency of different fields of inquiry (i.e., know information-gain possible per dollar of investment) contradicts the core of the RS strategy. A priori, efficiency is hard to predict; it depends on future outcomes, not current ones, and there is no true measure to compare the marginal or incremental value of information in one field with that of another. The historical pattern of claiming inefficiency in times of austerity and efficiency and effectiveness in times of prosperity suggests that this kind of marginal proposition is not really required in the decisionmakers' strategy. In a period of austerity, one could assert, alternatively, that less research will be done with fewer resources but that equity requires all resource claimants to suffer some pain. One could, at the same time, encourage experiments in changing input proportions in research and education to see if economies could be achieved.

While previous administrations had searched for technological innovation opportunities for the government to pursue, the Reagan administration believed that efficient markets would reveal all the technological opportunities of an economic nature, that is, those that would be provided and sold to industry or final consumers. To the extent that markets did not accomplish this, government interventions and regulations were at fault. The Reagan administration argued, therefore, that development and demonstration projects had to be cut back, but, like all previous administrations, certain projects — like nuclear power — were found appropriate.

RD.5 *Market forces provide better results in selecting development and demonstration projects than does the federal government.*

The transactions of actors in the marketplace and their revealed priority assessments provide guidance that is superior to centralized programming (OSTP 1982, 4). The liberating force of unhampered markets would increase research and innovation, compensating for any federal retreat. Retreat was, in fact, desirable to get rid of distortions created by the federal presence. The government's main business was helping to make private R&D markets work better through the right kinds of incentives. Macroeconomic policy and incentives create a proper business climate for innovation. The best thing that the government could do to improve market selection of technologies was to reduce its own pernicious regulations (OSTP 1982, 6).

Reflections on Strategy and Policy

The last forty years have, in the main, been rich and successful for the scientific and technological community. No one, except possibly Richard Nixon, has truly threatened the "contract" between science and government. The United States continues to invest as much in S&T as the major countries in Western Europe and Japan, combined. Of course, no level of investment seems sufficient to the scientific community. Sufficiency cannot be achieved, in the scientists' strategy, because of the power of its image of endless frontiers; there is always more research to do and there always will be. Diminishing returns on investments in science never appear, and, therefore, more dollars are always highly productive relative to the information to be gained. The only true limitation occurs when all scientists who want to do research and can do it are employed doing it and when all who have the desire and talent have been given the opportunity to do so. But it is the government's responsibility to remove even this limit by discovering and nurturing talent in the population.

From the perspective of the scientists' strategy, society short-changes itself by not providing the resources required to maximize the flow of scientific and technical information. If overall political and economic considerations make such a level of resources impossible, then society should provide, at a minimum, some real growth every year. This would be not only effective but also efficient. Stable expectations would permit researchers to plan their work more carefully and to avoid the costs of starting and stopping work (Staats and Carey 1973).

For most of the period discussed, decisionmakers have defined the budgetary environment for S&T as unprosperous, but they have not lost the hearts and minds of the science and technology community. Decisionmakers have maintained the implied contract made almost forty years ago. As long as that contract is maintained, budgetary levels are serious matters, but secondary ones. A procedure for presenting arguments has been developed. Decisionmakers can be lobbied each year to provide more resources; if they do not, there is always next year. Of course, when next year comes around, the same arguments that were not decisive the previous year may be presented again. But an opportunity exists, since decisionmakers change and their own budgetary logic is not credible. Everyone, including the decisionmakers, knows that the science and technology enterprise is "messy." Many inputs are not measurable, outputs come into existence years after inputs, and the production technology is partly unknown. The decisionmakers do not and cannot know exactly what they are purchasing.

A posture of stinginess may not be satisfactory in the face of these conditions. Very prolonged periods of austerity will begin to encroach upon the "contract." Then priorities would have to be set concerning intrinsic scientific payoff or extrinsic practical payoff, but no algorithm exists that will make persuasive trade-offs between different areas of science and technology. Given the scientists' credo that results are unpredictable, any such algorithm appears arbitrary, and decisionmakers know that it is arbitrary.

The public policy question is whether it is prudent to force the enterprise to make such trade-offs. If the enterprise is made efficient in the short run, important options may be excluded in the long run. The looseness in everyone's strategy concerning optimal or satisfactory resource levels means that there is tolerance for activity that could not now pass any kind of efficiency test. The looseness permits some hedging and insurance about what will pay off in the future.

The toleration of looseness in budgetary decisions means that we accept some special functions for the research enterprise that we cannot accept for, say, the health enterprise. The view is that the S&T enterprise is a provider of options, an enlarger of the social decision space. It permits new kinds of social and economic combinations and permutations. Short-run efficiency may imply long-run ineffectiveness; we may throw away long-run options, but we will not know we have thrown them away.

If this view is correct, there is policy virtue in decisionmakers taking a stand for efficiency and austerity, forcing the scientific community into continuous examination of information gain relative to cost. But there is also some virtue in forebearance, in not forcing the enterprise into complete short-run efficiency. The best analysis of efficiency that can be done today may be wrong. We are dealing with a system whose parts are interconnected, and we want the interconnections to change all the time. It is unlikely that efficiency at any particular moment will correspond to efficiency or effectiveness over time. If all we wanted was efficiency at one point in time, the resources currently devoted to R&D could probably be reduced. Given a messy system that is only partially understood, the needs to hedge, to buy insurance, and to permit changes in "connectivity" argue for a doctrine of "sufficiency."

There is no point estimate for sufficiency; rather, we have to be reasonably confident we are operating within the sufficient range. As long as we are within that range, we will probably not be able to observe any significant difference in the functioning of the enterprise, despite cries of pain from the scientific and technical community. Given the inherent and irreducible uncertainties about how the enterprise works, the best that decisionmakers can do will be to use multiple indicators. Compared to current practice, there should certainly be a harder look at information actually produced and, perhaps, less emphasis on the resources necessary to produce that information. It is doubtful that diminishing marginal returns do not exist somewhere in the enterprise. If the criterion is maintaining the connectivity of the system and the density of pathways, then, over time, some paths will become worn down and rutted, and new ones will need to be built. In making estimates of the sufficiency of resources and the effectiveness of their allocation, we can and should use jointly the classical indicators already mentioned: relative efforts, compared with those of other nations; relative investments, compared with other economic sectors; costs. We can probably make the indicators of social return more precise. If these indicators all point in the same direction when used together, we will have a rational case for adjustment.

While political pressures from the scientific community are self-serving – no one ever advocates less than he has – the substance of the case for more resources should be treated seriously. Debates about resources for science and technology have a stylized, rhetorical quality. The history of these debates shows continuous proclamations of crises by the scientific and technical community, many of which never materialized or for which the system was resilient. The budgetary language of decisionmakers, however, is too limited in scope and criteria. We need to talk much more about informational insurance and its costs, resilience and its costs, and density of information and its costs.

I have begun to describe languages, concepts, and procedures for bringing different strategies or policy models into contact. Strong adherents of traditional strategies will not be converted by such contact. But it can help to identify critical propositions and beliefs and, consequently, it should be possible to design some crude tests of their validity. In the highly stylized strategies for resource acquisition, that would be an improvement.

Appendix
Notes on the Economics of Research and Development
In this appendix I have tried to give the reader having only limited technical familiarity with economics some feeling for the ways economists think about R&D, economic growth, and productivity increase. I have not attempted to provide a comprehensive analytic survey of these areas and the associated technical and policy issues, since such surveys are available in NSF publications (NSF 1971, 1977a) and in various economics journals, for example, Griliches (1981). Readers who are generally interested in what happened to U.S. productivity during the 1970s and to its historical relationships with technological advance and R&D will find an extensive and capable nontechnical discussion in Denison (1979).

Conventional Theory
From the perspective of economics, the social performance of the market for R&D should be judged the way all other markets are judged. Markets should be efficient. This means they should provide sufficient quantities of goods and services so that the social benefits from having them are as great as they can be (without reducing benefits elsewhere),

and this is to be done at the least possible social cost. Markets can fail to be efficient for a number of different reasons. Monopolies and "externalities" are common textbook examples. Monopolies produce too little at usually too high a price, one probably well above the minimum that average production technology permits. Externalities exist when society incurs costs of production not included, for some institutional or technological reason, in the profit-maximizing calculations and decisions of private producers. Similarly, they exist when the total social benefits from production cannot be reflected in the private calculations of buyers and sellers. When private costs are less than social costs or private benefits are less than social ones, markets will not do the jobs they are supposed to do.

Markets may also fail, because some goods and services are hard to produce in a market environment. In some cases, the so-called exclusion principle does not apply. It is infeasible or too costly to bar the acquisition of goods and services by those who refuse to pay for them. Unless exclusion is possible, there will be little or no production, since firms cannot incur costs for long and be unable to recover them. Some goods and services also exist which provide benefits to consumers and producers but are not used up in consumption. The same goods and services provide benefits for any and all consumers and producers; in other words, there is a condition of supply undepletability. From a social perspective, once goods and services characterized by supply undepletability have come into existence, they should be provided to everyone who can benefit from them. Doing so involves no additional social costs, but there are incremental benefits.

Given goods and services characterized by nonexclusion and supply undepletability, it follows that private outputs will be too small. Consequently, the production of goods with such characteristics frequently involves government support, subsidies, regulations, or targeted incentives. When nonexclusivity and supply undepletability are both strong characteristics of goods and services, the government itself may have to supply them, employing its taxing powers to force citizens to pay for them. In other words, when society cannot easily find ways to provide important goods and services via the market, they will be supplied by government or other nonmarket institutions.

Information is a commodity that is frequently nonexclusive, undepletable, or both. New information, that is, information gained from R&D, has both characteristics. It is hard to stop individuals from using research information without paying for using it, and its use by one consumer does not diminish the quantity available for others to use. It follows that the production of information by the private sector will be too low. Since innovation depends on a continuing flow of new information, outputs of information that are too low will eventually translate into lower rates of innovation, and lower rates of innovation translate into slower economic growth and losses of comparative advantage. Recognizing this, the government provides partial exclusivity — patents — on new information in exchange for public disclosure. Patent policy tries to mediate the conflict between the exclusivity needed to induce private actors to produce new information and the social benefits of having no protection for information that already exists.

Basic research is said to lie in that part of the R&D spectrum most touched by nonexclusion and supply undepletability. A reasonably strong case has been constructed that there are divergences between social benefits and private benefits, although most of the technical economic analysis of R&D has not been able to disaggregate the effects of basic research from those of applied R&D and the later stages of innovation. Economists believe that social rates of return have been greater than private rates in the past, and there is reason to believe that this condition will continue into the future. If the rates estimated by private firms are low, then the levels of basic research undertaken by the market will be too low. In fact, since the basic research "product" is highly unpredictable in its arrival time and uncertain in its attributes, it seems dubious that markets can be easily formed which will equilibrate the amount of basic research currently "demanded" and the amount that will be supplied sometime in the future. This is why the main sponsor of basic research is the federal government — it sponsored an estimated 67 percent in 1983 (NSB 1983). And this is why universities, not private firms, are the main performers of basic research, defined in the strict sense as inquiry without a strongly prespecified applied objective. Efficient and effective conduct of science requires that nonexclusion hold for all interested researchers. More research does not deplete the stock of validated scientific information but enriches it. Consequently, nonmarket, nonprofit institutions like universities and "invisible colleges" are the main producers of basic research.

This logic of market functions and failures leads directly to the S&T policies preferred in the market strategy described in Chapter 3. Government should support basic research and, perhaps, also conduct limited amounts of it, because the economy underinvests in it. However, as basic research information leads on to applied research information and then on to development and demonstration and finally to innovation, the exclusion principle becomes easier to apply and supply undepletability becomes less prominent. It follows that government ought to be far less active in the D part of the R&D spectrum than in the R part, subject, of course, to government's need to have information for its own legitimate purposes.

Recent Modifications

The modern approach to the economics of R&D recognizes that under-investment is certainly one possible outcome, for the reasons discussed above. However, other outcomes are also possible. For example, as firms release information by "congealing" it in new products or processes, rival firms may rush to acquire similar information in order to maintain their competitive position. The social value of a "rush to invent" is low, since the information has already been incorporated in products or processes. Firms that are rivals may have no choice, however, but to engage in "defensive" R&D to maintain profits or market share. Since the firm's funds allocated for R&D are limited, a "rush to invent" around rivals' products leaves other important areas without sufficient funds. The upshot can be too much investment in some kinds of R&D and too little in other kinds (Hirschleifer and Riley 1979).

Because of its additional contingencies and complexities, the new economics of R&D makes public policy more difficult. Patents, for example, provide incentives for invention, but they are also signals of information "lodes" that others may rush to mine, even though society gains little from the mining. In fact, social benefits may decline, because the total variation in R&D activity may fall. For the same level of resources, leads that could have been pursued will not be pursued, because firms have to concentrate on defending their existing markets with all the instruments available to them, including R&D. However, concentration on existing markets may make rivals more vulnerable to unexpected breakthroughs. This implies that maintaining some variety in R&D is important.

Given a wider range of possible outcomes, it follows that S&T decisionmakers need more disaggregated economic and technical information than they currently have and need to have more policy instruments available than they do now. In general, they would have to operate with more technical and political sophistication; however, all bureaucracies have difficulty implementing sophisticated strategies. R&D bureaucracies have special difficulty, because their history, policies, procedures, and incentives are all geared to increasing the level of resources for everyone over time without worrying about whether increased resources are warranted for every sector or might even do damage to some of them. (The term *bureaucracy* is not used pejoratively but to describe well-known behaviors in public organizations.)

Empirical Results

Economists have used three different methods of investigating the effects of R&D on growth and productivity: (1) growth accounting (Denison 1962), (2) statistical estimation of aggregate production functions (Solow 1957), and (3) calculations of social and private returns to investments in research (Griliches 1958). The first two are macroeconomic. Their purpose is explanation of aggregate growth rates, increases of labor, or total factor productivity in the economy as a whole. The purpose of the third one is estimation of social and private rates of return to particular innovations to see if investments in R&D pay off to society and the firms that undertake them. In general, each method taken individually has shown that R&D is strongly and positively connected to the dependent variables that are of economic and policy interest.

From a forward-looking policy perspective, decisionmakers need marginal social benefits compared to marginal social costs, or marginal social rates of return on R&D compared to marginal returns on alternative investments. Decisionmakers have to know whether incremental investments flowing — directly or indirectly — from their actions or policies will generate sufficient incremental benefits. It is frequently very difficult for economists to deliver the necessary marginal computations, but the consistency of outcomes across all three methods considered jointly gives economists reasonable confidence that the causal statements they make about R&D are warranted. The very large contributions of R&D to macroeconomic growth and productivity and the exceedingly large differences between the social and private returns of past innovations suggest that R&D is a very good social investment, relative to other social investments. To show the reverse, errors in estimates and calculations would have to be so large as to be incredible.

Growth Accounting

The growth accounting framework, highly stylized, is as follows. For a selected time interval, one tries to explain changes in the growth of aggregate real output, real output per capita, or productivity (real output per man-hour) by examining changes in the growth rates of all the many different factors of production that determine these things. Chief among these, of course, are capital and labor of different quantity and quality. Suppose, for example, we list all the factors that we think make significant contributions to growth in real output. As a rough and ready approximation, suppose we assume that the aggregate production function can be characterized as a Cobb-Douglas type (inputs enter in a multiplicative manner; there are constant returns to scale; there are diminishing marginal returns to increased factor inputs; and average products are equal to marginal products). Suppose also that technological change enters the production function autonomously, depending on a stream of discoveries determined inside the research enterprise. In other words, technological advance shifts the entire production function outward. Then we can write:

$$\frac{\Delta Y}{Y} = \frac{\Delta A}{A} + \sum_i AP_i \frac{\Delta F_i}{F_i} \qquad (2A.1)$$

where $\Delta Y/Y$ is the growth rate of real output, $\Delta A/A$ is the rate of technological change and other nonfactor inputs that increase productivity, AP_i is the known average product of the ith factor, and $\Delta F_i/F_i$ is the growth rate of the ith factor over the relevant time interval. Then, if a factor grows by 1 percent, its incremental contribution to growth is AP_i percent. By making estimates of factor growth rates for different time intervals and subintervals and comparing them, we can determine those factors that are contributing more and those that are contributing less. Should the quantity or quality of these factors be susceptible to available policy instruments, directly or indirectly, then one can make recommendations for policies or actions that would bring about boosts in factor quantity or quality and, consequently, increase the rate of growth of real output.

Advances in knowledge (ΔA), of course, are one input; however, we do not observe them directly. We observe the rate of growth in real output and the growth rates of inputs. If the rate of growth in real output cannot be fully traced back to growth in inputs, then technological change and other implicit variables ($\Delta A/A$) must account for the rest of the contributions to the growth rate in output. In other words, the growth accounting framework treats advances in knowledge as a residual. After accounting for everything else that is economically credible in influencing growth, if the rate of growth has not been fully determined, then there must be a hidden contribution from advances in knowledge and improvements in daily know-how.

In his earliest work on growth accounting for the United States, Denison estimated that, between 1929 and 1957, technological change contributed 0.59 percentage points to an overall growth rate of 2.93 percent and was 20 percent of the total contribution of all inputs (Denison 1962, 230). For the period 1950–62, Denison estimated the contribution of increased knowledge as 0.76 percentage points and 23 percent of the growth rate of real output (Denison 1967). In work done just before the beginning of the 1980s, Denison found that a slowdown in R&D investments could not be regarded as a significant factor in retarding U.S. productivity growth, because the slowdown was not all that great. Even so, he argues that, on the basis of the rate-of-return literature, greater R&D now would promote further productivity growth (Denison 1979).

Statistical Estimation of Production Functions

The statistical estimation method, like the growth accounting method, assumes that the economy's total output can be represented by an aggregate production function that is analytically and statistically tractable.

It is usually defined as Cobb-Douglas in type or as one of the later generalizations of Cobb-Douglas. Given such a specification, the production function can then be estimated, using standard econometric methods. The advantage of statistical estimation over growth accounting is that the former provides formal confidence intervals for the effects of different inputs. One is not so dependent on the ad hoc adjustments frequently injected into growth accounting, because the economist holds additional relevant knowledge of micro or macro relationships that lie outside the framework.

The earliest statistical estimates showed that growth in the factors of production by themselves could not fully explain the historical growth in output or productivity. In each case, there was a large, unexplained statistical residual. Increase in knowledge, that is, technological advance, is certainly one reasonable explanation for these residuals. For example, Solow attributed 87 percent of the increases in U.S. labor productivity to things other than increases in capital and labor (Solow 1957). Such a startling result implied that technological change was a far more important cause of growth than were increases in capital and labor inputs.

Residual variance in a regression equation is clearly explained by all variables not included in the original specification. Technological change was a leading candidate as a cause of growth, but so were other things, for example, unaccounted improvements in the quality of capital and labor. If the quality of labor and capital increased over time, the effective amounts of these factors were greater than the reported amounts used in regression estimates. Thus, the contributions of the traditional factors of production were being understated. Faced with such possibilities, the natural inclination of economists was to work to reduce the size of the statistical residual by improving their estimates of the effective amounts of inputs, by disaggregating inputs, and by using more sophisticated estimating techniques. After all this had been accomplished, technological change still seemed to account for about 20 to 40 percent of total growth in output or productivity. For policy purposes, an estimate of 30 percent appears reasonable and would not draw the fire of too many economists.

Rate of Return Methods
The third method estimates the social benefits and costs of particular innovations and compares them with private benefits and costs. The purpose of such comparisons is to see when and how innovations pay off socially, and, using such information, to provide guidance on policy to achieve satisfactory rates of future innovation. The measure of social benefit is what people, collectively, are willing to pay for goods and ser-

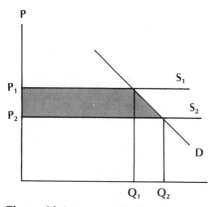

Figure 2A.1. Demand for X and consumers' surplus.

vices, compared with what they actually pay — the so-called consumers' surplus, the area under a demand curve above the going price.

Economists approximate the amount of consumers' surplus by estimating demand curves statistically. Alternatively, they may have some notion of changes in prices and changes in quantities after, say, a cost reduction due to some technological innovation. Then, if they have some estimate of demand elasticity, they can deliver an approximation of consumers' surplus. As long as they have some estimate of demand elasticity, economists can make rough estimates of the surplus without knowing the demand curve in great detail.

To take a highly stylized example, suppose that the supply curve for some commodity X is flat (constant returns to scale), and suppose that some innovation reduces the costs of production, shifting the supply curve downward. Then the innovation's marginal contribution to social welfare is the shaded area in figure 2A.1.

The total benefit is made up of the welfare gain from buying the old quantity at a lower price plus the gain from buying the additional quantities that have become possible. Geometrically, this is the sum of the areas of the shaded rectangle $[(P_1 - P_2)Q_1]$ and the shaded triangle $[\frac{1}{2}(P_2 - P_1)(Q_2 - Q_1)]$. Given a known elasticity of the demand curve, the entire welfare gain can be approximated by:

$$\Delta CS = kP_2Q_2(1 - \tfrac{1}{2}ke) \qquad (2A.2)$$

where k is the percentage change in cost and e is the absolute value of the elasticity of demand.

Given such a stream of benefits over time, the total amounts of social and private investment in realizing the innovation, and a discount rate, one can then compute the expected social rate of return on the investment and compare it with the known private returns. One can also make comparisons to other social investments and rank order the alternatives. The social rates of return to innovation that economists report have been so high that they dominate other forms of investment.

Private returns to prospective innovation, however, can be too low. If so, some policy intervention may be necessary (Mansfield et al. 1977). Of course, not all innovations with low private returns and high social ones will receive public policy treatment. Only those defined as socially important will receive such treatment; otherwise, government would continually be intervening in private markets. At most, differentials between social and private returns provide a necessary condition for intervention. Decisionmakers and policy analysts have to go on from there to see if intervention would be feasible and effective.

Although there are complex theoretical difficulties connected with the use of consumers' surplus and empirical ones in estimating demand curves or elasticities, one needs only rough guidance in making public policy — a correct direction, not an exact distance. The rate-of-return literature consistently shows that the social returns from R&D are very high, relative to private ones. Errors in estimation would have to be very large, indeed, to overturn such results. So economists feel reasonably confident that the results from the rate-of-return literature are robust and that investments in R&D are a good thing, at least up to the point where their returns fall toward those from other public and private investments.

The Search for Innovation Policy

3

Over a century ago Alexis de Tocqueville noticed the strong taste for novelty, change, and innovation in the United States. He observed that Americans linked the new with solutions to problems and did not hesitate to foresake old methods for new ones as long as the new ones promised a payoff (Tocqueville [1835] 1945, 1:443). New methods and products, in American belief, led to economic growth and development. Given this belief, the economic history of the United States can be interpreted as one of adaptation to technological, organizational, and managerial innovation. That history seems to show that, without many explicit policies for innovation, the U.S. economy generated a reasonable supply of them (Rosenberg 1972). Public policy for technological innovation could be identical to macroeconomic policies that encouraged investment and microeconomic policies that permitted innovators to reap reasonable, if not maximal, benefits from their investments. In the past, aside from patent laws, no special programs or targeted policies seemed necessary to induce innovation. The market for scientific and technical information seemed to work well enough, translating discoveries into goods and services. Among all the technologies that science made available, market processes appeared to select those that were economic or cost-effective; that is, there was demand for them and profits could be earned from supplying that demand.

The framers of the post–World War II "contract" between the federal government and the scientific and technical community felt little concern about an innovation problem. No direct government programs in support of industrial research were advanced by Bush in *Science: The Endless Frontier*; if the government supported basic research and science education, then industry would help itself (Bush [1945] 1980, 21). The 1947 report of the President's Scientific Research Board argued similarly that, if there were adequate basic research funding, U.S. technological leadership could be maintained. All that the United States needed was an industrial organization capable of doing and appreciating basic and applied research (PSRB 1947, 1:4). President Eisenhower's Science Advisory Committee reiterated the same view throughout the 1950s. The market worked well enough for ordinary capital investments that embodied known technologies, but the serious problem was finding new technologies that could be embodied in future capital stock (PSAC 1960, 2).

In the early 1960s, some decisionmakers saw industrial innovation as a way to attack national needs and get a sluggish economy moving. To the Kennedy administration, an unaided market did not deliver enough socially important goods and services at low enough prices, and some industries appeared to be making incorrect or improper judgments about innovations that would boost their own productivity or lower their own costs. For example, the administration defined adequate shelter for all at affordable prices as a national need. There appeared to be sufficient applicable technology to reduce construction costs. If the housing industry remained backward in its choice of construction methods, the defined national need could not be met by pure market processes or, if they could, it would take too long. If so, then it seemed appropriate that the federal government step in through S&T programs. Given the longstanding American faith in the effectiveness of technology for ameliorating problems, it was natural for a liberal administration to believe that many social and economic problems could be solved by bringing science and technology to bear.

In the 1970s and 1980s, slow growth, inflation, energy shocks, and declining productivity practically insured a look at greater innovation as a possible cure (Rothwell and Zegfeld 1981). Successive administrations tried to design federal programs to induce more innovation. Some decisionmakers believed that, if flows of scientific and technical information could be enlarged and universities and industry could be more closely coupled, then a greater volume and a more rapid rate of innovation would result; others emphasized the regulatory barriers the government itself had erected. In particular, many decisionmakers, economists, and scientists believed environmental, health, and safety regulations had skewed R&D away from new products and processes and toward "defensive R&D." While increased innovation was neither necessary nor sufficient by itself to cure major economic ills, more innovation would certainly not hurt the economy, although, as always, it might hurt parts of the economy.

Policies and programs to induce increased innovation immediately raise questions about economic and social policy. Compared with discussions about funding levels for research, decisionmakers, stakeholders, and the public are all involved. The variation in preferences and prescriptions for obtaining more innovation is naturally large, and the purposes of innovation, as well as the proposed policies for obtaining it, become an issue. Depending on the stakeholders, policy proposals can range from fostering a more favorable economic climate, reducing social and economic regulation, providing subsidies for industrial R&D, increasing the connectivity between the research enterprise and the industrial enterprise, and federal "lubricating" of R&D markets through information and awareness programs. The case for any of these, or some combination of them, depends primarily on judgments concerning (1) the purpose of innovation and (2) the appropriate role of the federal government in economic affairs.

Given the U.S. preference for a market economy, no persuasive general logic has been advanced for large-scale government intervention in the innovation process. The logic of economic choice via markets implies that any such interventions should be restricted to special cases, for example, in the provision of public goods, in some markets that are failing, or in situations in which the government itself is the major customer. But policies that apply only to special cases are difficult to accept if one sees disaster looming ahead from a chronic, pervasive, or systemic innovation problem. There are, of course, different definitions of disaster. Some decisionmakers, analysts, and actors see technological innovation as determining the place of the United States in the world and argue that its international political leadership depends on continuing technological leadership. Others are concerned about a poor quality of life and failing democratic politics; they argue that substitution of "appropriate" technologies for current ones would lead to an improved quality of life. Still others believe that technology is out of control and that gaining control requires large-scale institutional change. If one believes such things, arguments about federal provision of public goods or the treatment of market failures seem irrelevant, obscure, and obstructive.

In this chapter I will examine four strategies for technological change and innovation. I call them, respectively, the engineering, the market, the public interest, and the transformational strategies. The first has its roots in the existence of perceived social and economic problems that need solution. If they are not solved, national distress, it is predicted, will follow. Such problems are sufficient for direct government action; a higher innovation rate will, at a minimum, alleviate these problems, and it is up to the government to induce a higher rate of innovation.

The second strategy has its roots in perceived or actual market failure; the preferred policy is to make markets and private incentives achieve social purposes. Only if markets cannot ever be made to work better does justification exist for some direct government programs. But not all market failures deserve special policy treatment; such treatment is appropriate, if, and only if, there is something socially, politically, or economically important about the market claimed to be failing. Market strategists spend much of their time making such distinctions. For whenever government assistance or programs are at issue, there is an increase in the number of markets claimed to be failing and also to have social significance. Market strategists are short of powerful real-world tests for market failure.

The foundation of the public interest strategy is ethically correct social action. It is the central government's responsibility to foster correct or good types of innovation — those that benefit the public as a whole. But the government cannot identify good types of innovation; its perceptions are clouded. Special interest groups monopolize information and communication channels, and this monopoly prevents appropriate social evaluation of prospective technological innovations. By opening communication channels to groups who nominally represent the public interest or, at least, who represent views at variance with those of the special interests, decisionmakers will be able to choose and regulate technologies more wisely. Proper procedural safeguards in choosing technologies will insure good innovations and "appropriate" technologies.

The transformational strategy portrays technology as a large-scale, autonomous, and irresistible force. As innovation occurs, it imposes inappropriate life styles on individuals and creates unsatisfying conditions of work. In this strategy, everyday, incremental public policy instruments are irrelevant and ineffective. Incremental policies delude us because truly effective policy requires large-scale social change, not the incremental changes we are usually prepared to make and can make without too much political and social cost. Furthermore, government policy is itself both a product and a prisoner of the "technological order"; the government promotes it. The true job is the design and selection of technologies that will lead to a more humane society, despite the implicit or explicit opposition of government and bureaucracy. To the extent that adherents of this strategy are at all interested in public policy, they advise work on those systems designed to foster higher social values. For example, by making education more humane, some partisans of the transformational strategy hold that society can be made more humane.

In the United States, innovation programs and policies have been debated mainly between adherents of the engineering and market strategies. The public interest strategy, developed in the 1960s and the 1970s, has its conceptual roots in the environmental and consumers' movements. It is still relatively weak in the innovation domain, but it is strong in areas believed to limit the rate and type of innovation, in particular, environmental, health, and safety regulations. The transformational strategy, lacking any pragmatic, "marginal" recommendations, has had and can have little direct policy influence, but it does possess strong intellectual influence. It provides one endpoint in the spectrum of thought about technology and innovation. More than any other strategy, its claims about the impact of technology imply larger questions about the economic and social purposes of innovation.

Statement of the Strategies

Following the practice in Chapter 2, I will state the four strategies in propositional form. Propositions associated with particular strategies are again labeled and numbered. I have made an attempt to be comprehensive in these statements by showing what is logically entailed if one subscribes to one strategy or another. For example, if one believes strongly in direct government action to select and promote new technologies, one implicitly believes that government decisionmakers can know more than private decisionmakers and that they act differently. If government decisionmakers were expected to make choices similar to those resulting from market interactions, there would be little need for them. Although such belief in the superior knowledge of government agents is logically required to make an engineering strategy consistent and complete, a formal statement of it would not ordinarily appear during public advocacy.

The Engineering Strategy

E.1 *Innovation is an inherently desirable activity, since it solves or alleviates major social and economic problems.*

E.2 *The federal government is the prime agent for addressing major social and economic problems. Consequently, a federal interest exists in assuring a proper level and direction for innovation.*

E.3 *Increased application of S&T is a necessary condition for increased innovation.*

E.4 *The government must play an active role in promoting civilian technology.*

    E4.1 *Assessments of advanced technologies by the market will be incorrect, because the market lacks information and contains permanent institutional barriers that prevent correct assessments.*

    E4.2 *Since R&D delivers feasible new technologies continuously, the market is always making incorrect assessments, and the government's role should be continuous.*

E4.3 *Unless the government plays an active role over time in promoting S&T, U.S. economic and technological competitiveness will decline, if only because other governments do take
active roles and are effective at promoting innovation in
their industries.*

E.5 *The federal government is able to identify the right kind of science
and technology because:*

E5.1 *Federal agencies have access to greater information about
the present and future consequences of new technology
than do private actors.*

E5.2 *Federal agencies can make broader assessments of opportunities and take a longer run perspective than can private
actors.*

E5.3 *Federal agencies often develop advanced technologies that
are viable in the marketplace or that can be made viable.*

E.6 *Direct action by the federal government is superior to indirect
action.*

E6.1 *The government has control of its own activities and can
design effective programs.*

E6.2 *Indirect actions are less likely to be effective or controllable.*

E6.3 *The benefits of direct government action exceed their costs,
and any negative effects can be limited.*

E.7 *Policy preference: The federal government should design and
operate programs for the support of technological innovation.*

Historically, administrations of quite different political persuasion
begin their civilian technology policy with the "can do" engineering
perspective, sometimes called *technology push*. They discover,
however, that proposed program costs are too high, predicted effectiveness is too low, and political opposition is too great. They then shift
to a market strategy, sometimes called *market pull*.

The Market Strategy
M.1 *The market should always serve as the principal means of delivering goods and services.*

M1.1 *Market incentives and the price system produce "correct"
selections among current and future technological possibil-*

ities, when correct is defined relative to available resources and effective social demand.

M.2 *Markets will fail to assess technological possibilities correctly when, and only when, externalities, economies of scale, and very high risks and costs exist.*

M.3 *Failing markets can be restructured to achieve greater rates of innovation through incentives and disincentives offered to private actors.*

M.4 *R&D is a necessary condition for technological change and innovation.*

> **M4.1** *Society underinvests in R&D, since the market for R&D is simultaneously affected by imperfections, externalities, and high risks and costs.*

> **M4.2** *Government programs should be limited primarily to support of basic research because its production provides the clearest case of a market failure that is hard to correct.*

M.5 *Direct government activity in development, demonstration, and marketing should be highly limited.*

> **M5.1** *Social benefits of basic research exceed private benefits, but they narrow in later stages of innovation.*

> **M5.2** *Bureaucracies cannot make decisions about development, commercialization, or diffusion of new technologies which are superior to those made in the market. In all likelihood, bureaucratic decisions about civilian technology will be inferior or less efficient than those made by the market.*

M.6 *The federal government's own policies, programs, and regulations are major barriers to innovation.*

M.7 *Policy preference: The proper federal role in civilian technology must be primarily one of providing the private sector with information and incentives and/or reducing negative federal regulations. Regulation that enhances market incentives should be improved; negative regulation (i.e., health, safety, environment) should be reduced.*

In recent administrations, the engineering perspective has been represented by the OST, PSAC, and the Commerce Department. The market perspective in each administration has been represented by the OMB, which finds it convenient to invoke the market strategy in carrying out its major function — controlling agency expenditures. OMB is, of course, mainly staffed by economists, who by training prefer markets as the first solution to all problems. Although innovation policy impacts economic growth and productivity, the chief economic advisers in most administrations have not been consistently interested in innovation. Civilian technology policy is essentially microeconomic in character, although its effects eventually show up in the economy's aggregate supply of goods and services. The Council of Economic Advisers and the Treasury Department do not have a strong mandate to deal with microeconomic issues.

Advocates of the engineering and market strategies have not usually confronted each other a priori. The engineering advocates usually propose large government programs that are eventually vetoed by market advocates on grounds of appropriateness, efficiency, and cost. The set of low-cost, appropriate programs that satisfies the interests of both engineering and market advocates usually turns out to be federally funded information and awareness activity. Thus, the innovation programs actually pursued in different administrations are highly similar, although their design involves very different strategies and rhetoric.

The Public Interest Strategy
The public interest strategy has thus far had less direct programmatic impact in the innovation area than have the engineering and market strategies. Adherents of this strategy believe that procedural reform is necessary for good, substantive programs and that correct substance flows from more open, democratic, and participatory decisionmaking in the selection of technological alternatives. In this regard, the public interest strategy corresponds to the strategy of "competent communication" urged by some European thinkers. Social and political consensus can be reached through open, fair, and uncoercive public dialogue (McCarthy 1978, 272-357).

The preferred policy of this strategy is assured public participation and feedback in all government decisions that have significant technological content. Advocates further favor analytic techniques that incorporate public participation and address the interests of all parties to a technological decision. Thus, the technology assessment, risk assessment, and appropriate technology movements all owe a good deal to this model. Propositions for this strategy are:

PI.1 *Innovation left to market forces is indifferent to human values and does great social harm.*

PI.2 *Government actions to promote innovation should only be carried out to advance social objectives and avoid social damage.*

   PI2.1 *Any and all technologies supported with federal resources should be appropriate, relative to social objectives.*

   PI2.2 *Federal resources for technology should be directed to socially meritorious classes of industry, for example, small business.*

   PI2.3 *Government regulation, when properly designed and enforced, can promote socially desirable innovation.*

PI.3 *If parties currently excluded from technological decisions were included, then government would have wider information about consequences, and its decisions about technological development and deployment would improve.*

PI.4 *Substantive conflict declines with wider, deeper, and more accurate information, because stakeholders and the government will be forced to listen to each other and to adjust their views.*

   PI4.1 *Substantive policies can be designed to reflect mutual adjustments.*

PI.5 *Improved decision processes would necessarily show that support for small-scale, decentralized, and simple technologies would be cost-effective.*

PI.6 *Policy preference: The government should (1) assist excluded parties in participating in technological decisionmaking, (2) select decisionmaking procedures that guarantee extensive public participation and input, and (3) assist in developing newly revealed appropriate technologies.*

When the public interest strategy first appeared in the 1960s and 1970s, its view of technology was that it was a powerful force, but controllable by informed, activist citizens using newly opened communication channels. These citizens believed that reform of the economic and political system was necessary but that it could be accomplished by marginal changes in the design of U.S. institutions (Henderson 1978). From the public interest perspective, both the engineering and market strategies mislead us about the true nature of technology. The latter two strategies make a case for modifying, adjusting, or compensating for private calculations of gain and loss within a static market framework.

In the public interest strategy, however, technology is dynamic in its effects; it does not involve small trade-offs, but major social and economic changes. It alters market structures and changes connections between markets. It has powerful second- and third-order consequences that are not now considered in public and private calculations. For example, new industrial and agricultural technologies are frequently harmful because they do not take account of spillover on the environment or other social systems (Commoner 1971, 193). Without special attention to spillover, new technology will damage other things that are valued as highly or more highly than new products and processes.

Given the lack of systems perspective inherent in market systems, producers supply technologies that are inappropriate and consumers buy them, directly or indirectly. The appropriate ones are "soft," humane, small-scale, energy conserving, and environment preserving. The misdirection of technology can be cured by wider and more objective political and economic input (Ames 1978; Henderson 1978). Given wider participation and more and better information, public choices will improve and appropriate technologies will come to be socially preferred. More and better information does not result in more conflict because stakeholders, for a change, are forced to listen to each other and stand willing to adjust their views on obtaining wider and more accurate information. Substantive outcomes will reflect spillover and will thus be better.

Representatives of the public interest should be guaranteed access to the decision process and should be given the resources to participate seriously. Special interests, of course, have all the access and resources they need, contributing to the bias against appropriate technology. Furthermore, the government can and should obtain "objective" information about pending technological decisions, including impacts on existing and prospective stakeholders. This can be done by grafting analytic as well as communication procedures onto the decision process. For example, adherents of the public interest strategy believe technology assessment and risk assessment procedures can reveal relevant benefits and costs, public and private, and that such analysis has the power to distinguish between better and worse alternatives.

Given modifications and additions to the decisionmaking process, "softer" technologies will be chosen, and proper regulation of necessary but socially harmful technology will, in fact, take place. The will and competence of the government will be revitalized through better information and more intense interaction with those served by the government. Information strengthens resistance to special interest pleadings and increases sensitivity to the public interest. Like the engineering and market strategies, the public interest strategy contends that we can make new technology and innovation congruent with properly chosen social objectives, using marginalist measures.

The Transformational Strategy

In contrast with the three strategies already discussed, the transformational strategy has no formal policy program. According to this strategy, all traditional and incremental combinations of government programs and market exchanges are ineffective in choosing correctly among prospective technologies. Government is the captive of autonomous forces and conditions imposed by technology. Before one can come to any credible program, one has to be aware of the nature and impact of technology. There is a need for better strategic intelligence on the interactions between technology and society. Because technology is autonomous and systemic and imposes its own logic on political and economic behavior, policy prescription is less for the state than for the individual, although transforming certain systems like education may hold promise. The public policy problem, if this strategy can be said to have one, is to induce large-scale institutional change and much greater self-awareness so that one can cope with technology. The major propositions in this strategy are:

TR.1 *Technology is an exogenous, powerful force shaping industrial choice, institutional behavior, and personal life styles.*

TR.2 *Technological innovation, as evidenced in history, has imposed undesirable patterns of behavior on individuals and societies, and there is no evidence that these patterns can be altered in the future.*

TR.3 *Technology is not subject to control or direction by the policy instruments traditionally available to democratic governments.*

　TR3.1 *Governments are agents and servants of the current technological order.*

TR.4 *Policy preference: Society should develop new forms of social organization and individual behavior to counter the harmful impact of technology and to gain control of it.*

From the perspective of the transformational strategy, the programs of all three of the "marginalist" strategies are flawed. Basically, none of them recognizes that gaining control over technological choice implies systemic change and not marginal fixes. The technological order shapes the design of all other major social and economic systems – including the central government – so we cannot employ public policy in the conventional sense to regulate and direct technological development. Bureaucrats and politicians will inevitably design marginalist policies that will be ineffective at best and harmful at worst, for marginalist policy is too limited; it operates within the constraints technology has imposed. To gain control, large-scale reform is needed, and such reform cannot occur with marginalist measures.

Reform means living a different kind of personal life and operating the economy in a more decentralized way with smaller-scale, but highly economic technologies (Winner 1977). The program of reform, however, is not entirely clear or operational. Private rebellions, even on a larger scale – eating organic foods, pursuing crafts, living in communes or kibbutzim, do not clearly imply systemic political change or increased control. To the extent we retain an interest in public resource allocation, we can try to apply some rules that would deliver the required technologies. For example, we could try to allocate public resources to those technologies that (1) are intellectually accessible as well as physically available to users, (2) are flexible and changeable, and (3) make us less dependent on the large-scale systems now employed (Winner 1977, 322). But how such rules would fare in bureaucracies designed to promote autonomous technologies remains unclear.

A Comparison of Strategic Cores

Strategies for innovation differ in their value preferences and preferred policy instruments. We can gain some appreciation of the effects of such differences by placing their core preferences and perceptions side by side. A minimally complete strategy requires estimates concerning the effects of innovation, the rules for invoking policy action, estimates of government capabilities and effectiveness, and expressions of technological preferences. From these core estimates come alternative policies and action recommendations. The core estimates for the four strategies are enumerated in table 3.1.

On any given innovation dispute, decisionmakers face pressures from advocates of at least three of the four strategies. Prudent decisionmaking usually requires that stakeholders go away from disputes with perceived gains; at worst, damage to losers must be limited. Given the range in preferences and instruments, it is hard to find actions that meet the prudence test. Thus, the search for innovation, technology, or industrial policies tends to end in the same place, no matter the overall political and economic orientation of an administration. Federally funded information programs do meet the prudence test.

Three of the four strategies contain policy preferences and instru-

Table 3.1. Alternative Strategies for Innovation Policy

Core Concepts	Strategy			
	Engineering	Market	Public Interest	Transformational
1. Social consequences of innovation	1. Positive	1. Positive when market determined	1. Harmful without higher level of social direction	1. Harmful
2. Intervention rule	2. Meet national needs as defined by government	2.1 When markets fail 2.2 Delivery of public goods	2. If social objectives advanced	2. None
3. Government capabilities	3. Government knows more than private actors; Bureaucracies relatively efficient	3.1 Government knows less than private actors 3.2 Private incentives superior to bureaucratic action	3.1 Lacks relevant information 3.2 Lack of information implies bureaucratic action is misdirected 3.3 Competent bureaucracies would make situation worse	3.1 Structured to promote technology 3.2 Competent bureaucracies do social damage
4. Preferred type of technology	4. Usually large-scale and capital intensive	4. Market determined; Choose technology with maximum social utility	4. Small-scale; Decentralized; Non-complex; User friendly	4. None; Discover humane technologies
5. Preferred policy instrument	5. Government programs	5.1 Private incentives 5.2 Deregulation	5.1 Better information 5.2 Wider choice process	5. Countervailing power through reform of other major social systems
6. Policy preference	6. Augment and supplement markets	6. Limited federal activity	6. More open decision-making; Broader benefit/cost assessments	6. Direct personal efforts at social infrastructures — education, media, etc.

ments that are compatible with the way U.S. bureaucracies work. Many of their proposed instruments have already been debated and tried. There is a historical record; thus, we have some idea of actual outcome. There is no record of implementation for the transformational strategy. Strategies that call for the disestablishment of bureaucracies perceived as hostile rarely fare well with the bureaucrats who would have to do the disestablishing.

Even a transformational political administration, however, would find that the daily business of carrying out its mandates would eventually require bureaucracies and large numbers of standard, codified operating procedures. Thus, there is no direct way to judge how well a transformational strategy would work, were it tried. If it worked, there would be large discontinuities in social and economic behavior. However, we can examine the intellectual importance of a strategy, irrespective of whether it has been tried, and we can illuminate the marginalist strategies that have been tried by contrasting them with radical alternatives. We now consider the actual design and implementation of the marginalist strategies; we will return to the transformational strategy in the overall assessment at the end of this chapter.

The Kennedy Administration, 1960–1963

Aside from the special cases of atomic energy and aviation, formal policy proposals for general government support of civilian technology first appeared during the Kennedy administration. A push for an active role in civilian technology was consistent with the interests of both Kennedy's economic and science advisers. The main concern of his economists was to increase short-run economic performance, but they also retained an interest in issues of long-run economic growth. Over the long run, they knew growth and productivity increases were the ways to increased social welfare, but short-run, macroeconomic issues inevitably preempted the long-run issues. The president, in the summer of 1962, had established a Cabinet Committee on Growth, which included economics staff from the president's office and the secretaries of the departments most involved. The committee's work ran parallel to the science adviser's panel on U.S. technology but was broader in scope. Walter Heller, chairman of the Council of Economic Advisors (CEA), involved his staff in both the Cabinet Committee on Growth and the OST's Civil Technology Panel. In fact, the presence of CEA economists during the deliberations of the science and technology advisers helped to sharpen and clarify the issues at hand while increasing their complexity.

The president's economic advisers believed that technological advance was necessary if the economy's long-run growth rate was to be improved, but they perceived barriers to such an acceleration. In some cases they believed firms and industries were myopic, underestimating the benefits they themselves would receive from employing new technology. In other cases, they believed firms made correct benefit/cost calculations for themselves but did not and could not take into account positive benefit/cost outcomes for their industry or society (Cabinet Committee on Economic Growth 1962, 11). Even if firms made correct estimates of the returns from alternative technological ventures, the advisers thought they would be too low, from a social perspective. The forces of the market, Adam Smith's invisible hand, only worked well when there were no externalities, clearly not the case for important new technologies.

Since divergence between private and social rates of return was likely to persist, it was up to the government to accelerate the adoption of new civilian technologies. The president's economists did not lack faith in the competence of the government to design effective programs for doing this. In fact, echoing the concerns of the science adviser, the economists argued that the absorption of scientists by expanding space and defense programs made positive programs necessary for civilian technology (Gordon 1962). The economists even went as far as designing and promoting a new civilian technology agency that would have monitored the progress of other R&D agencies and would also have run its own programs.

The interests of the CEA and the Cabinet Committee on Growth ran parallel to the interests of the science adviser's Panel on Civilian Technology. The panel was essentially PSAC, augmented by technology experts; thus, it was natural for it to find the engineering strategy congenial. It summed up its views in its report to the president, *Technology and Economic Prosperity* (Hodges, Heller, and Wiesner 1962), and told the president that he needed new programs to maintain technological leadership and to boost output. The nation was properly committing resources to R&D in space and defense, but the panel argued that these did not contribute directly to economic growth. The results of military and space R&D were not easily adapted to those civilian industries that could boost growth. Because the government's own programs were absorbing so many scientific and technological resources, U.S. industry was handicapped. Consequently, the government had to stimulate civilian technology and, through education, greatly expand the pool of scientific and technical talent. More government involvement in civilian technology was necessary to maintain a dynamic free enterprise system and to achieve high-priority national objectives. Industry could not maintain a reasonable rate of innovation because the government was monopolizing scarce research talent and channeling it into activities that had no immediate economic relevance.

(Ironically, a little later, spillovers into civilian technology became one of the justifications for continuing a large-scale space program.)

The panel noted that there was ample precedent for an involvement with civilian technology. Most Western industrialized countries had such programs, and the United States itself had been successful in its one prior large-scale effort — support of agricultural research, development, and demonstration programs. The panel believed that textiles, coal, and housing deserved special attention. From the perspective of national decisionmaking, they seemed to (1) be relevant to basic needs, (2) have low innovation rates, and (3) have significant potential for science and technology applications. The panel gave different reasons for recommending these three for federal action and designed different programs for them. The textile industry suffered from inadequate basic engineering because it was short of up-to-date technological manpower. This situation implied targeted grants and contracts for research. The difficulty with the coal industry was its high cost of transportation. Costs could be reduced with R&D on coal slurry pipelines. In the case of housing, the panel saw a fragmented industry, operating at an uneconomic scale. This meant it did not pay construction firms to acquire and use state-of-the-art technology. The situation implied the creation of an industrial extension service analogous to the agricultural extension service.

Given the consistent views of its economic and science policy advisers, the administration designed the Civilian Industrial Technology Program (CITP). The CITP included industry-university science and technology centers, data collection, and technology assessment. It was to foster innovation in industries whose output the government defined as critical in meeting national needs and whose performance was seen as inadequate. The administration believed that housing construction met the criteria, but CITP drew the strongest negative reaction from this industry. While the government took an engineering perspective, the housing industry maintained a market perspective. The administration's assertions of government interest and responsibility for R&D were countered by assertions that what the market did was economically correct. Where CITP proponents saw a fragmented building industry underinvesting in R&D and innovation, the industry itself saw a significant rate of innovation, consistent with market signals (Nelkin 1971). Indeed, to the industry, federal funding of building research threatened the validity of those signals. The government would be selecting some industries and firms for special treatment in R&D, but nothing suggested the government could do research or subsidize it any better than the private sector could. Because of poor political tactics and the substantive and political opposition by the nominal beneficiaries, CITP could not get through Congress, but in 1965 the Johnson administration succeeded in passing a derivative program, the State Technical Services Program (STS).

The Johnson Administration, 1963–1968

The Johnson administration stressed technology for "socially profitable" purposes. Innovation, on its face, was "socially profitable," and there was never enough of it. Consequently, federal programs to increase industrial innovation seemed necessary and appropriate, and President Johnson directed the government to join business and industry in speeding the diffusion of new technology. Since those who had designed CITP in the Kennedy administration remained in their positions, it was natural that CITP's concepts would be modified to take into account the substantive objections and political opposition; STS was the result.

Rather than proposing to do government-supported research on behalf of industry, STS stressed the delivery of technical information. It was to support industrial extension work, education, and demonstrations. Based on plans developed jointly by industry, universities, and the states, such activities could be considered as smoothing the work of the market. Donald Hornig, President Johnson's science adviser, stressed that STS was really an experiment in the provision of information. The government would deliver information on best practice through selected state and local agents. Information on best practice would, thus, be tailored to local conditions and would be more attractive than existing practice (Katz 1978, 170). Hornig, like past and future science advisers, assumed that what was technologically best was economically efficient and that, if only industry's technological and economic myopia could be cured, "correct" judgments would follow.

The STS experiment did not end the concerns about the government's role in promoting civilian technology (Pierce 1965). Throughout 1965, 1966, and 1967, the OST continued to promote programs for greater government involvement. There were, by that time, a number of different government studies on productivity, innovation, and growth. A White House panel led by Charles Zwick, director of the BOB, was established to sift and evaluate the recommendations of all of them (Zwick 1966). Not surprisingly, given the strain now being applied to the president's budget, the panel produced a minimal set of recommendations primarily oriented toward patent policies and procedures. It argued that more evidence of a "maldistribution of capital" was required before the government should provide technical assistance to the private sector.

The limited market approach of the Zwick panel did not satisfy the science adviser, or he did not read the signals of constraint the adminis-

tration was sending. Throughout the Johnson years, his office consistently sought to expand its domain of action, holding that urban problems, education problems, and so forth would all benefit from science
and technology advice and programs. The science adviser argued that
"healthy" technological change should be established as a national goal
(Hornig 1967c). He proposed (1) use of federal government purchasing
power in housing and transportation, and the linking of systems development and evaluation with procurement; (2) reducing barriers to
entrepreneurial risk taking through business assistance centers; (3)
strengthening of engineering schools, universities in particular, in
nondefense areas; and (4) expansion of long-range R&D programs in
critical civilian fields such as urban development, transportation, tun-
neling, pollution, water resources, and so forth. In 1968, the OST
pushed hard to make the White House and the Department of Housing
and Urban Development (HUD) more sensitive to problem solving via
R&D. The OST supplied HUD with a number of programs and proposals in housing, transportation, and planning. Hornig told the
Secretary of HUD that he intended to involve the OST in programs and
issues relevant to "urban innovation," implicitly assuming the administration would remain in office (Hornig 1968).

The grounds Hornig found for such programs were first, that the
federal government's own decisions to buy goods and services and
finance purchases by others determined the market for public technology, thereby weakening private incentives for development of civilian
technology. Second, the market for public technology was imperfect. In
particular, potential risk-takers in civilian technology lacked necessary
information. Third, there were institutional and regulatory barriers in
the market which were either created by or could be overcome by
federal action.

These arguments, derived from past OST work, received no interest
or support in the waning days of the administration. But the OST's
expansion into areas where technical factors were weak and political
and economic ones were strong caused a growing disregard for the OST
and contributed to its demise during the Nixon administration. The
design of technology policy continued to draw attention, however,
because of the growing realization that economic growth depended
more on innovation and new technology than on anything else.

The Economics of Innovation

As discussed in Chapter 2, the scientific community used economists'
findings on the effects of technical advance and divergence between
private and social rates of return to make a case for more basic research
funding, but there were logical and empirical gaps. The studies

measured the impacts of technological advance, taken as a whole and compared with the traditional factors of production. They showed, more or less persuasively, that innovation and technological advance were relatively more important. While economists had traditionally been interested in growth through capital deepening and increases in the quantity and quality of human capital, the studies suggested that new knowledge deserved equal and maybe more attention (Mansfield et al. 1977; NSF 1971, 1977a). The studies were relatively aggregated, however, and they did not identify those returns that could be uniquely associated with investments in basic research. The gaps were filled by assertions that basic research was now a necessary condition for innovation. Technology, in other words, was becoming more science based.

The new economics of innovation could not specify the form and direction of technical advance and related R&D. These remained as open as ever, and, therefore, subject to policy dispute. The studies themselves could not provide much policy guidance. Statistical modeling was based on past experience that would not necessarily hold in the future, and the results were probably not very robust, should there be severe shocks to the economy. The theoretical work did not really incorporate the effects of practical policy instruments. Nor did the finding of significant impact when technological advance occurred provide rules for decisionmakers seeking to produce such advance or tell them what to avoid. Decisionmakers were left to learn by doing.

The Nixon Administration, 1968–1974

The Nixon administration, surprisingly like the Johnson administration, felt that the purpose of federal R&D was to help solve social problems. Much of its science policy efforts went into trying to reshape the government's portfolio of projects. This president wanted to apply research to national needs, and he felt that his administration could rank the needs. In 1972 — in the first S&T message from any president — he gave priority to problems of the environment, health, energy, and transportation (Nixon 1972).

Since the government had already been spending substantial R&D monies in these areas, the administration believed that the R&D agencies must have developed technologies that could be converted into projects attractive to the private sector. With this kind of view, the science adviser had to continue the OST's thrust into the civil sector. For example, Edward David, Nixon's second science adviser, found himself arguing for increases in civilian R&D budgets in order to make clear the administration's commitment to solving domestic problems. Since the United States has no a priori process for setting the R&D budget, it was not surprising that bureaucratic inertia produced budgets similar to the ones produced before Nixon's new priorities had been announced. R&D is supposed to be relevant to each agency's mission, so it shows up as part of each agency's budget submission, not in a grand R&D budget. The OMB and the science adviser construct an ex post R&D budget from the general agency submissions and try to see if it is consistent with White House priorities and is technically sound. On doing so for FY 1971, David found that the budget did not make clear the priority given to civilian research (David 1970a). He went on to suggest that more funds be provided for health care, the environment, energy, air traffic control, weather, rapid excavation, and applied technology. Since the budgetary climate was a constrained one, he appeared willing to take reductions elsewhere. In general, David tried to make clear to the scientific community that it would be treated relatively well with respect to resource levels but that the resources had to be directed toward national needs (David 1970b).

To go with its civilian R&D priorities, the administration tried to derive a civilian technology policy. Typical of such a venture, it began with an engineering strategy. Its 1971–72 search for new technological opportunities (NTO) was supposed to elicit technologies developed with government resources, which could then be transferred to industry and sold via normal market channels. Since the prime directive for any R&D agency is budget maximization, the agencies responded to NTO with technologically feasible proposals that were highly costly. They included development of new nuclear power systems for commercial ships, development of offshore ports for deep draft tankers, mapping and explorations of the continental shelf, high-speed rapid transit, a campaign against kidney diseases, and so forth (Barfield 1972, 757).

This search for technological opportunities, however, coincided with the administration's very strong requirement for budgetary constraint. Its fiscal objective in the early 1970s was a full-employment, balanced budget, with no increase in tax rates. Reaching this objective would be difficult, according to the OMB, unless budget decreases could be found to offset the increases (Weinberger 1971). Consequently, the NTO proposals would meet resistance on budgetary grounds. Budget constraints meant that the OMB would raise questions about the NTO's relationship to the private sector, since such questions could be used to resist claims for new resources. The director of NTO found that he was not prepared for questions concerning the relationship between markets and government programs. Questions that might have been addressed during the search for opportunities erupted after the search was over — questions concerning appropriateness for government, social benefit/ costs, and how to terminate programs, once started (Barfield 1972, 759). The legitimacy of any claim for resources can be reduced, if the OMB can show that granting the claim may reduce incentives for private sector activities. The NTO, whatever its substantive merits, involved supporting the development of technologies that the private sector eventually would be selling profitably. If this was the case, there was no persuasive reason why the private sector should be allowed to avoid the development work; thus, NTO was found to be inappropriate.

The OMB also demanded cost-effectiveness studies of the new opportunities. Of course, they would have been ambiguous at best and infeasible at worst. But the lack of demonstrated or persuasive cost-effectiveness was convenient, since, on budgetary grounds, the administration did not want to go forward with the NTO program. The nominally objective demand for evidence permitted the OMB to "buy off" some of the proposers of initiatives by giving them some marginal funds to get the evidence at some future time. The administration eventually approved a few "experimental" programs in the Bureau of Standards and at the NSF, as well as some small-scale research programs. The questions to be addressed were never very clear, and the agencies were hard put to design "experiments" that would have answered them. In any case, agency claims for resources could not be pressed until the evidence arrived and that would take at least several years. Strong positive evidence probably could never be produced, and this would provide barriers to new proposals. In sum, civilian technology programs were infeasible because of cost and worries about preempting market decisions. These difficulties dominated the administration's strong belief that it could use technology to solve social problems.

The Ford Administration, 1974–1976

The Ford administration was far more oriented toward a market strategy. This was so, perhaps, because of the perceived failures of many Great Society programs, the wage-price controls of the early 1970s, and growing concern about regulation of the economy. Whatever the cause, by the mid seventies, belief in the efficiency and effectiveness of government programs and the general competence of government had declined. The federal government, if anything, was the major deterrent to innovation and growth.

Whereas the Ford administration believed that basic research funding had been too low in previous years, it saw no particular need for civilian technology programs beyond those keyed to the government's own mission requirements. The pervasive presence of the government in many markets and the disincentives created by government regulation hampered the growth of civilian technology. President Ford had many of the same feelings about government intervention in markets that Eisenhower had. For example, he told his department and agency heads that government should intrude in the free market only when well-defined national needs could be met or when barriers had been erected against a free, relatively unregulated, competitive market system (Ford 1975).

Given the president's general preference for market processes, OMB sought principles for federal R&D support consistent with a market strategy. The OMB, as usual responding to the tastes of a sitting president, found that federal support was appropriate when, and only when, (1) government was to be the primary user of R&D, or (2) there were externalities or resource constraints that prevented the private sector from producing satisfactory levels of R&D, or (3) there was a strong consensus on some national need the market was not satisfying (OMB 1978). These criteria meant that the government could continue to do whatever it had defined as appropriate in the past. For example, research on military aircraft met the first criterion; basic research met the second criterion; and energy research met the third one. However, new ventures would have a more difficult time. Rules had now been stated explicitly, and the administration would hold new ventures to a higher standard of proof.

To complement its "positive" criteria, OMB developed a negative set. The government was to avoid preempting the private sector in getting new technologies to market. Where some government development work had taken place and a technology was ready for commercialization, cost sharing would be required or, at least, strongly encouraged. And always trying to avoid fixed budget commitments over the long run, the government was to avoid investing in technology for which future funding would be a significant issue (Loweth 1976).

Given these positive and negative criteria, the Ford OMB felt that government investment in any technology that was approaching commercialization in the short run was inappropriate and could even damage the expected market outcome (OMB 1976). True to a market strategy, OMB and the president felt that incentives and the removal of disincentives inevitably produced by government were the best ways to increase the rate of innovation. The federal government was to ensure that its policies and programs stimulated private investment in S&T and encouraged innovation by the private sector. Too much direct government support for civilian technology would displace private sector initiative. Market mechanisms, like tax incentives or more rapid patenting procedures, avoided such displacement (Ford 1976).

If anything deterred the private sector from investment, it was ubiquitous government regulation. Regulation reduced incentives to innovate and did not let the price system operate so as to direct R&D to most needed areas. President Ford clearly believed that his deregulation actions were also innovation programs. He wanted to deregulate the energy, transportation, banking, and communications sectors. He wanted to get the federal government out of setting rates and prices and was in favor of relaxing government constraints on entry and exit in regulated industries. Government, he felt, perpetuated monopoly and high prices (Ford 1975, 3).

The Carter Administration, 1976-1980

On balance, President Ford's technology policy was to provide increased support for basic research activity well within his administration's tastes and guidelines and to free the marketplace of government-induced distortions so that private economic agents would make correct technological choices. The Carter administration continued the policies of the Ford administration with respect to basic research, but it also wanted to promote civilian technology. Here its major effort was a review of policies and programs for increasing industrial innovation, similar to Nixon's NTO, but larger and broader in scope. In keeping with post-Watergate concepts of open government, advisory committees representing industry, labor, and the public presented their views to an internal federal group conducting the review. Although the design of the review gave greater weight to industry positions, labor and the public were permitted to critique those positions. Certainly, the White House believed the design of its review provided a wide enough spread of information and views (Carter 1979b).

In the end, President Carter chose a few programs that were consistent with a market strategy, although the lead agencies for his review, the Office of Science and Technology Policy and the Department of Commerce, were in favor of more aggressive government action, consistent with an overall engineering strategy and budget maximizing objectives for science and technology. As might now be predictable from the other cases, proposed programs for innovation ran into the president's need for fiscal constraint. Given that the OMB imposed a constraint of zero or little cost increase on all proposals, the only feasible initiatives involved procedural reforms so that markets could work better. Better regulation would result from using cost-impact analysis more widely, strengthening the patent system, using performance rather than design specifications in federal procurement, and providing missing economic information to relevant markets.

The administration defined one case of market failure. To it, there appeared to be underinvestment in "generic" technologies. These were potentially important technologies for which no particular industry could capture all the benefits. Thus, the administration and industry believed there was underinvestment, making government support necessary (Carter 1979b). While such underinvestment is a necessary part of a case for intervention, it is not sufficient. One needs to show why private returns are too low to induce the desired innovation. Aggregate social benefits (returns) indeed might, as the administration argued, have been greater than private benefits in the case of generics, but the administration made no attempt to demonstrate why the latter were too low. The examples the administration often gave involved combinations of computer and machine tool technology. Although such combinations might prove to be a deterrent, if there were low but positive incremental returns, the innovation would be undertaken by the market.

Because of inflation and budgetary stringency, the initial package of innovation proposals could not involve significant incremental costs. As the OMB scrutinized the Commerce Department's proposals, the issues of cost-effectiveness and private sector performance appeared, as they had in prior searches for innovation policy. The actions the administration eventually accepted diverged from the ones preferred by the main beneficiary — industry — as well as those preferred by guardians of the public interest. To industry, the innovation problem was part of an overall economic problem of tax disincentives for investment, so it wanted changes in general tax policy. But the president was in no position to overhaul tax policy for the sake of industrial innovation. Furthermore, government's own regulation acted as a disincentive. To industry there was regulatory "drag"; if the federal government would only remove disincentives and provide incentives, innovation would take care of itself. Although much had happened to the U.S. economy since the 1960s, industry found a correlation between the decline in productivity and the rapid increase in environmental and safety regulation. This new social regulation decreased the relative competitiveness of U.S. products abroad, while requiring large amounts of domestic resources (Advisory Committee on Industrial Innovation 1979).

In its science policy preferences, industry wanted increased university-industry "coupling," federal support for technology-based ventures, and support of generic technologies. Industry's budgetary expectations for generic technology were high; support was to begin with computer-integrated manufacturing and eventually extend to advanced manufacturing technology. But the administration's ambitions had to be low.

Although adherents of a public interest strategy were far outnumbered by those subscribing to engineering or market strategies, the Carter review permitted formal presentation, if not serious consideration, of public interest positions. From a public interest perspective, if government were to set innovation policy in any formal sense, it had to know and could know the goals or ends of innovation. The direction of innovation was a far more serious question than its rate. The market did not give any preference to innovations that were socially meritorious, or that delivered some higher goods (Public Interest Subcommittee on Economic and Trade Policy 1979). These goods existed and were known; they could be found in social legislation, in surveys, and through true social accounting. If higher-order social goods could truly be identified, then innovation could be guided toward providing more of them. But current government policy and programs actually reversed the preferences expressed by citizens. For example, although the public rated national defense much lower as a priority than health, education, and law enforcement, the former received the lion's share of federal R&D expenditures and still does.

The public interest strategy generates concern about the type of technology that government support fosters. Government support of technology has fostered increasing reliance on centralized, capital intensive industries (Advisory Subcommittee on Public Interest 1979). Increasing capital intensity produces monopoly, unemployment, increased use of energy, and environmental damage. Thus, public funds should only be provided for technology that is "appropriate." Appropriate technologies, according to the public interest strategy, are decentralized, comprehensible to workers, and pose no threat to the environment. Such technologies are feasible now, and the government has a responsibility to disseminate information about them to local groups and communities.

While industry found that government regulation, both the classical economic type and the new social type, hampered innovation, the public interest group found deficiencies in industry's view of regulation. The public interest group felt that regulations provide benefits for all in the form of a higher quality of life; they are a means of channeling innovation in the right direction. The problem lay not in regulation but in industry's slow and unimaginative responses (Public Interest Subcommittee on Environmental, Health, and Safety Regulations 1979).

Despite these assertions of the public interest, President Carter selected a minimal program consistent with a market strategy. He decided to develop resources currently missing in the private sector or else to provide incentives to private decisionmakers (Carter 1979b). Like the other presidents, Carter imposed a zero or low-cost constraint on any possible programs. Increasing technological information flow and the provision of incentives were legitimate low-cost government activities within a market strategy. The few direct action programs in the president's portfolio were justified in terms of market failure, for example, perceived private underinvestment in generic technologies. Industry-preferred proposals to solve innovation problems through alteration of tax policies immediately raised larger considerations of general economic policy and had to be deferred.

The Reagan Administration, 1980 through 1984

Even Carter's minimal program was not implemented. The election of President Reagan led to significant budget reductions and shifts in economic and innovation strategies. President Carter's proposals involved too much government activity for the new administration. The latter believed strongly that the market was the preferred mechanism for making any choices about innovation. Consequently, it wanted to make much sharper distinctions between public and private functions in S&T. The belief that the federal government had become too large and intrusive, budgetary stringency, and preference for market solutions all meant disinterest in an explicit search for a federal technology policy. Technology policy was the small set of things appropriate for the federal government to do, and support of basic research was one of the few things that the government could do well. Although the variance in its returns was high, eventually they did come (OSTP 1982, 4). The grounds for this position were traditional. In the case of basic research, the incentives for private sector support were believed to be weak because the information from basic research was, by its nature, always widely available and appropriable by anyone.

Government support for development, however, compounded the innovation problem. It caused market difficulties, if not outright failures. Bureaucratic attempts to correct market failures led to bureaucratic failure and to market distortions. The innovation problem was really one of making markets work better by reducing uncertainties produced by the government (OSTP 1982). The administration argued that uncertainties about future federal policies with regard to taxes, patents, antitrust interpretations, and regulatory requirements caused uncertainty in the private sector. Given the desire to avoid risk, the private sector invested too little. Uncertainty could be reduced by removing the most onerous regulations and by a high threshold for triggering enforcement of the remaining ones.

The administration truly believed it could discern a difference between "defensive" R&D and "productive" R&D. Regulatory reform would reduce defensive R&D (OSTP 1982). The administration, however, failed to deal with such questions as why auto emission control or fuel efficiency standards produced "defensive" R&D when, to some firms, they provided incentives to engage in "offensive" R&D, producing new and improved products in response to the market pull of such regulations.

Perhaps the best way to improve the economic climate for innovation was to remove government from the marketplace. When general economic conditions improved sufficiently, sales would rise, pulling industrial R&D up, and once more generating the high levels of innovation historically characteristic of the U.S. economy. To boost these market effects, the administration was prepared to provide some tax incentives; the Economic Recovery Tax Act, passed in 1981, included tax credits for R&D, accelerated depreciation schedules, and the transfer of R&D losses by unprofitable firms to profitable ones. Whether incremental amounts of R&D will result and whether they can be attributed to these measures is an open question.

Assessing the Strategies

The policy debate about the government's support of civilian technology is less clear and far more open than is the debate about its role in supporting research. In the latter case, most parties agree that the government should support basic research in general and some applied research that is relevant to assigned agency missions. The residual issues here are determining the level of government support and the strategy to be used in distributing the volume of resources selected.

In the civilian technology domain, no general a priori case for government action can be constructed as long as the United States retains its preferences for a market system of resource allocation. In the case of civilian technology, the choice between strategies turns much more on the value propositions in the strategies. The two most prominent strategies in the policy history so far examined — the engineering and the market strategies — implicitly accept traditional principles of consumer and producer sovereignty. Innovations, whether supported by the government or not, should eventually meet tests of effective demand and cost. Neither of these strategies contains extramarket propositions about the "goodness" or "badness" of prospective new technologies.

The other two strategies hold that higher-order social objectives can be discerned beyond those expressed in markets or defined by myopic bureaucracies. The public interest strategy maintains that technological choice can be guided to realize these transcendent social objectives; new political or analytic procedures would permit this. The transformational strategy holds that individuals and institutions almost unconsciously adapt to the requirements for operating large-scale technological systems. Selecting technologies consistent with transcendent social objectives requires greater awareness of technological dynamics and causation and more attention to human values. The latter can be identified a priori and used as measures of the worth of prospective technological innovations.

The four strategies differ, not only in their value propositions, but also in beliefs about the utility of information. Given an information state, they differ about the kinds of actions that can be effective. The engineering strategy holds that central R&D bureaucracies have more information about innovation than do individual actors in the marketplace. In the first place, these bureaucracies are nominally charged with making policy to internalize the externalities that are common in the innovation process, and individual actors are not so charged. In the second place, bureaucracies have access to greater information than does any single actor in the marketplace. If necessary, bureaucracies can create information, and, in the case of innovation, information has to be created and then disseminated. There is no guarantee unassisted markets will develop such information, and even if this happens, it may never be put in a form permitting wide dissemination.

With the market strategy, individual actors hold relevant but partial information. Because they are seen as closer to market conditions than are bureaucrats, they should ordinarily know more about the demand for prospective innovations than would central R&D bureaucracies. If the market truly suffers from a breakdown in information flows, then the government's role is not to supplant the market with its own innovation programs but to correct the breakdowns. Once corrected, the government should stay out of the way, with a minimum of direct action programs and regulation. Private incentives should be sufficient to generate technologies that can meet the only proper test — effective demand supplied at a price at which industry maximizes profits.

The public interest strategy holds that the information structures the government or markets use screen out important concerns about values. Without attention to values, neither government nor the market will deliver technologies consistent with collective, transcendent social objectives and preferences. It is up to the government to force consideration of these preferences by mandating analytic procedures such as technology and risk assessment, grafting more democratic procedures on bureaucracies, or regulating the market.

In the transformational strategy, individuals discover the true state of technological affairs through self-awareness and competent communication with others. An aware individual can compare technologies with "good" properties, for example, small scale of operation or noncomplexity, with those with "bad" properties. When enough individuals have realized the true state of affairs, they will rebel and design new institutions and policies to guide technological choice toward discernibly correct paths.

The historical cases examined in this chapter have demonstrated that U.S. decisionmakers shift between marginalist strategies, depending on their overall economic beliefs and budget conditions at the time. Innovation strategies and programs are usually examined in the heat of the budget season. The OMB invokes market considerations as the nominal reason for not proceeding with proposed innovation programs, but saving money is its real reason. At no time in the history discussed here has there been tough, critical, systematic third-party analysis of the proposed policies and the means of implementation. And at no time has there been consistent comparison of alternative strategies and their costs. The U.S. search for an innovation strategy has been marred by faulty design or, more accurately, by no design. Analysis has usually been placed in the hands of those with something to gain or lose. Alternative strategies have not been articulated or debated clearly, and values, facts, and predictions have never been clearly distinguished.

Intellectually, innovation policy falls somewhere between S&T policy and economics. Bureaucratically, it falls somewhere between an administration's economists and budget advisers and its science and technology advisers. Neither by themselves are equipped to address it. And so U.S. innovation policy has usually been left to slip to those minimal core programs that garner universal agreement or avoid nasty disagreements; these are usually information and awareness programs. Perhaps the considerations that lead to this outcome are cogent and persuasive; perhaps not, but it would pay to know. Unlike basic research policy, public policy for civilian technology is still unformed.

Science Education

4

Strategies concerned with federal support of research require complementary strategies for science education. The scientific and technical community developed an educational strategy right after World War II. It tied education and research together as the joint inputs and outputs of the science and technology enterprise. Given increasing returns to investments in research and continuous, but unpredictable payoffs, an adequate supply of scientists and engineers is necessary. If the government wants the best science for its investments in research, it has to be concerned about the education of scientists and engineers. But education is a "roundabout" process; it has long lead times. If, in the long run, the only true limit on research output is the number of skilled scientists and engineers, then talent should be identified early, and those with talent should be given the necessary incentives and resources for later participation in the scientific enterprise. To do science later, skills and attitudes must be acquired early. If so, a sufficient flow of manpower for research entails a federal interest in science education at all levels.

These human capital and manpower justifications for federal involvement in science education were buttressed by faith in the relevance and utility of some science and engineering knowledge for all citizens. The scientific community asserted that any smoothly functioning democracy requires informed citizens. This, it said, is especially the case for an economy that depends on scientific and technological information for growth and innovation and for a polity that is constantly and heavily affected by technological developments. Citizens needed technical information in their daily lives; without it, they would fail to make sensible public and private choices. Furthermore, public decisions could not be made or would not be accepted without background technological knowledge. Although the polity had developed means and institutions to cope with citizens' lack of knowledge in many other domains of public choice, and well-functioning markets economized on the information required for private choice, the assertion here was that decisions with heavy scientific and technological content were special or different and could not, or must not, be handled by traditional means. So the desired "civic culture" of a democracy lent force to the scientists' demands for a federal presence in science education, based on human capital arguments.

While the production of scientists or informed citizens is roundabout and lengthy, it takes immediate resources. The availability of resources usually depends on current perceptions of supply and predictions and expectations of future supply. For most of the period considered here, decisionmakers, manpower analysts, and forecasters felt the market was producing too many scientists and engineers. Given technical manpower markets with excess supply, it was natural that the scientific and technical community and the collateral community of professional science educators would eventually find themselves at odds with those in charge of the federal science budget.

Part of the difficulty was bureaucratic and organizational; those in charge of education budgets and programs had little responsibility for science education. Those in charge of science had responsibility for science education but had little inclination to make trade-offs in favor of education. The scientific community had always insisted that decisions about science and science education had to be made together and that science education should not be divorced from practicing scientists. But, given that its first-order preferences were to preserve basic research, the scientific community always acceded to reductions in science education budgets whenever overall policy required them.

Part of the difficulty was conceptual. The scientists' arguments about the level of federal support for science education were unbounded. Given the needs and jobs seen by the scientific community and the science education profession, and given the size of the U.S. educational establishment, no budget could ever be sufficient. No concept of sufficiency could even be put forward. From a research perspective, there is no internal limit on the numbers that should be practicing science and engineering; more practitioners means additional valuable information. Decisionmakers, however, could argue that equilibrium in manpower markets was a reasonable criterion for economic sufficiency. As markets changed over time from conditions of excess demand to excess supply, decisionmakers would feel impelled to reduce federal programs for developing human capital. If federal support was necessary because all citizens had to have exposure to science education, then any level of federal activity would appear to be too small. Any proposed program could be perceived as below "critical mass" and therefore, ineffective and worthy of elimination.

A third difficulty, a political one, arose later because of the federal government's attempts to make the scientists' strategy cost-effective. The strategy called for federal efforts to improve science education at the elementary and secondary levels. But federally supported science curriculum projects, and attempts to implement their results, eventually mobilized citizen groups with views very different from those of scientists and educators. These groups were strongly opposed to any federally developed science curriculum but especially to those with strong biological and social science content. Ordinary political and bureaucratic prudence, in response to these citizen groups and combined with decisionmakers' well-established desires to reduce budgets, made the federal government's role in science education questionable by the end of the 1970s.

This chapter examines the educational strategy initially formulated by the scientific and technical community and shows what happened as that formulation was challenged. That strategy focuses primarily on the development of human capital for the practice of science and engineering, the production of materials for use at elementary and secondary levels, and the provision of scientific and technical information for the general public. As before, I will first state the strategy and its implications for action. Then I will discuss the competing policy alternatives and finally, the outcomes associated with the arguments. The chapter closes with some suggestions for improving debate over science education.

Scientists and Science Educators Produce a Strategy

The educational strategy grew from the same perceptions as did the research allocation strategy described in Chapter 2. Like the latter strategy, it appeared early in the postwar era and was held tenaciously, whatever the actual state of the market for scientific and technical manpower. If excess supplies of manpower blunted demand for greater numbers, then the quality of scientists and engineers could always be improved. In any case, the strategy held that production of knowledgeable citizens always requires investments in science education.

The contents of this strategy are listed below and numbered *SE.1, SE.2,* and so forth. The references cited at the end of some statements are early and late works that illustrate the constancy of the strategy and the language associated with it.

SE.1 *The effective manpower base for performing science and engineering must be continually increasing, either in quantity or quality and preferably both (Bush [1945] 1980; PSRB 1947; NSF and DOE 1980).*

Sometimes scientists assert a stronger version of *SE.1,* that is, a nation can never produce enough scientists and engineers. The test of adequacy should not be the numbers determined by market forces, but potential scientific and technical discoveries. Since there is an unlimited number of these, society should provide for a continued inflow of practitioners, no matter what the market indicates. Society reaches an upper bound in the number of scientists and engineers only when it can profitably employ all those who have the talent in scientific occupations and when all those who can develop the talent are in a science or engineering educational track. The actual number is then always too low, and it pays society to do the things that will move the actual number toward the upper bound.

SE.2 *Unaided market forces will not deliver a sufficient quantity or quality of researchers in time to meet national needs (Bush [1945] 1980; PSAC 1962; NSF and DOE 1980).*

If the market happens to supply enough quantity, it never produces enough quality. From the scientists' perspective, as the technological complexity of the economy increases, larger inputs of high-quality scientific and technical talent should be employed, if maximum economic growth is to be achieved (NSF and DOE 1980). However, the possibility that increasing technological complexity could reduce the demand for scientists, engineers, and technicians is not admissible in the strategy, although economists have constructed plausible scenarios that this could be the case.

The quantity-quality duality in *SE.2* makes the strategy resilient against claims by decisionmakers and others that programs can be reduced, because the labor market clears or delivers excess supplies of trained manpower. Such outcomes can be granted, and an appeal can then be made to an always unsatisfied quality dimension. This appeal to quality is often coupled with the need for special concerns about the flow of young scientists and engineers. Increases in quality do not come from upgrading the average skills of the entire scientific labor force; rather, they come through the continuing introduction of new practitioners with higher than average skills and energies.

SE.3 *Students with latent ability for research are discouraged by inadequate instruction (PSAC 1959; NSF and DOE 1980).*

SE3.1 *Elementary and secondary curricula are obsolete.*

SE3.2 *Science teachers are poorly prepared.*

SE3.3 *Action implication: The federal government should act to reduce the institutional barriers between researchers and* *teachers so as to produce better curricula, teaching aids, and teachers.*

SE.4 *Citizens' knowledge of S&T is a necessary condition for sound and accepted public decisions (PSAC 1959; NSF and DOE 1980).*

   SE4.1 *Action implication: The federal government should secure some knowledge of S&T for every citizen.*

Human Capital

What one would today call a "requirements" approach justified the human capital part of the strategy; a large number of national needs that had to be met or jobs that had to be done were specified. Relative to those needs, the expected market supply of scientific and technical manpower was constantly projected as too small by government and private forecasters. The predicted excess demand was to be reduced by federal programs and resources. In such projections, the government usually has no budget constraint, and all needs seem equally worthy. Thus, predictions and projections do not ordinarily generate assessments of the incremental benefits and costs of doing different jobs or of doing the same jobs in different ways.

A key task of the 1950s and 1960s was the supplying of human capital to a growing R&D sector, especially the university component. If the universities had neither the faculties nor the physical capacity to train the manpower required to meet projected national needs, then they would be a bottleneck, thwarting satisfaction of national needs. For this reason alone, more scientists and engineers appeared necessary. Since national security and economic progress were also linked to the supply of human capital in all sectors, and both of these needed to be increased, even more scientists and engineers were necessary (PSAC 1962, 3). If the argument of sheer numbers did not carry enough weight, then one could always appeal to the need for quality; there is always a shortage of exceptionally able scientists. Given the images of research and education feeding each other and an expanding agenda of national needs, public and private forecasts of the need or demand for scientists and teachers were naturally large. That markets might work to eliminate the excess demand or that programs could end were not conditions projected in the strategy.

The Eisenhower administration proved quite sensitive to such predictions. Predictions of shortages and shortfalls in the technical competition with the Soviet Union were strong themes through that administration. Early on, the president and his cabinet began a long series of meetings on scientific and technical education, so many that the president would refer to science education as the "perennial" subject. In the spring of 1954, the president instructed his cabinet to see what could be done about developing more scientists and engineers. HEW Secretary Arthur Flemming was assigned to design feasible programs and to develop cooperation among relevant agencies. Flemming's Special Interdepartmental Committee argued that (1) there was excess demand in many fields of science and engineering, (2) shortages of scientists and engineers endangered national security, and (3) the shortages were self-perpetuating because of the roundabout nature of the training process. The scientists needed to train scientists, and engineers were in short supply (Flemming 1954).

Flemming proposed broad public and private programs designed to influence career decisions, reduce teacher shortages, provide more career counseling, and improve college courses for science teachers. But consistent with the president's very strong preference for private sector solutions to national problems, the role of the federal government was to be limited. A presidentially appointed committee was to be set up to increase public awareness and coordination. (In this domain, as in others, the Eisenhower administration believed coordination was a process that inherently led to greater effectiveness.) Through its work, this committee would induce public and private groups to take the needed actions. The president was also to try to persuade federal agencies to take a hard look at their own responsibilities and programs to see if more assistance to science education were possible. However, education was not recognized as a truly federal responsibility. More scientists and engineers would result by creating more awareness in the private sector and by giving incentives to the local organizations that actually controlled resources (Flemming 1954).

Eisenhower's appointment of a science adviser and the creation of the President's Science Advisory Committee (PSAC) meant that the scientific community could argue from within that the government's role in education had to be more than just inducing sensitivity and awareness in other sectors. At a minimum, PSAC was prepared to argue that externalities at the graduate level entailed federal support. Even though state or private universities trained physicists and engineers, they were doing it in part to satisfy a federal customer. Since the local "producers" could not capture all the benefits, output was too low (PSAC 1959). For other levels of education, PSAC told the president, excess demand for teachers was increasing and curricula had to be improved. Better curricula could help reduce the excess demand for teachers, since the effectiveness of each current teacher would be increased. Substantively, there was too much of a lag between the material presented in textbooks and knowledge at the scientific frontiers. From a learning point of view, students were not instructed in science as a process of discovery, but only as facts already discovered (PSAC 1959). In PSAC's view, the investment of a few million dollars in science teaching materials would upgrade the quality of instruction markedly, provided that practicing scientists helped design and produce the materials.

Although the production of more modern curricula was the most important single action that could be taken to improve elementary and secondary science education, PSAC also proposed talent identification programs, the upgrading of the status of teachers, science-for-citizens courses, and the general upgrading of graduate schools of science and engineering. Although no budget estimates were attached to these recommendations, very large national programs were seen as necessary; trade-offs with other expenditures would have to be made (PSAC 1959).

The administration climaxed its long interest in education by obtaining passage of the National Defense Education Act (NDEA) in 1958. The act included a large number of science fellowships and scholarships and other assistance for science education. It was seen as a realization and vindication of the scientists' strategy, in particular the explicit provision for direct federal support of education. According to Eisenhower's science adviser, it was a precursor for bringing the federal government into a permanent relationship with the educational system (Killian 1977, 196).

In the short run, the NDEA could do nothing to alleviate the expected shortages of manpower. Predictions of shortages were even more distasteful to the incoming Kennedy administration, which had a large social agenda. President Kennedy learned of the state of science manpower even before he took office (Wiesner, Kistiakowsky, and Brooks 1960). He was told that educational resources were not growing fast enough to meet all the expected demands, and, furthermore, that the growth in government programs alone was causing excess demand for scientists and engineers. If so there was a direct case for government action to insure at least the minimum number required for its own demands.

The new administration was committed, in any case, to greater activity in education. According to his biographers, education was a domestic issue that mattered greatly to the president (Sorenson 1965). But the administration's education program had been halted in Congress. Stressing the relationship between education and economic growth was a way to soften congressional resistance to general education programs; the connection between scientific and technical education and economic growth could be sustained and sold to Congress. The president's economic advisers told him that the quality of human capital was positively related to growth, even though difficult to measure, and that quality was a function of educational investments. Improving the quality of human capital was not different, in principle, from improving the quality of tangible factors of production like land or capital (Heller 1961). Technical education was the key to innovation, which was the key to growth. Growing countries were characterized by the "technological dynamism possessed by their scientists, engineers, and managers" (Heller 1961). This condition for growth implied that the federal government should take on even more responsibility in the education field. Education upgraded skills but, just as importantly, it helped in adjusting to rapid structural changes in the economy (CEA 1962). Whatever the past constraints on federal programs, keeping the supply side of the economy healthy justified an expanded federal role in education. Insuring a healthy civilian economy created the same need for federal manpower programs as did space, defense, and health requirements. Just as the United States needed scientists and engineers with skills relevant to solving space, defense, and health problems, it also needed them with skills useful in attacking the problems of the civilian economy (Cabinet Committee on Growth 1962, 16). Given the excess demand for manpower that the federal government itself had created, there was a shortage of those technical skills that would most benefit the civilian economy. A broad mix of federal assistance — fellowships, grants-in-aid, and research support — would provide incentives for the development of those scarce technical skills. Such assistance had always been favored by the scientific community. It was seen as complementary to the larger-scale, more costly measures that were desperately needed. PSAC, for example, favored upgrading of educational instruction, more equal opportunity, expansion of physical plants, more technical and vocational education, more on-the-job training, and so forth.

Within the administration's broad views on economic growth, PSAC focused on programs for meeting the increased requirements for engineers, mathematicians, and physicists. PSAC defined these requirements or demands very broadly: providing for economic growth, national security, space, health, education for an informed citizenry, and responsiveness to technical change. Not surprisingly, given these primary demands, the derived demands for scientists and engineers were large. Moreover, an augmented numerical supply of scientists would not be sufficient, for an increased supply had to be of sufficient quality. Thus, any increase in numbers also required upgrading existing institutions and creating new centers of excellence. If enough students chose careers in S&T, capacity would become a constraint, a problem that could not be solved in the short run. Consequently, the government had to take action now to avoid future constraints on plant and equipment.

Unlike its previous efforts in manpower planning, PSAC did try to cost out its strongly preferred maximal program. Based on contributions from all sectors of the economy, estimated annual costs rose from $580 million in FY 1964 to $760 million in FY 1970. PSAC did not try to cost out any smaller programs, nor did it consider trade-offs. The president himself had expanded the number of national needs that the federal government was to meet. Since the expansion implied more budget and manpower for the S&T enterprise, PSAC had no incentive to question whether the administration's entire menu of needs was too large or whether some items on the menu were inappropriate. If the federal government wanted its apparently fixed requirements to be met, it would have to finance the necessary additional human and physical capital. It seemed clear that the private sector would not be able to support the required levels of investment. The huge projects that the government was undertaking meant that it had to take charge now in order to have sufficient engineers, mathematicians, and physicists over the long run. Because the production of human capital had such long lead times, the government could not postpone investments on the supply side without jeopardizing its abilities to perform the tasks it had set for itself.

Thus, Kennedy's economic and science advisers both argued that there would be significant payoff from additional investments in education, particularly science education. And, in fact, investments in science education started to climb during the administration's tenure, but not fast enough to meet the perceived demands. Toward the end of the administration, the science adviser remained uncomfortable about the nation's ability to achieve all the objectives that had been defined earlier, but he was unwilling to make trade-offs between objectives or to drop some of them (Wiesner 1963).

Between 1963 and 1965, the science adviser and PSAC made strenuous efforts to increase resource flows to education and research programs. The duality between research and science education allowed OST and PSAC to argue for increases in basic research, because they were needed for educational purposes. President Johnson's strong tastes for federal education programs meant that educational reasons for action now dominated the traditional economic reasons derived from high social returns in the future. PSAC, OST, and the BOB proposed that federal investments in academic research be increased by 15 percent each year. Each 1 percent increase in graduate enrollment implied a 1 percent increase in academic research. (Economists would say that the elasticity of the research budget, with respect to enrollments, was unitary.) Thus, a 10 percent budget increase was justified in terms of increased Ph.D. enrollments. Increased "sophistication" of inquiry justified another 5 percent. As noted in earlier chapters, technologies for inquiry were always becoming more powerful, but necessarily also most costly. Consistent with the kitchen-sink mode of policy argument, the OST provided 11 different reasons why an annual 15 percent increase was a "conservative austere minimum" (OST 1964).

By 1965, the possibility had emerged that the future might bring excess supplies of scientific manpower, rather than the excess demand that was driving the scientists' educational strategy. However, OST argued that the market was myopic; it could only account for expected or predicted contingencies, and these were always based on current experience. A continually expanding academic research budget would create sufficient demand through assured but unpredictable new opportunities. A highly educated labor force would create new institutions and opportunities, and these, in turn, would create an increased demand for education. The United States, having embarked on a general expansion and being certain that it would definitely pay off in the long run, should not be overly sensitive to short-run fluctuations in demand. If the United States wanted a Great Society, it needed more scientists and engineers, no matter some short-run excess supply (OST 1964). In any case, excess supplies of manpower in the research sector could always be absorbed through increased demand by other sectors. Training in science and engineering equipped people to do other things better. (This argument has had a long life, appearing most recently in the Carter administration's review of science education in 1980.)

Although President Johnson did not provide the 15 percent increase that OST desired, he did instruct all government departments to assess the institutional impacts of their research budgets. Since each department bought research products from the universities, their aggregate demand strongly influenced academic research capabilities, and since the agency demand for new information was increasing, like everything else in the Great Society, the president wanted to use agency research budgets to increase the number and geographic distribution of first-rank research universities (Johnson 1965). But this expansionary objective could not last. In 1965, the president's economic advisers were already seeing inflationary pressures arising from the Vietnam War. Believing that inflationary pressures would increase, the advisers wanted tax increases and budgetary stringency; however, President Johnson refused to increase taxes, and with no tax increases, he had to cut his budgets well below what he preferred. A budget that allowed for the war and favored Great Society programs left little that was truly "controllable." Out of a $135 billion budget, BOB estimated that there was only $10.6 billion that the president could affect. Even though science education and academic research might well have qualified as favored Great Society programs under less budgetary pressure, they were among the more truly discretionary items within the controllable budget.

Budgetary pressure downward coincided with the discovery that the president could not simultaneously increase the existing set of first-class research universities while creating new ones in parts of the country that did not have them. Whereas more research universities would, over the long run, maintain and enhance scientific and technical leadership, in the short run the best existing research universities provided this quality. Commitment to creating new centers of excellence was costly and was not a substitute for maintaining the fiscal health of the current system (Hornig 1965). By 1967, the budget was so tight the science adviser was warning the president that he was forcing existing universities to retrench to a point where they could no longer train students effectively. Given the universities' inability to change their input proportions, maintaining effectiveness implied a constant ratio of inputs as enrollments rose (Hornig 1967b), but the rate of increase in inputs did not match the 10 percent increase in graduate student enrollments.

By 1968, the substance of the manpower problem was changing. The predictions of the early 1960s about excess demand for scientists and engineers proved incorrect. Newly revised predictions stated that there would be an excess supply of scientists in most fields by 1980. Among decisionmakers, particularly those in the BOB, the positive image of the federal government alleviating excess demand for scientists and engineers changed to one of a government contributing to excess supply and a waste of resources. Given budgetary stringency for the science enterprise overall, the completion of some national S&T objectives, and political doubts about the federal role in education, manpower programs were bound·to decline drastically, and they did.

The *SE* strategy contained provisions for just such a contingency through its quality statements. If there was now no general need to fill the "pipeline," there still was and always would be a need to insure sufficient quality. The very best students deserved both incentives and praise for excellence, so the NSF and the National Institutes of Health (NIH) managed, with some struggle, to retain their graduate fellowship programs. The possibility that some reasonable fraction of high-quality talent would make significant breakthroughs was deemed sufficient to justify support of some new talent, no matter the amount of excess supply, and the concept of quality included an age factor that was linked with research productivity. Unless a flow of young talent into the scientific enterprise was assured, that enterprise might wither or become less productive. The joint nature of research and education implied this, and the R&D agencies and the scientific community tried to show what the "optimal" fraction of young talent had to be in order to maintain the desired level of productivity. Budgetary stringency meant that the current fraction of young talent was always below the optimal fraction.

The retreat to a quality argument meant that the most persuasive justification for federal funding of science manpower programs was greatly weakened. Compared with "hard" numbers demonstrating or predicting excess demand, shortages based on quality were subject to challenge. Faced with a shortage of quality, a flexible market economy would adjust its factor proportions over time to alleviate the shortage. A greater number of lower-quality science and engineering professionals might be deployed. If trade-offs between equipment and labor could be made, that would be done. If current low-quality factors could be upgraded by additional training or retraining, that would also be done. In any case, while the country and the scientific community knew how to produce greater numbers of scientists and engineers, they did not know how to produce smaller numbers of higher-quality professionals. These had been produced by "fallout," so to speak, from the large numbers the nation had been producing. Thus, the strong desire of the scientific community for a guaranteed flow of young talent could easily be challenged by decisionmakers in the OMB and the White House, and it was.

By the early 1970s, the science manpower problem was one of excess supply, although unemployment rates for scientists and engineers were lower than the general unemployment rate. In fact, the Nixon administration felt it had to embark on reemployment programs for experienced scientists and engineers and also assist new graduates with Ph.D. degrees. The specialized skills of unemployed scientists and engineers were to be put to work on the priority problems of society, as defined by the administration. These were no longer space and defense, but domestic problems such as energy, the environment, and transportation.

During this period of excess supply, the administration saw universities as oblivious to the messages the market was sending. The OST saw the agency that represented the universities — the NSF — as the home of a stodgy bureaucracy unwilling or unable to cope with overproduction of research Ph.D.s. The roundabout nature of Ph.D. production meant that it was hard to turn off the programs that had been started, in response to market fluctuations. Sunk costs matter to universities as well as to bureaucracies. Any bureaucracy whose main clientele was universities would hardly be willing to cut programs that furthered research, no matter the market for Ph.D.s. The situation could be rationalized by the belief that society could always absorb excess supply in the research sector by using more people outside research and by upgrading the credentials required on the outside.

The short-run unemployment among scientists and engineers could be overcome by accelerating their flow to jobs in urban renewal, mass transit, and pollution control. Unemployment, to the administration, was transient, reflecting the time it took to shift workers from space and defense to the domestic areas that now had higher priority and could benefit from larger inputs of scientists and engineers (David 1970a, 1971b). The prospect of excess supply over the long run implied reduction in manpower and training programs. Such reductions were prudent and necessary from a bureaucratic perspective, but reductions in education also implied a budgetary threat in the research area. If Ph.D. production decreased, then research funding ought to be reduced. And if research budgets were reduced, the government contract with science would be strained, if not broken (Handler 1971). Although the budgetary rules for the *SE* strategy are symmetric — increases in Ph.D. production imply greater research budgets and vice versa — practically and politically, they become asymmetric. Increases in research budgets as a result of increased educational demand are welcomed, but budget decreases, in response to decreasing demand, are not. Even if there were less need for human capital, there will always be needs for higher quality in informed citizens.

The OMB, however, maintained downward pressure on science manpower programs throughout the seventies and into the eighties. OMB used a market criterion for sufficiency, and all national projections of scientific and technical manpower continued to show excess supply (NSF 1977b, 1980). Later projections even showed the excess supply increasing overall, although they also highlighted spot shortages for particular skills, for example, computer scientists and engineers. Even so, it was hard to make a case for specific, critical labor bottlenecks as long as market substitutions of related manpower and on-the-job upgrading of skills were permitted.

The scientific and technical community countered predictions about excess quantities with arguments about higher quality, with anecdotes about crises in particular fields, and with the observation that statistical projections wrongly assume that society will not require scientists and engineers to be used with greater intensity. Greater scientific labor intensity would benefit the nation, because technologies not now known would be invented.

Technical objections were also offered. Some of these concerned the possible inability of aggregate projections to identify those specialties that might prove to be true bottlenecks, with respect to national objectives. For example, when the Carter administration embarked on the construction of synthetic fuel plants, there was concern that there were not enough scientists and engineers trained in the necessary skills, but this deficiency would not be picked up by aggregate projections. Of course, these fears arose, because the R&D bureaucracies, wanting larger budgets, argued that the market would not make the relevant substitutions.

Nevertheless, aggregate and independent projections made by different groups consistently suggested that there would be rough equilibrium or excess supply for science and engineering manpower up to 1990. But prospective market equilibrium did not deter the scientific and technical community from suggesting new programs. Thus, in 1979, despite what their own analysis suggested, the Department of Education (DOE) and the NSF proposed new programs that would allow qualified undergraduates to transfer from their current field to one where shortages were expected and would also provide programs for graduate traineeships in fields where there were shortages of personnel. In the case of computer science, the agencies would provide incentives for Ph.D. candidates planning to remain in university research careers and for university faculty and graduate students in computer science to stay on campus. Whether the Carter administration would have taken these proposals seriously is unknown. No cost figures were attached to them, and they were made in a period of budgetary stringency. The OMB implied that any such programs had to be accomplished without incremental funds.

The arrival of the Reagan administration changed the definition of appropriate educational activities. The operation of free markets and the choices of actors in those markets were to determine educational content and structure. Markets were supposed to send signals of excess demand or supply, and consumers and producers of scientific and technical labor were supposed to make adjustments. If they did, then markets would eventually clear (Keyworth 1981; OSTP 1982). There was no federal responsibility to make markets clear. Although the administration saw some difficulties in engineering education and precollege science education, it was not felt that the federal government should address these problems with other than information and "jawboning." Thus, manpower programs in the NSF were disestablished except for a few residual ones of great symbolic value to the scientific community.

By the time of the FY 1984 budget, the Reagan administration had identified one market failure in elementary and secondary education that was worthy of federal correction; this was the "failure" of the market for elementary and secondary science and mathematics teachers. Industry had been outbidding the schools for those with science and mathematics training, leaving unfilled places or places filled with underqualified instructors. The administration perceived a nationwide shortage of such teachers on the one hand, and a large number of unemployed workers with some science and mathematics training on the other. By providing matching grants for state, city, and industry training and retraining programs, the administration hoped to eliminate the excess demand at minimum cost, and by encouraging exposure to science for all citizens, it argued that productivity, technological growth, and military strength would all increase over the long run.

Precollege Science Education

The government's original entrance into precollege science education was logically entailed by the *SE* strategy statement. Given the objective of upgrading elementary and secondary education and given the desire to involve practicing scientists in that upgrading, the development of curriculum materials seemed a cost-effective way of achieving the objective while satisfying the desire. The knowledge base was changing all the time, sometimes year by year, and, as science changed, educational materials ought to change. There would always be some gap between knowledge and school curriculum, but it had to be made narrower (PSAC 1959). Federally supported curriculum development and implementation insured access to the most current scientific knowledge and to the spread of that knowledge throughout the entire system. Although the private sector produced and sold curricula, there is little evidence that the proponents of federal curriculum development worried very much about a market failure or what the trade-off was between direct federal support for development of educational materials and possible subsidy to private developers. The science and education communities implicitly assumed that private developers did not have access to the most current knowledge and, furthermore, that it was not in their interests to revise educational materials at the rate science changed. Consequently, a national need existed for federally developed curriculum.

Given that there was sensitivity about a federal presence in elementary and secondary schools, federally sponsored materials initially had to make their way in the open market without too much investment in implementation and promotion. For example, the NSF tried early on to prevent its teacher-training summer institutes from using the texts it had supported (Lomask 1976). But from a cost-effective perspective, there was no particular point in using federal dollars to develop curriculum without knowing that it would be used. Consequently, one would expect federal decisionmakers eventually to exert pressure for implementation and use, but programs to insure use would increase perception of an augmented federal presence in state and local education.

By the 1970s the federal government had invested in an extensive portfolio of science curricula. The NSF held most of the portfolio but not all of it. It contained projects in the major fields of science taught at the precollege level, including the social sciences; however, there was no explicit design or needs assessment guiding the choice of projects. The economics of curriculum development and the alleged needs that led to the investment were not subject to any formal checks. University-based developers asserted need and the peer review process certified it, but that process was designed to elicit technical merit rather than need.

Need was not a dominant criterion, because curriculum change was less of an objective than was the creation of alternatives that were far more current and accurate in scientific content. The NSF hoped that the technical superiority of its curricula over those in the market would induce needs, but there was no guarantee for adoption. If there was no guarantee, then the front-end investments could be questioned. Consequently, it was relatively easy for decisionmakers to present an alternative strategy of science education and of curriculum development in particular. That strategy can be stated as follows:

DE.1 *The federal government's proper role in precollege science education is to be a change agent (David 1971c).*

DE.2 *Educational innovations should be correlated with national priorities.*

DE.3 *The measure of innovation is the extent of adoption within a finite time period.*

> **DE3.1** *Investments in education cannot be cost-effective without implementation activity (NSF 1974).*

Since the budgetary climate continued to be one of constraint, the OMB used this *DE* strategy, along with the excess supply of scientific manpower, to make large reductions in science education programs and changes in design. Although curriculum projects were not derived from federal needs, there was emphasis on producing educational material relevant to the national priorities defined by the administration. Since the NSF was involved in the maintenance and upgrading of the skills of precollege teachers, it was easy for the OMB and the OST to argue that teacher training should be tied to curriculum implementation (McElroy 1971; David 1971a). In fact, the NSF was to support only training that fostered the use of newly developed curricula. The NSF's institutes had always been predicated on upgrading individual skills; the participants' home schools were not involved. But now the home school's certification of the likelihood of curriculum adoption was involved in the admission process (House Subcommittee on Appropriations 1972).

While the OMB and OST pursued their strategy of appropriate programs, the issue of curriculum content became entwined with the larger issue of the federal role in education. The *SE* strategy entailed the development of curricula in the biological and social sciences as well as in the natural sciences. At least some of the former, and possibly some of the latter, could be expected to offend groups and citizens involved with elementary and secondary education. Given that politicians generally care a great deal about education and gain much from exhibiting their caring, it was inevitable that controversy would arise over the federal role in precollege science education. And given that the agencies involved in developing curricula had never made independent estimates of either economic demand or educational need for the alternatives they were developing, it was inevitable that questions of procedure and judgment would become entangled with those of substantive content.

It is not the intention here to explore science textbook controversies but to present the strategy deployed by the critics of the *SE* strategy (Nelkin 1977). That strategy (the "citizens' education" strategy – *CE*) can be stated as follows:

CE.1 *At least in the biological and social sciences, the presentation of values along with specific content cannot be avoided.*

CE.1 *– Strong Version: The presentation of any kind of content verified only according to the internal logic of science is sufficient to raise value issues.*

CE.2 *Instruction in values is a matter reserved to citizens in the first instance. To the extent public agencies need to be involved, at most, they should operate only at state and local levels.*

CE.3 *Citizen input is a necessary condition for the design and development of precollege curricula (Science Curriculum Implementation Review Group 1975).*

Directly or indirectly, exposure to curriculum teaches children values. In fact, such instruction is one of the purposes of education. Instruction in values has large spillover effects, and so neither parents nor the government can be indifferent to such instruction. Consequently, parent input was necessary at all stages of curriculum development.

CE.4 *The free market for curriculum better reflects the tastes and preferences of citizens and localities than does demand from the scientific community expressed through federal agencies.*

    CE4.1 *Private sector publishers and developers are better equipped than federal agencies to supply curriculum that* *is matched to community preferences and is scientifically valid.*

CE4.1 is the educational analogue of the debate about who knows more about the prospects for technological innovation — firms or bureaucracies. Publishers were far closer to local community sentiment than were university-based educators or federal R&D agencies and close enough to scientists and science educators who wrote textbooks to be far more preferable producers of curriculum than were "faceless bureaucrats."

CE4.2 *The market failures of federally funded curriculum entail federal attempts to promote curriculum.*

Failures in federal programs, unlike failures in the private sector, do not cause agencies to cut their losses and stop production. Rather, they call for renewed efforts and expenditures to achieve success. Visible cutting of losses has very strong and negative implications for agency budgets.

To the OMB, mandating curriculum implementation was just a sensible way of insuring the cost-effectiveness of a federal investment. From the OMB perspective, curriculum was a special case in the economics of information — once information has been produced, it pays society to disseminate it as widely as possible. In the citizens' strategy, however, such dissemination appears to be an improper intrusion of the federal government. The citizen groups complained, for example, that the NSF never had clear authority to establish implementation activities or to impose constraints on teacher training institutes in order to insure adoption. The NSF, however, was in no position to air its disagreements with the OMB and OST over increasing federal implementation activities.

Curriculum development had lower priority in the NSF than did other activities. Caught between contending policies and worried about "spillover" effects on the budget for more highly valued programs — basic research — it was prudent for the NSF to reduce its commitments in curriculum development and implementation and change its procedures. Under direct pressure from mobilized citizen groups, and the Congress, the budget for this activity fell from a high of $16 million to $2 million, and the approach changed. The agency tried to take a rational systems approach to curriculum development. Instead of relying on developing proposals to make a case for need, the agency commissioned third-party analytic needs assessment. It broadened its peer review process to include informed citizens and parents and also adopted a prototype approach so that the agency could judge predicted outcomes with more information in hand at any point in the development process (NSF 1977b).

Despite pressure from competing alternatives and evidence of failure, strategies change slowly over time, but the value propositions hardly change at all. In spite of the decline of curriculum development activities, the desire remained, and despite the important victory in upgrading curricula for the natural sciences and mathematics, there was still the challenge of curricula for ordinary students who needed to become informed citizens. The scientific community still believed that daily encounters with science and technology-based products or decisions required substantive exposure to science and technology (NSF and DOE 1980). Given limited resources for science education and this kind of perspective, one can expect the NSF and the other education agencies to start up curriculum programs once more. Per dollar of expenditure, they expose more citizens to S&T than does any other alternative. In fact, the most recent consideration of curriculum development, a study commissioned by the National Science Board, the NSF's policy and governing board, argues the national need for NSF to return to curriculum development and dissemination (National Science Board Commission on Precollege Education in Mathematics, Science, and Technology 1983).

Science Literacy

There are more than enough axioms and propositions in a strategy to maintain a core, even when portions of it are destroyed or damaged; believers will shift from destroyed or damaged propositions and statements. So it is with the *SE* model. If federal support for science education could not be maintained upon manpower grounds and if reaching out to elementary and high school students was inappropriate, then there was still a need to create informed citizens.

Adequate information is a necessary condition for participation in political and economic decisions. Voting, at least in ideal theories of democracy, should require immersing oneself in issues. And markets work properly only when consumers and producers have knowledge of relevant prices. But these prices must truly reflect technological conditions, resource constraints, and qualitative properties of the goods and services being exchanged, including the risks associated with their use. If they do, producers and consumers ordinarily do not need any special knowledge of S&T to go about their business of exchange. The scientific and technical community felt that markets miss important information when they have to handle goods, services, and processes that have high S&T content. If some relevant information is not conveyed by markets, then the amounts of goods and services the economy produces could not be optimal and they will not have desired properties. This makes a case for government literacy efforts. The additional claim raised in the *SE* strategy is that some property of policy issues with high science and technology content inherently prevents citizens and their representatives from obtaining the requisite knowledge for informed decisions. This barrier to knowledge has to be overcome by special educational efforts aimed at the public.

To the extent the public is involved in decisions about the conduct of science itself, it needs to know something about what scientists do, how they do it, and with what canons. And to the extent that the public must make decisions about the deployment or regulation of technology, it needs to know what the technology does, how it does it, and what the social and economic impacts might be. So federal programs in support of science for citizens could include explanations of scientific undertakings and also the presentation of debate and analysis of technological issues. For example, the NSF has supported the television show, NOVA, which does both jobs, and it also has provided funds for citizens' groups to acquire experts on issues of concern so that they might educate themselves and become more effective intervenors.

But what is so peculiar about S&T that public choices require special intervention by the federal government? The scientific community believes that, because S&T is operating everywhere, even the choice of consumer goods requires some knowledge. That such choices go on all the time without such knowledge is no deterrent to such a view, for actual choices would be better if citizens had such knowledge. Because scientific information is complex and because it is held by small groups with years of specialized training, it does not, in such a view, flow in the right directions or to the right people without help. This condition is permanent. But we can surmount it in the long run by improving our educational system. Important technological decisions have to be made in the short run, however, making special literacy efforts necessary. The scientific community knows or can discover the kinds of scientific and technical information citizens really need in the short run in order to make informed decisions and can, without too much difficulty, make citizens understand the missing information and its relevance.

This view of citizens as lacking scientific and technical information and, therefore, being incapable of making informed decisions has persisted for a long time. But there has never been a clear statement of the nature of public decisions nor of whether increased doses of science literacy would make any difference in the quality of decisionmaking, ex ante, or in actual outcomes. The language of exhortation common in science education debates suggests that all citizens have a need for science literacy and a right or entitlement to it. Such a right characteristically raises unbounded claims for resources, and such claims always cause difficulty in obtaining reasonable funds and programs for science literacy. Those programs that are feasible, practical, and politically possible will always seem ineffective, relative to the numbers that claim to have the right or to hold the entitlement. If there can be only ineffective programs, then why have any?

On the other hand, notions that a lack of scientific and technical information is the root cause of poor public decisions do not exhibit much sophistication about decisionmaking. In many, if not most cases, there is more than enough information; it is the analysis and inferences that are faulty. But improving public policy analysis and "strategic" intelligence are not matters that can be helped by increased deliveries of information from the scientific community. They are matters of institutional design and communications linkage.

Where does such a situation leave the science literacy movement? Its intellectual foundations are in much the same shape as those of the curriculum development movement. No doubt a persuasive intellectual case for some science literacy effort by the federal government could be established. But the reasoning would need to be more complex than the kind scientists and educators are accustomed to using whenever they venture into policymaking, and their claims for resources would have to be bounded.

Strategies for 1984: Education as Economic Warfare

Since World War II, American education has seen several waves of reform, each designed to correct important deficiencies. By 1983 the nation's educational system was perceived once more as a failure. The cognitive quality of American education was questioned because of continuously declining test scores, and it certainly had difficulty meeting the social objectives assigned to it. Each reform movement hoped to improve education in some dimension, but somehow the collective outcome of all of the efforts at reform was a failure. A rising tide of mediocrity seems to have been the result of the combined efforts to improve the system (National Commission on Excellence in Education 1983).

Conceiving of education as a necessary contribution to an economic race with other nations, many consider this mediocre education to be the cause of a current or immediately prospective U.S. decline in commerce, industry, science, and technological innovation. The growing economic competitiveness of other nations is, at root, a matter of their superior and more intense educational systems. Comparing education to war, the National Commission on Excellence in Education (1983, 5) argues that continued adherence to the current educational system is "an unthinking act of unilateral disarmament." We are also, according to the commission, disarming ourselves as individual citizens, because shared education is essential to a free, open, democratic society. In a technological age, shared scientific and technological knowledge is seen as essential. The commission finds that the "cafeteria style" curriculum diverts attention from main courses to appetizers and desserts, from hard substantive learning in mathematics and science to physical and health courses and personal development.

The Twentieth Century Fund, at exactly the same time, reported similar views for similar reasons (Twentieth Century Fund 1983). It found marked deterioration in the quality of mathematics and science instruction, in particular, and major deficiencies in science literacy. Science literacy is necessary for two major reasons. First, the students of today are the human capital of tomorrow. The quality of future human capital rests on the scientific and technological literacy that is built today. Without high-quality capital, the United States will lose out in its competition with other nations. Second, without science literacy, citizens cannot participate intelligently in controversial political decisions about, for instance, radiation, pollution, or nuclear energy. These are essentially the statements from the *SE* strategy. The Twentieth Century Fund report makes the usual general recommendation that the federal government "emphasize" programs of science literacy for all citizens and programs to provide advanced training in science and mathematics for high school students. It sees proposed administration programs of $50 million to do these jobs as too small, and even the more ambitious proposals of the Congress — $400 million to $500 million — are seen only as moving in the right direction.

At the same time and in a similar vein, the National Task Force on Economic Growth contends that the United States needs profound changes in its system of education, if it is to keep pace with Japan and other competitors. This task force cites high-quality human capital as necessary for domestic growth and international trade (ECS 1983).

Concern about education is certainly well placed and necessary without reference to economic competition or public decisions. But to decide to change the system in a reasonable way, one needs to examine the policy language science educators are using and assess declared economic and social warrants they are offering for action. After all, it was just such language that led to making the changes that have now resulted in bad outcomes. The language, as is typical, is crisis language, and the forecasts of the future without powerful social intervention are grim indeed — unilateral disarmament in the face of determined economic adversaries, if not enemies, and bad public decisions by uninformed citizens.

These reports present one economic justification for improving education and one political one. The quality and intensity of education, particularly at the precollege level, are seen as determining international economic competitiveness. At times, the reports appear to argue that improved education is both necessary and sufficient for economic competition. Goods and services are merely congealed knowledge, and that knowledge finally resides in a highly educated labor force. Japan's economic performance is usually cited as a good example of the connection between education and competitiveness.

A moment's reflection should convince us, however, that this connection is not at all clear. Science educators claim the Soviet Union has a high-quality, intense system of precollege education with very heavy emphasis on mathematics and science. It was fear, once again, that the Soviet Union might be outracing the United States in science education that led a number of scientists and educators to urge President Carter to reconsider his science education programs. Yet the domestic economic performance of the Soviet economy is exceedingly poor. One might argue that the Soviets allocate their highest-quality human capital to military R&D. But here the United States claims qualitative, that is, technological, superiority over the Soviet Union, and there is evidence that that claim has some substance.

Other Western industrialized countries, where much more mathematics and science education is provided than in the United States, have also seen their growth rates fall precipitously and have also lost economic competitiveness. West Germany has certainly been no slouch at precollege education, but it has faltered economically. Japan's growth rate, in fact, has also fallen, although it is still respectable. We have seen developing nations win trade wars without highly educated populations, and we should expect this to happen. Somewhere a nation highly endowed with uneducated labor will have a comparative advantage in goods and services that can utilize that labor. Nations can make their way in the world without highly educated populations, however desirable they may be. And relatively uneducated populations, by Western standards, have shown that they can produce high-technology goods and services.

Education is neither necessary nor sufficient for economic growth and competitiveness. Much of economic competitiveness rests on macroeconomic fluctuations in price levels, interest rates, and exchange rates. While these factors may have some connection with the quality of human capital and the science literacy of citizens, it is indirect and complex. Improving science education, on economic grounds, is not a clearly superior alternative to working directly on prices, interest rates, and exchange rates. Economists and decisionmakers have some notion of what works with respect to these.

If one believes that the true source of U.S. comparative advantage is innovation, then what is needed is a labor force that can shift in and out of different lines of work as the United States loses comparative advantage in some products and services and creates it in others. Higher-quality, more intense science education might very well make human capital more flexible, malleable, and resilient. But that demonstration has not been made.

I have already addressed the science literacy issue. The extrinsic arguments for it have remained remarkably constant. Either bad public decisions will be made, or citizens will not accept reasonable decisions that are made. These arguments are certainly strong ones. The assertions of the consequences of lack of science literacy are truly appalling, but nowhere is there a specification of the content of science literacy and how that content helps citizens make better decisions. As explained in Chapter 7, public policy debate does not turn on the science literacy of the participants; it is about the performance or regulation of public programs or systems. Debates about the performance of public systems do not depend on information held internally by the scientific enterprise, that is, knowledge about physics, chemistry, biology. The variables in policy debates are costs, effectiveness, externalities, side effects, distributional effects, political and organizational feasibility, and so forth. Technology, and presumably the science behind it, certainly sets boundaries on the performance characteristics that have to be considered seriously. For example, if citizens want to involve themselves in issues of nuclear strategy, they probably should know something about variables such as weapons radius, circular probable error, and reliability, and how they relate to one another and to predicted outcomes. Outcomes that decisionmakers talk about seriously are predicated on the values assigned to those variables, but citizens do not have any clear need to know the science and engineering principles that determine them. This means that citizens can participate effectively in public policy debate. Requiring science literacy, in the sense of knowledge of scientific principles, would prevent participation. However, even though we want effective citizen participation in public debate, we should not be prepared to argue that courses in public decisionmaking and policy analysis replace courses in physics and chemistry (*Wall Street Journal* 1983). Citizens need scientists and engineers to tell them what effectiveness they can expect from a system, and they may need economists to tell them about the economic efficiency of alternative systems. They may even need philosophers to tell them about the justice of alternative systems. But they do not need to know the internal language of natural science, economics, or philosophy or to have deep technical knowledge. If science literacy in the strict sense were truly required for decisionmaking, no decisions would ever be made.

Where does this leave proposals to reform the educational system, and particularly proposals for the reform of the science and mathematics curricula? It leaves them weak on utility as the justification when utility is argued as casually as it is in macroscale studies and reports on education. Utilitarian statements are offered to make a case for federal responsibility, dollars and programs, and interest, and they are stated as self-evident. But given the history and the design of the U.S. education system, there exists a rebuttable presumption that education, and especially precollege education, is not a matter for the federal government. Given good enough reasons, citizens should be prepared to rebut this assumption. To advocates of improved education, it seems easier to rebut the presumption with utilitarian arguments about losses in economic competitiveness, the relatively superior education systems of allies or adversaries, and poor or undemocratic public decisions. But such arguments as now presented must be considered unsophisticated and not truly persuasive.

Utilitarian arguments to rebut the presumption can no doubt be constructed, but they will have to be more complex and indirect than those seen for the last twenty-five years. In particular, the incentives and disincentives created by educational agents themselves need to be addressed. Educational reform movements traditionally begin with a perception of poor performance on some desirable or valuable dimension. They propose a general cure or reform and implement it. As the reform is implemented, some other dimensions of the educational system become affected, and the system overall continues to perform poorly. In other words, reform has diminishing returns. There are only so many things that can be taught, desirable as they all may be, and cognitive, economic, and political limits all affect the educational system.

Educational reform movements never encompass the tragedy of trade-offs. If they did, it would be hard to maintain the enthusiasm and certainty required to make changes. As reform movements achieve their objectives, the limits and trade-offs come into play, and yet another deficiency emerges. If high-level science and mathematics are taught, they take time and attention away from our attempts to instill basic skills. If substantive learning is emphasized, that takes time away from attempts to make children good citizens or, for that matter, good people. Since we cannot agree, collectively, on the purposes of education, some educational crisis will always be emerging. And since the educational system cannot solve its own crises, there will be continuous calls for outside forces to intervene. Government should take responsibility or industry should, but not without wariness about the inherent limits of reform inevitable in the large, complex, highly differentiated educational system that the United States has developed.

In addition, a careful examination of the incentives and disincentives produced by the federal government is probably in order whenever one is trying to solve an educational crisis. After all, while the National Commission on Excellence in Education sees the mediocrity of the schools as an outcome sufficient to rebut the presumption of no federal presence, President Reagan sees the mediocrity as caused by twenty years of intrusion into the schools.

The government's tastes for its own presence in the educational system have ranged from the jawboning of the early Eisenhower administration to the promotion of curriculum in the name of efficiency and effectiveness during the Nixon administration to the laissez-faire attitude of the Reagan administration. Whatever administration has been in power, federal programs have all operated with the rebuttable presumption intact, that is, programs and resources must be limited. Since federal resources can never be large, programs have to be designed for what bureaucrats call maximum leverage. Leverage, for example, drives the government to support of science curriculum development. For a given level of resources, curriculum will reach more of a targeted clientele than will other programs. If we believe a crisis is great enough, we may wish to drop the rebuttable assumption altogether and stop straining for leverage. Few, if any, of our adversaries and allies hold to it. But if we decide to enlarge the federal role in education, we may as well address educational issues in their own terms. What is it as a whole that we want the system to do? What can we not do? What do we have to drop? Above all, we need to think about education with more precision and with a finer degree of resolution than we have so far been able to accomplish.

The Uses of Scientific and Technical Information

5

The stock of scientific and technical information (denoted STI) that society creates has a triple role: (1) providing the base for further scientific and technical advance, (2) creating new possibilities for industrial innovation, and (3) aiding in the solution of public policy problems. Within the S&T enterprise itself, it makes sense to think about information processes as reflexive and adaptive. At any one time, scientists and engineers employ currently available information to change the substantive relations between fields and areas, generating additional, usually more complex, and higher-cost information in further rounds of inquiry. Although the enterprise has its own traditional procedures for validating and disseminating its outputs, public investment in the production of research always raises questions about correlative policies and investments for its dissemination. There is little point in producing information without disseminating it, and once produced, it should be disseminated as widely as possible. Even when monopolies in information — patents — are granted, they are temporary and require that now-protected information be disclosed in exchange for the monopoly so that others may learn from it.

The rate and volume of information transfer between the scientific and technical communities and industry are now a public concern since most industrial innovation strategies assume, at least for recent periods, that information from basic and applied research activity is a necessary condition for innovation. Here we have to ask whether the "internal" science information market has sufficient links with the "external" market in industry. If not, what arrangements need to be made to insure that more scientific and technical knowledge is available for incorporation in physical plant and capital equipment or new products and services?

STI is needed not just to make things, but to make public policy. Available STI determines, in part, feasible choices for domains outside of S&T. In fact, new STI may create policy issues where none may have previously existed. For example, some previously undetected health effects of the environment will raise new questions about regulation. We may want to know the effectiveness of current policies, for instance, in the health or energy domains. The only way to know this is through the collective ordering and analysis of available STI. Using STI for decisionmaking is a more complex task than using it to produce goods and services. To have utility for decisionmaking, information has to have, or be made to gain, properties beyond those it naturally has as a product of scientific inquiry. In addition to being valid, information has to be timely, relevant, and actionable. Otherwise, it will have little value for pending decisions, although information without these properties may increase the personal sensitivity and awareness of decisionmakers about the issues they confront.

Finding or creating STI with the necessary properties is not easy. Even validity is conditional. Public policy issues will often be of concern in areas where science is uncertain. Validity depends on further inquiry and checking by the scientific and technical community, and this takes time. But decisions have to be made now. Furthermore, relevance to public policy issues is not a norm for the practice of science, and some people think such a norm would be destructive, both to science and public policy. Relevance, in this view, reveals itself over time in deeper ways. Satisfying the short-run needs of transient decisionmakers may prevent such revelations and may misallocate resources. Information keyed to the short-run policy instruments that decisionmakers command is hard to find, and information that can be keyed to long-run instruments is hard to predict accurately. Thus, the status of STI in decisionmaking is ambiguous at best and uncomfortable at worst. Given that there has to be some translation between the language of science and engineering and the language of public policy and decisions, we need to ask about reasonable uses of STI in policy debates and decisions.

In this chapter, I will explore the strategies and perspectives that have been used in debate over STI itself. The analytical procedure will be similar to that in previous chapters. I will construct or reconstruct the strategies that important actors have used in making information policy and will try to show how they influenced actions or decisions. At the end of the chapter, I will suggest some alternative ways of thinking about STI problems.

The Internal Market for STI

Results from basic research traditionally reach their audience via word of mouth and publication in refereed journals. Dissemination is so ingrained as a norm of scientific inquiry that its effectiveness and efficiency have only been sporadically examined (Polanyi 1968). The classic texts of science policy, so rich in argument and advocacy, devote little, if any, discussion to information issues. *Science: The Endless Frontier* briefly refers to a government role in enhancing international flows of STI. Vannevar Bush presumably saw some barriers to free flow here, whereas he could reasonably believe domestic information flows were well channeled by the ordinary standards and norms of scientific practice (Bush [1945] 1980, 74). His principal action recommendation — federal support of research — presumably took care of any domestic information problem, but not necessarily of the communications between U.S. scientists and those of other countries. Yet he did not go on, as he might have, to draw possible conclusions about comparative advantage and national specialization in research, if STI flowed freely across national borders. The report of the President's Scientific Research Board similarly made no comment on any problems about domestic information flows, although it noted the need for the United States to help reconstruct European laboratories and increase the international flow of students and professionals, implying that international barriers existed (PSRB 1947).

During the Eisenhower administration, federal coordination of the resources for research became a salient issue to the president and his budgetary advisers (see chap. 2). The demand for greater coordination forced the scientific and technical community to be more explicit about its perceptions of information flow and the organizations that promoted it. Those perceptions stemmed from the craft rules of science and engineering. The rules implied that a decentralized, atomistic "internal" market would be an appropriate choice, provided it did not grow too large and complex. If producers and users (other producers) did not have to invest significant time and resources in searching for existing information, rather than producing new information, then traditional mechanisms would suffice.

Until World War II, scientists believed that the trade-off between searching for existing information and producing new information was highly favorable to the latter. However, as the scientific enterprise expanded, they saw the internal market beginning to break down. The sheer increase in production meant an increased literature that had to be searched. Given limited time and resources, no one would be able to keep up, thereby reducing efficiency and effectiveness. If no one could keep up, research might have diminishing returns. To prevent this possibility, additional federal efforts were seen as necessary, just as they were in science education.

The strategy for information dissemination (denoted *SID*) can be stated as follows:

SID.1 *The standards and norms of science demand that investigators offer the information they produce to others, freely and quickly. Investigators, in turn, should follow and check the work of others, quickly and eagerly.*

The publication of research information is absolutely essential to every working scientist for two reasons: (1) It is the means by which he announces significant results for his own work, establishes priority where appropriate, and invites the evaluation of other scientists; (2) It is also the means by which he keeps abreast of what others are doing in his field. (PSAC 1958, 1)

SID.2 *To be effective and efficient, scientists need all information relevant to their inquiries.*

SID.3 *The internal market for information coordinates the overall directions of basic research and allocates society's resources to the most promising lines of research.*

This internal market had its own clearing mechanism. Damage to reputation and standing was the price to be paid for low-quality research or unknowing duplication of effort. Consequently, scientists who engaged in basic research had to keep up. With such motivation, the internal market sent correct signals, and there did not have to be any extramarket coordination (Waterman 1956).

   SID3.1 *Corollary: The allocation of federal resources for basic research can and should be done by consulting those investigators who know the internal market well. Levels and direction of research support should be consistent with assessments of the internal market by knowledgeable practitioners.*

SID.4 *The internal market for science information breaks down because (1) scientific progress increases the volume of information that each producer has to track, and (2) the number of practitioners increases over time.*

The problems created by the ever-rising flow of scientific and technical information have been strikingly illustrated in individual fields by showing that it would be impossible to keep abreast of all relevant information even if a scientist devoted virtually every waking moment to reading. (NAS 1969a, 178)

SID.5 *The internal STI market works best when it contains a broad mix of suppliers — government, nonprofit, and private vendors —*

who aggregate and arrange research output, making it of greater use.

SID5.1 *To realize the benefits from its own investments in science, the federal government should augment the resources available to the internal market but not alter the character of information suppliers and vendors.*

SID5.2 *Coordination of the internal market can be done by indicative planning — agents letting each other know their intentions — rather than by central directives.*

SID.6 *There is no reason to believe that scientific progress is limited to any single nation, but nations erect barriers preventing the free flow of STI across borders.*

SID6.1 *Federal resources should be used to overcome barriers to free international flows of nonproprietary STI.*

SID6.1 applies primarily to basic research. Since high-quality basic research can arise anywhere, the federal government should make sure that U.S. scientists have access to it. Scientists engaged in basic research need not, of course, concern themselves with proprietary STI. However, the United States has a long history of trying to preserve the international rights of U.S. firms that hold proprietary STI, especially those whose technological information is the ultimate reason for trade. For example, the U.S. government has long been resistant to demands for a new international economic order (NIEO) by developing nations. NIEO depends on more favorable access to proprietary technological information held by Western firms, particularly the large multinational corporations.

How the Strategy Worked

Debate over the structure of the internal market for STI has not engaged many public or private stakeholders. Choices over its structure can affect future economic performance and the conduct of public policy. So the public had some stake, and there were private suppliers of STI services, for example, libraries and abstract and information services, whose welfare was seen as threatened by federal interventions in the STI market. But, in the main, debate about alternative structures was more concerned with technical and economic factors than with passionately held and opposing values about what should be done with information.

Since U.S. scientists and engineers were highly dispersed and decentralized, they preferred decentralized federal information services. In the Eisenhower administration, PSAC argued that centralized information systems were only consistent with a centralized organization of the research enterprise, although other pairings were theoretically feasible. The internal market reacted rapidly because it was not hampered by central bureaus. Investigators could use whatever means of getting information they liked, subject to any resource constraints they had. Since they knew their fields and their own constraints well, whatever searching they did reflected directly the utility that that information had for them. Turning STI over to government bureaus would mean bureaucratic utility, not that of investigators, was being maximized (PSAC 1958).

Based on PSAC's views, President Eisenhower chose a decentralized delivery mode for STI. He directed the NSF to support private indexing and abstracting services as well as to support research on new methods and technologies for handling information. He also directed the agency to review and coordinate the science information programs of other federal agencies, since, to him, coordination was always the path to effectiveness. The president amended Executive Order 10521 (referred to in chap. 2), authorizing the NSF to do the coordination. (He does not appear to have recalled his previous experience with the NSF in a coordinating role.)

The NSF responded to its STI mandate by setting up an internal information office and an interdepartmental committee. The one thing it did not do was coordinate other agency STI programs. In highly predictable, rational bureaucratic behavior, the interdepartmental committee assigned to the director of the NSF the role of alerting agencies to emerging STI problems (Adkinson 1978). Since the NSF could not know agency practice in using STI, this assured that the NSF would not do much coordination, a situation desired by the NSF and the agencies. The same structural difficulties and policy reluctance that prevented the NSF from coordinating federal research programs also prevented it from coordinating the dissemination of research.

With the advent of the Kennedy administration, the new science adviser decided to have PSAC do more analysis of the issues. PSAC developed the Crawford report in 1962 and the Weinberg report in 1963 (PSAC 1962, 1963). PSAC, unsurprisingly, found that a clear government interest existed in the dissemination of STI, because dissemination was necessary for research. Following the lines of the SID model, PSAC argued that science was fragmenting into a mass of repetitive findings and practitioners were now incurring significant costs of time and resources in accessing information. Despite its finding of government interest, PSAC was unable to agree on the level of effort for information dissemination. It recognized that claims to resources always outrun their availability, but its strategy contained no propositions about reasonable levels of investments in dissemination, let alone the optimal level (PSAC 1963).

PSAC went on to recommend that a central coordination role be given to OST and that the government keep track of planned and current research. A government-wide central clearing house would report research results of federally supported work and would provide access to federally supported data bases. Whatever the level of resources, PSAC saw a need to support specialists who would integrate information and argued that such specialists were necessary for maintaining research productivity. It urged distinguished practitioners to allocate some of their scarce time for reviews, interpretation, and evaluation of existing findings. If they did not, average research productivity would decline (PSAC 1963, 14).

The Johnson administration saw the STI problem in much the same way as had preceding administrations. The supply of STI was outrunning the ability to handle it, and handling costs were now budgetarily significant, estimated at $500 million a year. Federal information systems remained decentralized and employed private vendors for specialized uses, but decentralization had its costs in duplication. For example, systems were not interconnected, and this meant that all information relevant to a question or an issue could not be accessed through a single system. It was necessary to have all recorded information in one system in order to avoid duplication and perceive significant relationships. While there did not have to be a single operating service, there was a need for central coordination and exchange. The federal interagency coordination committee for STI (COSATI) saw a need for centralization in the midst of decentralization (COSATI 1966).

To remedy this situation, COSATI recommended to President Johnson that the various federal systems be networked and that there be tighter links between users and the various operational information systems. Tighter linkage would make for improved STI practice and policy. But just as research funds were being cut because of the cost of the Vietnam War, funds for information systems were also being cut. The administration decided to take another look at the issues, and in 1965 commissioned a lengthy examination of STI by the National Academy of Science (known at SATCOM) (NAS 1969a). Completed in 1969, SATCOM produced fifty-five different recommendations for improving STI. Although many of these were not decision oriented, some bore on public policy and the structure of the internal market.

The federal government had by now recognized the importance of STI dissemination by allowing publication costs to be a legitimate charge in research grants; however, SATCOM saw incipient market failure. Information remained fragmented and unintegrated. What was required and what would reduce the costs of search were integrated evaluations that would make new and old information clear. Science and technology were growing so complex that the standard reference lists then produced by STI services were difficult to use. To maximize payoff, STI had to be organized and translated according to user criteria (NAS 1969a). Thus, SATCOM wanted the federal government to support information consolidation activities and state-of-the-art reviews and evaluations. Consistent with this need, SATCOM wanted to develop cross-disciplinary information systems with greater standardization so that all information relevant to a given inquiry could be derived from a single search. With respect to organization, SATCOM wanted to maintain the traditional, decentralized systems for disseminating STI but wanted some central coordinating activity. Since SATCOM saw the federal government as a source of funds for maintaining internal STI flows but not as an operator itself of research information systems, it proposed that the National Academy of Science establish a commission that would coordinate private suppliers of STI and provide a single forum in which the federal government could suggest its preferred policy. Coordination would emerge not through federal dictation but through indicative planning. Each agent would adjust his actions as he learned about the plans of other agents.

These improvements in domestic information flows were to be accompanied by improvements in international flows, since, for maximum effectiveness, any given national S&T enterprise had to be able to capture the information produced in another enterprise. Every nation had comparative advantage in some basic research field, and the world's output of research increased by exchange of results — when one knew about them. National STI services, each with their own rules, could be neither efficient nor effective in disseminating results (NAS 1969a, 31–32). So SATCOM wanted government support of private international exchange programs, a priori agreements on how information from jointly conducted international research projects would be stored and transferred, and representation of the private sector in internationally managed STI projects.

Writing during the high tide of the Great Society, the SATCOM authors and the scientific community recognized for the first time that STI had to go to nonresearch scientists and to problem solvers in industry, agriculture, and the public sector. So a statement connecting the internal and external markets for STI was added to the basic strategy.

SID.7 *STI produced in the internal market should be transformed and translated for use in the external market.*

These nonresearch practitioners also needed consolidation and integrated reviews and assessments. But the different perspectives and utilities they attached to STI meant that consolidations designed for active researchers might not serve other users. Consolidation had to be tailored to particular "spot" demands for evaluated, interdisciplinary information. The spot demand usually arose because users did not have information linking different disciplines. Finding or inferring linkages and interactions between fields implied that specialized services, "light on their feet," might be able to help (NAS 1969a).

Although SATCOM had no direct action consequences, it kept the disposition of STI alive as a policy issue and maintained visible continuity in the STI preferences of the scientific and technical community. The SATCOM authors noted that they were writing in the same tradition as the earlier Crawford and Weinberg reports. This tradition held in subsequent examinations of STI. In 1972, the NSF commissioned yet another STI examination – the Greenberger report. With respect to the classical issues concerning the internal market for scientific and technical information, the Greenberger report carried on SATCOM's thrust for information consolidation and evaluation. It argued that evaluated, consolidated information economized on search time and suggested that such evaluations be a legitimate cost of federally funded research projects (Greenberger 1972, 37).

Picking up the SATCOM theme on STI use by nonscientists, the Greenberger report argued that deliveries of ordered information from the internal to the external market were growing more important. Merging finally into science education concerns, Greenberger asserted that properly educated citizens would have to be taught how to be efficient information seekers; this was a forerunner of the computer literacy movement.

The Greenberger report saw all public issues as having S&T content; thus, STI problems merged into more general concerns about the information available to make public policy. Since most of the current supply of STI was produced by and directed toward the traditional disciplines, there appeared to be a structural mismatch between the public demand for STI and its supply. The public did not understand the process that turned basic research information into results relevant to policy, and so it was not aware of either the possibilities or the limits involved in using STI for policy purposes. The scientific and technical community, however, was not interested and had no comparative advantage in producing information for the external policy market rather than the internal market. The incentives for producing for the internal market were certainly far more powerful than those for producing for the external market.

The Greenberger report also found deficiencies in STI policy and management. The government simply had not addressed itself to rules for intervention in this market or to the basis for subsidizing private suppliers, and it had not established any policies on international transfer. Echoing the themes of earlier reports, the Greenberger report advocated an information policy board that would reside at the NSF. (It did not recognize the NSF's checkered history in coordinating any federal S&T activities.) This information policy board was to conduct strategic intelligence and analysis work on the development of the market for STI and provide a forum for public and private agents in STI (Greenberger 1972).

The Greenberger report's most important message was the reorienting of STI so that it could be brought to bear on the numerous policy problems that had some S&T content. Since nearly all problems were so defined, this recommendation was unbounded. Highly general, unbounded recommendations are difficult to translate into concrete programs and bureaucratic operations; thus, lack of federal action was predictable. The scope of the recommendations, the technical difficulties in implementing them, the prior and fragmented investments in the public and private sectors, and the interests of information bureaucracies in remaining uncoordinated meant that the Greenberger report's message would receive little attention at best and resistance at worst, and so it turned out.

In 1975 the Greenberger report was followed by a broader study of the National Commission on Libraries and Information Science (NCLIS 1975). NCLIS injected entitlement and equity notions into information strategies. It proposed that equality of access to information become an important design principle for information systems and suggested that an integrated, federally supported network holding general-purpose information would be cost-effective. Such a network would provide equal access for all at a reasonable cost. By extension, STI systems ought to have the same properties. Equality of access to STI systems meant that there would have to be either a massive translation and sorting of STI to meet the requirements or creation of special intermediate services, tailoring information to users' needs and their technical and fiscal abilities to access information.

The next specific look at STI issues occurred in 1977 when the director of the NSF commissioned his Task Force on Science Information Activities (Task Force on Information Science 1977). Although it was primarily oriented toward the highly limited NSF operating programs, it had to consider the whole STI industry to make its principal point. The Task Force argued that the information industry had developed to the point where it no longer needed federal subsidies for STI operations. However, the information industry was in need of research; therefore, agencies dealing in STI, particularly the NSF, should support research in information science rather than subsidize the operations of private vendors.

In the early eighties, the traditional concerns about STI continued to be expressed, although no one could argue that STI issues were taken very seriously. To some, the STI explosion continued to be a problem with which no federal entities were coping. Fragmentation and poor coordination continued to be characteristic of the federal government. The situation existed because no one was interested in central policy-making or capable of producing it (Hilman 1981). Others argued that the need for central policymaking had declined markedly because of technological advance and cost reductions.

Assessment of Policy Prescriptions for the Internal Market

The most striking thing about the STI strategies just examined is their lack of impact. Twenty-five years worth of ongoing studies all argue that a significant information problem exists. Information flow, they all say, has been too fragmented and disaggregated. Substantively, they have all tried to legitimize consolidation, integration, and evaluation as critically necessary functions of the STI system. But no such functions have clearly emerged. Similarly, national coordination and oversight have been the organizational solutions preferred for solving the problem, but no such coordination exists. The market for STI continues to work without benefit of the national framework that the studies believed was necessary.

A number of reasons help to account for this curious situation. First, the perceptions of the STI community about the way scientific research is done may not be correct. Second, the perceptions and assumptions about the way nonscientists use STI may also be questionable. Third, the need for coordination may have declined because of advancing information technology and the evolution of private markets.

It is not my intention here to go deeply into the ways scientists do their work or use information. But the portrait used to justify integrated, consolidated, networked STI systems may simply be wrong. In this portrait, scientists search out all the relevant literature, collect and integrate it in their minds, and then decide what unresolved research questions to tackle and what procedures to use. Such behavior may tell someone where to do incremental, routine science, but not necessarily where to go for breakthroughs.

If the scientist is at the frontier of his discipline, he already knows the breakthrough research that has been accomplished recently. His "invisi-ble college" of colleagues and competitors has already sent this message long before it can be captured formally in any STI system. These col-leges adjust research, priorities, and training as new information arrives. Those with good standing in the invisible colleges know what is happening at the frontiers of their discipline long before new results trickle out to the whole cadre in a discipline via printed publication or some other formal STI mechanism (Kranzberg 1980). Because adjustments of the internal market are so rapid, the original presumption made by STI systems designers — that to be effective, scientists need access to all relevant information — may not hold. The function of STI systems may be archival and historical. Given current information from invisible colleges, scientists may "backtrack" from a breakthrough to the relevant literature and citations leading up to it. The fact is that few research scientists really use the available STI systems in the way envisioned by their designers. Actual use is messy and unsystematic.

The STI systems designers may believe, however, that there are significant social and individual costs in not using the information captured in the STI data bases. Society may incur some duplication costs, for some research may be funded that has already been done elsewhere. An individual scientist may damage his reputation and career by repeating someone else's work unknowingly, although repetition is supposed to be an important canon of scientific method. Such costs have to be weighed against the operating costs of searching data bases when they exist and the costs of creating them when they do not exist. The data bases do not ordinarily provide any index of quality for the literature they report, and it is probably high-quality information that scientists need most, rather than large quantities. Much of the high-quality information for the internal market is disseminated rapidly and orally via the invisible colleges.

If one believes that the STI market functions well, then the data bases that do emerge and are viable satisfy effective demands for both quality and quantity. If so, the extramarket coordination, so typical of STI strategies, is inappropriate. After all, the purpose of extramarket coordination is to give actors relevant information the market cannot deliver in the form of prices, because of imperfections or failure. If new technology and a changing market structure ameliorate the imperfections or failure, there is little point in central coordination and "national" policies. One can argue that technology is, in fact, now changing market structures and eliminating imperfections.

In the past, the STI community believed that a central agency had to coordinate the market and make it efficient. The utility of central coordinators in other science policy domains has always been strongly questioned (see chap. 4). A rapidly growing stock of information and the continued diversification of user groups led the STI community to believe that the dispersed, decentralized systems that served so well in the past were breaking down (NAS 1969a). Given this breakdown, some form of voluntary cooperation and coordination seemed necessary. But markets do not always break down in the face of expanded activity; they may even function better because of the economies of scale that are made possible. The costs of handling large volumes of information have, in fact, come down and give every indication of going lower. The advent of the microcomputer and personal computers may well be widening access to STI. New computer technology allows individuals and institutions to tap STI data bases at relatively low cost without much intermediation and coordination.

Even if the internal market can adapt to an increased volume of information for strictly research purposes, STI discussions, over time, broadened perceptions of need. There was growing concern for professional and technical users who were not themselves researchers. For them, "raw" STI has to be repackaged and translated to make it relevant to problemsolving. But the *SID* strategy never achieved a fully articulated connection between information and problemsolving. It contains little analysis of the information practices of problemsolvers. It did not ask whether translation into problemsolving language was feasible or would make a difference, if feasible. Feasibility and desirability were matters of faith.

Some of the STI strategists wanted to go even beyond technological problemsolving. They wanted to make STI much more relevant to public policy. As noted, information for decisionmaking must be at least contingently valid, but it has to have other properties as well. Most STI does not have these other properties. Its validity may have to be established by additional research, compromising timeliness. Decisionmakers define relevance and actionability when they have a problem, but such attributes cannot normally be attached to STI, a priori. So there is a question about the ways in which repackaged, general-purpose STI truly would be useful, as opposed to limited search and inquiry focused on specific policy issues.

Decisionmakers' need for information, particularly STI, has been taken as an axiom, even though decisionmakers can be seen to act without it, and indeed, because decisions and information flows are not closely matched, have to act without it. There is a trade-off between acting now and waiting for information to arrive and then acting later; it is not clear that the trade-off is in favor of waiting while getting more information, as opposed to careful deliberation with the information in hand.

The External STI Market: Industry, Universities, and the Federal Government

We now know that technical progress is probably the greatest contributor to growth and productivity (see chap. 2). From an information perspective, technical progress means that the external market for STI imports information from the internal market. Producers of goods and services incorporate or "congeal" STI into new or higher-quality outputs, inputs, and more efficient processes. Ordinarily, the external market will also export STI to the internal market, since interesting research problems frequently turn up as producers transform information into goods and services. In constructing any overall industrial policy or strategy to enhance technical progress, one needs to examine one's notions of the trade relations between the internal and the external markets. Since universities and the scientists they employ are the main agents in the internal market, and firms, industries, and the researchers, engineers, and professionals they employ are the main actors in the external market, it is necessary to examine beliefs about the flow of information between universities and industry.

The classics of science policy are largely silent about such traffic. In those classics, universities have a comparative advantage in the production of basic research information because they face no pressures of "commercial necessity." Yet, there is increasing industrial demand for the university product, because production processes and new products and services are becoming more "science based," that is, more information intensive. The information problem seen by the classical STI writers was that the internal market would be too small and would not be capable of meeting industrial demands. The time to utilization of basic research information was falling, and so the United States had to make greater and greater investments in basic research and had to make large increases in university capabilities. Industry could easily use up the current stock of STI, and the internal market would be too small to replenish that stock very quickly (PSAC 1958).

By the 1960s the scientific community perceived an "information explosion" inside the internal market. The problem was not an insufficient volume of information, but the information was too disaggregated for scientists, let alone users. Beginning with the SATCOM report, there was worry about the trade between the internal and external markets. The main problem perceived was that the outputs of the internal market were not being tailored for customers in the external market.

SATCOM's solution was to design a new product — research consolidations and assessments — without too much analysis of industrial demand. For example, research on industrial research emphasizes oral communications and information "gatekeepers," people who know where information is and how to get it (Allen 1977). But SATCOM did not propose any direct measures to increase either the number of gatekeepers or their capabilities. On the other hand, the Greenberger report, written from a Great Society perspective, stressed the importance of user demand in the a priori design of information systems. However, it addressed itself primarily to organizational changes to improve the utility of government information services.

From the perspective of decisionmakers interested in innovation, the trade between the internal market and the external market has always been too small. Decisionmakers in practically all postwar administrations have perceived the inability of industry to capture or use information as a principal barrier to innovation. Various markets for goods and services failed to incorporate the best available technology because firms had incapacities in evaluating information or, alternatively, because the STI imported from the universities was not packaged properly. Consequently, information dissemination was always a prominent feature of government programs designed to increase the rate of innovation. If industry, in general, or at least certain critical industries did not have the competence to make appropriate valuations of research, or if information was not packaged properly, it was legitimate to supply those missing factors.

Using analogies to the agricultural extension service, the information problem, as decisionmakers saw it, was to set up new institutions that would facilitate trade between the internal and external markets. Information for industrial use is as much embodied in people as in paper, so industrial innovation programs often contain university-industry exchange provisions. By showing industries "best practice" techniques and what they could do, the average quality of technology use would rise. Even if firms and workers already knew what best practice was but were irrationally resistant to it, additional contact with university-based researchers would help overcome that resistance. The government would be providing a missing factor of production – people – who were on top of current trends in basic research and who could also make a translation to the language of industrial technology, the language of the "bottom line."

President Kennedy's proposed civilian technology program contained a university-industry extension service that was to be people-intensive, and the STS program in the Johnson administration expended significant amounts of its available resources on information dissemination via university-industry "networking." The STS premise was that many firms did not have access to national information markets, but universities did. Some combination of university-industry-state cooperation would provide access to national markets, thereby boosting state economies. By 1966, STS claimed it had 600 projects, including information dissemination, referral service centers, field units, and federally supported information analysis centers (NAS 1969a).

The Nixon administration stopped the STS program, but it continued to support experimental partnerships between states, universities, and industry. To the Nixon decisionmakers, states possessed greater knowledge than did the federal government about the structure and competencies of local industry and the capability and willingness of universities to become involved in technology transfer. From such "experiments," it would be possible to learn what kinds of information transfer arrangements and incentives would make the greatest contributions to innovation.

In its search for an innovation policy, the Carter administration emphasized STI transfers strongly, believing there was too little trade between the internal and external markets. The gap between the internal and external market had two causes. First, industry did not have or had not chosen to create a capability to use STI. Second, it was unaware of readily available STI that it could use. Generic technology centers at universities with a two-way flow of people would address both problems. Participation in such centers meant that capability would be formed via learning-by-doing, but industrial staff would also acquire awareness of relevant university research. The centers would form a new invisible college, a practical one that acquired and transmitted "bottom-line" information rapidly.

The Reagan administration has had a strong market orientation concerning government support of technology. Although STI has never been a major concern to this administration, one would expect it to believe there is no compelling justification for government STI programs. If firms are successful, they do not have any incapacity to discern and process STI relevant to their operations, and government does not have to place information into formats that successful firms and industries will find useful. Firms must have the capacity to acquire and process information effectively, since they know the demand for their own products. It is this demand that gives signals about what kind of information would be useful. Since firms get such signals firsthand, they know better than anyone else which information held in the internal market can be transformed into saleable goods and services. Supplying firms with government-produced or -supported technical information is then an unnecessary and inappropriate subsidy.

Given this perspective, one would expect the administration to emphasize the virtues of voluntary industry-university cooperation. Since industry is not myopic, private industry-university contact should work well. For example, in the case of genetic engineering, the time elapsed until application of the results of university experiments has been very short. Firms, at least in this case, are farsighted about basic research. The demand for collaboration with university scientists and their students is growing larger. And this would be true wherever industry sees a positive bottom-line outcome. There is no reason, in the administration's view, why this situation would not obtain wherever universities and their labor force — scientists and students — hold STI with prospectively high payoff. Industry's motivation toward short-run profits may create conflicts between universities and industry in doing research or revealing its outcome, but a priori discussion by the interested parties should lead to reasonable rules of thumb without government intervention. The government's role, in the Reagan view, is to do what it does best – support fundamental research. It should stay out of the way of natural market processes that will lead to cooperation or, at most, provide incentives for cooperation.

STI and Public Policy

The strategies for resource allocation and science education that were considered earlier contain no clear statements about the relations between S&T and the determination of public policy. Although S&T seems to infuse everything in these strategies, the opportunities and problems posed by decisions turning on STI escaped the originators of the strategies. Neither Bush, the PSRB, PSAC, nor White House science advisers ever discuss the use of research and STI to make public policy. The scientific and technical community has long been concerned that citizens have sufficient knowledge of the benefits of science and technology that they are willing to support expenditures for it. For example, PSAC always wanted citizens to understand why public resources were flowing to research (PSAC 1958, 5). PSAC reports have even contained some worries about the scientific literacy of citizens in choosing competing products for their own use. But PSAC rarely dealt with making research and STI relevant to decisionmaking in nonscience domains.

Succeeding official reports on STI successively broadened notions of its role, but they did not present any clear perceptions of how STI was relevant to decisionmaking or the algorithms by which STI was to be made relevant. More STI was seen as necessary, implying that decisions would be better. Public policy, at least from a rational, analytic perspective, crossed disciplinary boundaries and required that STI from different disciplines be connected. STI from the natural sciences had to be made relevant to economic and social choices. STI derived from the social sciences, which might have been relevant, was not, because university incentives for relevant policy analysis or research were weak. In any case, social scientists believed their true business was creating the background, strategic knowledge that would eventually change the general climate of opinion and the conceptual orientation of decisionmakers coming into power in the future. So no one dealt with the critical questions, the ways in which STI was to be given the attributes needed for use in decisionmaking and how uncertainty in available STI was to be treated.

The issues of connecting STI with decisionmaking became acute in the 1960s and 1970s, when health, environmental, and safety regulation became a prominent feature of the U.S. economy. For example, standard setting and rule making require estimates of environmental or health damage, and these estimates depend on knowing the impacts of chemicals or pollutants, individually and jointly. By increasing the volume of research, particularly basic research, in those domains where society wished to imitate public policy, the scientific community argued that understanding would be increased and greater understanding would lead to improved policy. For example, in the case of environmental pollution, PSAC argued that technical ignorance constrained ability to deal effectively with pollution problems. There was incomplete knowledge of the causes of pollution; consequently, more basic research was necessary (PSAC 1965).

But this view did not rest upon any analysis of how decisionmakers used STI or ought to use it, if only they could achieve greater technical understanding. Rather, it was an extension of the statements in the strategies for obtaining basic research funds (see chap. 2). Public policy problems were a vehicle for increasing basic research budgets. Increased demand for STI by decisionmakers would reveal the relevance of information currently held in the internal market, and incremental investments in basic research would provide unexpected insights into policy. There was no more reason to doubt unexpected payoffs in public decisionmaking than in other domains, and so no special requirements had to be imposed on research designs or actual research practice. The difficulty was in curing the decisionmakers' lack of interest in funding basic research oriented toward problems, rather than the kinds of information scientists produced. Whatever the policy problem, more basic research always seemed necessary. Thus, one might state an augmented *SID.3* statement:

SID.3 *Augmented: The collective but decentralized search for information within the internal market coordinates the overall direction of basic research and allocates society's resources to the most promising lines of research. In the case of information for decisionmaking, an unconstrained and decentralized basic research approach will uncover policy-relevant and policy-actionable results.*

Since decisionmakers' understanding of their problems is inherently shallow — they never have time to gain understanding of "deep structures" — the need for basic research in problem or decision areas is almost self-evident. Thus, public policy concerns did not induce significant and discernible changes in the direction of research nor in research designs. Eventually someone or some group would put conventional

STI together in a meaningful package for decisionmakers, but who that would be was not at all clear.

Advice

In the short run, the way to make STI relevant to decisionmaking is by tapping the expertise embodied in science and engineering professionals. This involves seeking advice and usually collective advice. The form of the advice may range from calling in some knowledgeable experts for informal discussion to commissioning formal benefit/cost analysis or technology assessments. A full history and exposition of advisory mechanisms or benefit/cost techniques is beyond the scope of this inquiry. The rise of the benefit/cost techniques as decision aids has been discussed extensively, as have their limitations (Stokey and Zeckhauser 1978; Porter et al. 1980; Majone and Quade 1980; Mishan 1982). Rather, the concern here is what conceptual strategy leads decisionmakers to use them.

Perhaps the most common way of obtaining STI for policy purposes is through the scientific advisory committee or panel. Such committees can be found inside and outside the federal government's formal organization. A common form for policy with STI content is the ad hoc, external, blue-ribbon committee. The federal government often charters the National Academies of Science, Engineering, or Medicine to convene such committees. PSAC was an example of a standing external committee giving its views and advice to the science adviser, who, in turn, usually presented them to the president. Usually, but not always, the science adviser, through an iterative process, was able to adjust the final advice to recommendations that were technically feasible and politically acceptable.

The process of advice begins with decisionmakers recognizing that they have a problem or an issue with significant science and technology content. The feasibility of some technology may be at issue, or researchers may have reported some newly discovered, deleterious effects of chemicals on the environment or on human beings. A decision must be made by a certain time, or a situation must be defused. Political, administrative, and substantive prudence all require justification for any pending decision. In a short time, it is not practical to design and implement new studies or research bearing on the issue at hand, and so decisionmakers set up scientific advisory committees in the hope that these committees will carry out the integration and evaluation of research and data needed for sound and acceptable decisions. From a decisionmaker's perspective, the comparative advantages of advisory committees over other mechanisms lie in their temporary nature — their ability to recruit highly qualified members and staff; their ability to command a wide audience for their findings, on the one hand; and the decisionmaker's ability to accept or ignore their recommendations, on the other.

From a decisionmaker's perspective, committees project an image that is comprehensive, rational, and substantive, an image that, however inaccurate, it pays a decisionmaker to cultivate. The scientific and technical community believes that committee work is a cost-effective way of providing advice. It is a process similar to committee judgments on research priorities or on tenure, and given reasonably competent supporting staff, advisory committees do not take too much time away from research. Thus, a committee procedure can make the interests of decisionmakers and the scientific community consistent.

Individual or committee advice, as a way to deliver STI for policy analysis and decisions, has not been examined too closely. We have few "theories of advice," and there are almost no cost-effectiveness studies of the process. The value of the information the committees produce has rarely been established, although decisionmakers will frequently point to a committee's recommendations as the reasons they took or avoided action.

While we have the memoirs of many policy advisers and even know the institutional constraints and interactions that led them to give certain kinds of advice and behave in certain ways, we do not have the means to distinguish adequate from inadequate advice, and we do not really know the attributes of adequacy (Goldhamer 1977; Boffey 1975; Kissinger 1979). So far as advice with high STI content is concerned, it is possible to encompass the scientific community's perceptions by adding some statements to the science and information dissemination strategy (*SID*).

SID.8 *On any policy issue with science and technology content, the joint expertise and joint positions produced by a committee process are sufficient to connect currently available STI with the policy question at hand.*

   SID8.1 *Corollary: Since there will be residual uncertainty about magnitudes, effects, and causes, a committee process serves as a check and balance on uncertainty, providing the best estimates of individual variables and overall effects which can be obtained in a short time.*

SID.9 *An open committee process provides protection for the scientific community against possible claims and actions by decisionmakers allegedly based on scientific and technical findings.*

These additional statements for the case of public policy advice flow naturally from the prior *SID* statements. The most qualified scientists and engineers possess the most current information about research results (from the invisible colleges). A committee process (given a competent chairperson and staff) forces rapid articulation of the information. Scientific committees are, presumably, not subject to the kinds of distortions and biases common in committee processes. The working habits of scientists, the scientific and technical content of the issues, and the canons of scientific discourse are assumed sufficient to prevent dominant personalities, logrolling, bargaining, and the other phenomena known to afflict committees in most other domains.

The difficulty with the advisory approach to public policy is that the rules or procedures used to draw out the STI from the persons who hold it and aggregate it are usually obscure, and the decisionmaker usually has no way to discover these rules. They are not usually stated explicitly in the design of committee work but tend to evolve as a committee works. Thus, it becomes difficult to know how much weight to give to the final collective advice. We ordinarily do not know how committees treat conflicting information and antagonistic scientific positions or, what is more difficult to handle, conflicting values. For the decisionmaker, trust in the results is equivalent to trust in the competence of the advisers and those who selected them plus trust in whatever review and oversight mechanism the advisers may have set up. But the review mechanism will, in all likelihood, be a second set of knowledgeable experts. There will not ordinarily be time to design and implement new research to check the conclusions of an advisory committee, and there is no good way to derive a committee's results and advice from its joint premises or from the individual premises of its members. Some scientists and decisionmakers prefer, when possible, a more explicit, analytical approach in support of policy.

Benefit/Cost Analysis

Benefit/cost analysis, benefit/risk analysis, and technology assessment are formal, analytic ways of bringing STI to bear on policy problems. Many, but not all, in the scientific and technical community and many, but not all, critics of technology believe that these analytical devices, when employed properly, are valid ways of linking STI to public policy. However, there are also those who strongly believe such techniques are inherently, inescapably, and irreparably flawed as tools of public policy analysis. To them, these techniques address the wrong questions with the wrong procedures. Whatever one's belief, they have become familiar and, in some cases, are mandated. So it is necessary to be clear about what they do. They are all a priori, rational, comprehensive techniques for structuring and obtaining policy-relevant STI and then using the STI to present action or policy recommendations. Their purpose is to reveal the consequences of deploying or restraining new technologies, expanding old ones, or pursuing new policies. They are supposed to give us systematic information before we act, and after we act, they are supposed to tell us how well we did.

The line between the various techniques is a fine one. One can argue that technology assessments do not assign values and costs to the consequences they have assessed, but only provide information on available alternatives. But this conflicts with the view that the purpose of technology assessment is to evaluate alternative technological paths to a given objective and compare all public and private costs over time (NAE 1972). If we believe technology assessment involves the evaluation of alternatives and add a discount rate to the assessment notion, we have a more or less classical definition of benefit/cost analysis. Benefit/cost analysis can be defined as an analytic approach used to evaluate alternative policy or expenditure decisions. Its conceptual force lies in systematic comparison of all benefits delivered against all costs incurred, directly and indirectly, now and in the future (Stokey and Zeckhauser 1978). But such comparison is also the business of technology assessment and benefit/risk analysis. For our purposes, we can treat them all as formal, a priori techniques for appraising policy with STI content. What we need is the strategy that would lead us to employ such techniques. This strategy can be stated as follows, with *BC* denoting any and all analytic techniques where benefits are weighed against costs, however measured.

BC.1 *The development of new technologies and the expansion or deployment of old ones should be subject to public influence and control.*

BC.2 *Current procedures for making public and private decisions with high scientific and technical content are inadequate, because (1) affected or impacted individuals, groups, or systems are excluded from the calculus of private markets or public agencies, and (2) the expected future consequences of technology are never weighed heavily enough in the routine procedures currently used to make public or private decisions.*

BC.3 *Nth order consequences cannot be regulated or controlled at the time they occur but must be anticipated. Nth order consequences are not reversible when they do occur.*

BC.4 *Neither markets nor bureaucracies are responsive enough to early warning about the long-run consequences of current or immediately prospective technologies.*

BC.3 and *BC.4* exclude some "learning by doing" or "muddling through." Because presumed future effects of technology are systemic and irreversible and institutions slow and inflexible, we cannot wait and see if predicted impacts occur, weigh their seriousness, and then take action. We have to make decisions about technology now in the same way we have to make decisions now about any other effects and outcomes that are expected to be irreversible (Fisher and Peterson 1976).

BC.5 *Social consequence: Society will not adopt new technologies or expand old ones in an optimal way. Adoption will be too fast, too slow, or subject to "unnecessary" conflicts.*

BC.6 *There exist a priori methods for estimating the benefits, costs, risks, or effects of current and prospective technologies, which possess validity and credibility for decisionmakers and interested parties.*

> **BC6.1** *Criteria for distinguishing valid, sound, actionable benefit/cost analysis exist or can be specified.*

According to *BC.5* and *BC.6,* a priori, systematic analysis of the future today, followed by resolute action, will improve outcomes tomorrow. This improvement does not rest on one or another criterion of scientific validity or truth that might be used — say, the falsification of predictions. According to *BC.2* and *BC.3,* one cannot wait to see if there is falsification. And even if one could wait, the purely scientific or technical parts of a benefit/cost analysis are difficult to test. The technical parts usually concern estimating the effects of natural and man-made systems, and we only partially understand these. Some properties of complex systems may not be understandable within the time and resources available or may never be understood. So the worth of benefit/cost analysis rests less in providing greater truth than in forcing our attention now onto the nth order future consequences. In this sense, benefit/cost analysis is valid if it does its job, which is focusing the attention of decisionmakers and the public on more or less desirable futures.

The source of political conflict in benefit/cost analysis is perceived to be lack of a common conceptual framework or a common information base, rather than different interests and values. That having such a common framework and information base might sharpen conflict is not an admissible possibility. After invoking benefit/cost analysis, even if we disagree, we will know systematically why we disagree, and this will reduce conflict and be an improvement in the decisionmaking process. Thus, we have the last required statement justifying benefit/cost analysis.

BC.7 *Common knowledge and estimates of nth order consequences will reduce social conflict and improve public decisions.*

The STI data bases found in benefit/cost analysis are a mixture of empirical facts, validated, but usually probabilistic scientific or technical judgments concerning causes and effects and subjective judgments and estimates of future consequences. Estimates of causes and effects can be "back of the envelope" or involve extensive formal modeling. Judgments and predictions may be offered up loosely or in one of the structured formats for eliciting personal judgments, characteristic of "futures" research.

Although some of the facts and relationships encountered can be checked or tested according to scientific canons, the predictions of nth order social and economic impacts cannot. Here the STI problem is not aggregating presumably valid pieces of research and telling a coherent story for use by other practitioners; rather, it is providing some rules for aggregating partial, uncertain, and often conflicting, technical information. The decision analysis problem is to join the STI to the judgments and preferences of concerned or impacted agents and to come to some view of the merits of proposed action recommendations. There are no particular canons for doing this. We can apply craft rules or rules of best practice that have evolved over time and make checks on how well experts agree or how sensitive the predictions are to slight changes in assumptions. We can observe whether "pitfalls" have been avoided (Majone and Quade 1980). And we can discover the reasons experts may disagree and sharpen debate by calling out and refining points of disagreement. Such craft rules are discussed in Chapter 7.

STI and Benefit/Cost Analysis

The 1960s were a period when belief in government competence ran high. Bureaucracies, it appeared, could take a more comprehensive and enlightened approach to public problems than could market processes motivated by "greed," that is, individual utility and profit maximization. While there was a well-developed theory of market failure, there was no corresponding theory of nonmarket failure (Wolf 1979). Markets have difficulty making correct choices about new technologies. The federal government was seen as able to correct or compensate for the market's inability to handle new technology properly by injecting the right kind of information or by requiring bureaucracies to provide it, for example, mandatory technology assessments or environmental impact assessments before policy implementation.

That the right kind of information could be produced was not doubted, and there was confidence that the newly available tools of systems analysis or policy analysis, if used carefully, were the proper framework for making STI relevant to decisions. Without some prior analysis, the wrong kinds of technologies would be deployed, or the right kind would be deployed too late. The issues were too important to be left to individual markets or the collective judgments of committees (NAS 1969b, Brooks and Bowers 1970). The way to improved public policy was through a priori, analytic estimates of the benefits and costs of alternatives. If technical barriers to obtaining relevant information and logical barriers in inferring correct consequences could be overcome, we would equip ourselves with the tools that would give us systematic and unbiased analysis of new technology and the social risks associated with it. Of course, we do not have this kind of STI capability. However, even though the benefit/cost advocates are not as active in the eighties as they were in the seventies, benefit/cost approaches to technology have become institutionalized, especially in decisionmaking concerning the environment, public health, and safety.

Benefit/cost analysis makes the kind of large-scale demands for integrated information that have long concerned STI systems designers. From an STI perspective, it may simply be too costly or too time consuming to construct the linked STI data bases that, in principle, benefit/cost analysis requires. So, despite improvements in techniques and information bases, uncertainties of fact and inference will probably continue to be characteristic of knowledge about the effects of old and new technology. Furthermore, we will probably discover that we still have no compelling logic to take us from facts and preferences to correct conclusions about technological impacts and risks. We may never be able to construct such a logic. No matter how hard we try, our choices will be colored by uncertainty. If so, then we have not so much an analysis problem as a design problem. How can we design our institutions to respond quickly and flexibly to new STI as it arrives from the internal market? How can we design institutions that can reverse or adjust their course when emerging STI indicates they are in error? There are no easy or permanent answers.

Summary

I have traced STI concepts first in the internal market of science and engineering itself. Here STI is used reflexively by the research enterprise to transform itself. I have also examined whether any information-flow problem exists and, if it exists, whether it is perceived correctly. Since the technology to produce STI has changed dramatically, the traditional problem of handling large volumes of information may not be so severe now. The ability to acquire pertinent information quickly has improved. We still face the problem of extracting high-quality information from large data bases, but the informal channels for acquisition of STI deliver adequate signals of quality at disciplinary frontiers, if not within frontiers.

In the case of the industrial enterprise, the STI problem is the rate of transformation into marketable goods, services, and processes. The preferred strategy for deploying STI depends on general concepts of how markets work and when they work. If firms do not have the capacity to acquire or evaluate STI relevant to their operations, or alternatively, if they have no capacity constraint but there is a shortage of relevant STI, then we usually elect to have government serve as an information broker. Government information or extension programs have been the components of all the industrial or innovation policies tried so far. The difficulty comes in trying to judge whether there is, in fact, industrial incapacity or shortage of information. Since industries differ, one should expect to find incapacity in some, shortages in others, and significant capacity without shortage in yet others. The public policy problem is first one of discovering which condition holds. Given the identification of a particular condition, we then need to choose among alternative STI programs. But we have no one in government to do this now, and no one prospectively, since STI is not an issue for which expected bureaucratic and personal gains are very large.

Finally, I have examined the role of STI in making public policy. There is reflexivity of a sort here too. Our economy transforms STI into goods and services via changes in technology, and the improvements in technology often have negative spillovers. Desirable social outcomes tragically come with current social costs or damage or expected costs and damage in the future. We try to use our stock of STI to make sensible decisions about the direct effects of technology and the spillovers. In making policy for the social control of technology, the STI problems are of higher order than those encountered in the internal market or in external markets for goods and services. We need relevant STI, but it has to be formated. The format joins information to decisionmaking. We can certainly do better than we have, but there will be circumstances in which, no matter how hard we try, we will not get many unambiguous clues about correct decisions. In that case, a priori rationality helps some, but not enough. We have to design our information and decision systems to be responsive and flexible simultaneously as we acquire new information and try new policies.

Trade and Aid in Science and Technology

6

In the production of basic research, the S&T community of the United States has viewed itself as part of a worldwide enterprise. The objective of domestic inquiry has been to contribute to the collective output of the world enterprise, not necessarily to maximize national output. The basic research enterprise is like a large multinational firm with many branches, each producing similar (information) products. Since branch products are similar, it pays to encourage information flow among them. The physics of France is not different than the physics of the United States. Although French and U.S. scientists may decide to produce information with different processes or methods, there is no dispute, because of nationality, as to what information has value. Different approaches strengthen each subsidiary enterprise, since each has no difficulty using the information produced by the others.

Attempts by nation-states to control the flow of basic research information are seen as impediments to be removed. Scientists believe governments should positively support their exchanges with foreign colleagues, because each national enterprise is strengthened as the world enterprise is strengthened. Governments, however, have their own reasons for promoting exchange, and these reasons are not always consistent with maximizing flows of information between national science enterprises or increasing the world output of scientific information. But basic research has characteristics which make it useful as a diplomatic tool. Because it has less direct social and economic utility than applied research or working technology, nations care less about it. Since they do not care so intensely, they can have productive negotiations over its exchange. They can easily assert common interests and reach agreements. Information and know-how developed by a nation's scientists can thus serve as foreign policy instruments. Since exchange of information abroad involves both scientists and diplomats, it has to satisfy some minimal mix of scientific and political criteria.

124

Unlike the scientists who produce basic research information, producers of technological know-how gain direct and immediate benefits. Technology is a prime determinant of domestic economic welfare and growth, and differential holdings of technological information are a source of comparative advantage in international trade. So international transfers of technology are far more controversial than transfers of basic research. There are more stakeholders, and the political and economic content of prospective transfers is higher.

To the extent a nation's economy depends on international trade, stakeholders believe technology transfer to current economic competitors should be monitored and, in the extreme, regulated. However, advanced technology has always been seen as a very desirable tool for promoting economic development. Developing nations, for many years, have demanded access to advanced technology on favorable terms, that is, terms other than those presented by international markets. Developing nations have tried to persuade the developed ones that the latter have moral obligations to provide advanced technologies to all who desire them, even though receiving nations may become economic competitors in the not too distant future. Even if this occurs, a case for transfer can be made. Newly developed nations will provide markets for the output of the transferring countries, thereby mitigating any short-run losses from the original transfer. Technology transfers to developing nations will benefit the transferring nation's trading position in the long run, whatever economic damage the transfers do in the short run. But damaged stakeholders can protest strongly in the short run, while advocates for the long run are scarce. Thus, decisionmakers have to be able to mediate between short-run damage and long-term benefits.

In this chapter, I will explore the strategies the United States has used concerning support of international S&T transfer. I will examine the conflicts involved in promoting international scientific activity, on the one hand, to sustain one's own research enterprise and, on the other, for use as "bargaining chips" in foreign affairs. Although I have touched on problems of information transfer in earlier chapters, I now want to examine this issue directly. How has the United States viewed exports of scientific and technical information? If exports of information reduce comparative advantage and create economic competitors, what policies has the United States used to try to stay ahead? How has the United States viewed the export of the technical knowledge it possesses in relation to economic development?

Basic Research and International Relations

For exchanges of basic research information, the international relations strategy (denoted *IRS*) preferred by the scientific community can be stated as follows:

IRS.1 *A greater world output of basic research benefits any and all national research enterprises because each can capture incremental information at zero or very low cost.*

IRS.2 *Any and all nations have a potential comparative advantage in some field of basic research.*

IRS.3 *There exist barriers of distance and time, which make the actual output of the world scientific enterprise lower than its potential output (given the technology available to do science).*

IRS.4 *Exchanges of information and people reduce barriers to increased output.*

IRS.5 *Private efforts by national scientific enterprises to further international exchange will be too low relative to potential output, because each lacks sufficient resources.*

IRS.6 *Scientific exchange should be a valuable foreign policy tool, because scientific inquiry promotes values that all nations can share.*

    IRS6.1 *Scientific productivity is a necessary condition for diplomatic and political effectiveness.*

Scientific exchange provides the means to reach common objectives and does not carry within itself issues that divide nations. Scientific work can be directed toward the achievement of important political objectives if it has credibility to scientists and engineers of the countries involved. For example, improvements in agriculture via basic research poses interesting scientific questions. Given technical credibility, scientists from different nations can work productively on such questions, and such work enhances political good will and prestige and also makes bilateral political relations worth having (Killian 1964). On the other hand, research and exchange without credibility, done purely for the enhancement of political and diplomatic relations, will be self-defeating. The best scientists will refuse to work under such conditions.

IRS.7 *Policy implication: The U.S. government has an obligation to promote international exchange of basic research information and personnel.*

    The *IRS* strategy can be thought of as an attempt to assure scientists that exchanges will be technically productive and contribute to their disciplinary objectives, while cautioning diplomats about signing exchange agreements for purely political or diplomatic reasons. But, by statements *IRS.1, 2,* and *3,* any country has a comparative advantage in some field of science or can create one. So any and all scientific exchange agreements can be viewed as being potentially productive, and they are so claimed by the diplomats and science advisers who sign them. Demands by scientists for technical productivity do not serve as an effective check on political and diplomatic requirements. Purely political exchanges may be self-defeating because the best scientists will refuse to participate. However, the scientists' belief that science is a universal activity and that every nation can find some science to do means that objections to exchanges on grounds of scientific productivity cannot be persuasive.

Diplomats and decisionmakers see pure scientific exchange from a different angle than scientists do. They may well believe, along with scientists, that bilateral or multilateral scientific inquiry, because of its very nature, contributes to international amity and comity. But their reasons for involving governments in the process of international scientific exchange have to be pragmatic and oriented toward diplomatic requirements. From a diplomatic perspective, exchanges are a low-cost tool for achieving "linkages" with friends and adversaries. The diplomat's strategy (denoted *IRD*) can be stated in the following form:

IRD.1 *Scientific exchange is a signal from one nation to another or to many others that it wants to strengthen communications and linkages.*

> **IRD1.1** *Scientific exchange used as a diplomatic signal is clear and is not subject to misinterpretation, as are signals in more overtly political domains.*

> **IRD1.2** *Scientific exchange used as a diplomatic signal is limited in scope and is quasi-private in nature.*

IRD.2 *Scientific exchange creates valuable but limited stakes for participating nations.*

IRD.3 *Scientific exchange is a reversible signal, and it can be reversed at lower cost than other signals.*

IRD.4 *Scientific exchange can serve as a low-cost precursor to more extended relations in nonscientific fields.*

IRD.5 *For diplomatic purposes, the costs of scientific exchange are always attractively low. Costs will not have to be borne by the*

Table 6.1. Strategic Perspectives

	IRS	*IRD*
A. Expected benefits from exchange	Increase world scientific output Increase home country output	Send clear and limited signals of positive political interest Send signals of diplomatic disapproval
B. Scope of exchange	Scientists of any nation that actually or potentially produces basic research	Any nation where diplomatic relations need improvement
C. Costs	Shifted to U.S. government	Shifted to U.S. government's R&D agencies
D. Uncertainties	Degree of scientific payoff	Available resources for agreement

diplomatic establishment, but by U.S. scientific and technical agencies.

In table 6.1, the *IRS* and *IRD* strategies are shown side by side. The strategic perspectives of scientists and diplomats are shown in the rows, which are related to some categories one might want to use when doing an ex post evaluation. Row A, for example, enumerates the benefits expected by scientists and diplomats.

The Dualities of Exchange

The United States has a very large number of agreements for international scientific exchange, and they vary in form. Each of them illustrates the duality induced by the simultaneous operation of the two strategies. Decisions to sign agreements involve satisfying different constraints. Although each agreement has sufficient ambiguity to enable bilateral exchanges, the different valuations and perspectives they provide cause difficulties in budgeting, implementation, and evaluation. A history of U.S. scientific exchanges is beyond the scope of this work, but I will proceed by example to illustrate some of the difficulties (CRS 1976b).

In 1972, when the United States first pursued detente with the Soviet Union, it signed eleven agreements in subject areas considered "safe," from a national security perspective. These agreements provided for government-sponsored exchanges and continuation of the quasi-private exchanges of the National Academy of Science and other societies. Scientific cooperation had a dual purpose, one relevant to incremental research knowledge and the other to politics and diplomacy. Secretary of State Kissinger noted that apolitical research agreements have diplomatic content, nevertheless; governments receive joint benefits. Both parties gain technical knowledge simultaneously, and these joint benefits produce constraints on the international behavior of friends and adversaries. Agreements create stakes that can be used diplomatically. As Kissinger put it:

> [Prior to 1972] there were no cooperative efforts in science and technology. Cultural exchange was modest. As a result, there was no tangible inducement toward cooperation and no penalty for aggressive behavior. Today, by joining our efforts in even such seemingly apolitical fields as medical research or environmental protection, we and the Soviets can benefit not only two peoples but all mankind; in addition, we generate incentives for restraint. (Kissinger 1974)

The Carter administration renewed the 1972 agreements in 1977. When the Soviet Union invaded Afghanistan in 1979, the administration sought credible but limited signals of its displeasure. So it turned to the science agreements. President Carter sought to exploit the stakes he thought the Soviet Union had in the agreements by restricting high-level policy meetings and explorations of new work but letting existing technical work go on. Since the United States also believed it had a stake, it worked to preserve the framework of the agreements. The president believed he was sending a signal that the Afghanistan invasion would cost the Soviet Union a substantial sum in terms of lost information. However, the United States also lost some information and continued contact with the Soviet research community, which was thought to be politically valuable and also provided an intelligence window (Carter 1980).

In holding the Soviet Union responsible for repression in Poland, the Reagan administration refused to renew the existing agreements. Refusal to renew the agreements, the administration believed, sent a signal that the United States was willing to give up at least a limited stake over Poland. The signal was not as strong as it might have been, because the administration argued that the United States was getting insufficient scientific return. Refusal to renew did not imply the United States was giving up something highly valuable to itself. It was thought that the benefit-costs of the agreements were unfavorable, because the Soviet Union did not permit true scientific exchange. It controlled the access of U.S. scientists to their Soviet counterparts (OSTP 1982). Even if the United States did not lose so much, canceling the agreements gave the administration a chance to show its displeasure while maintaining more important political and economic contact and negotiations.

In the case of the recognition of the People's Republic of China, scientific exchange served as a precursor. Prior to recognition of the

PRC, President Carter's science adviser, Frank Press, went to China to hold discussions about common scientific interests. Afterward, the Chinese came to the United States to sign, what was at the time, a "private" agreement between the two governments. This private agreement set up a "national" program of exchange. Subsequent to U.S. recognition, many U.S. agencies signed agreements with the PRC under the auspices of the Office of Science and Technology Policy (OSTP) and the science adviser. The administration sought to bind the Chinese by proliferating the number of agreements and by providing various forms of technical assistance.

In the case of relations with small countries that are not strategically important to the United States, the low-cost nature of scientific exchanges, their limited scope, and their relative clarity lead to wide use as a diplomatic tool. For example, the NSF alone administers approximately forty agreements, and other R&D agencies administer agreements nominally relevant to their missions. The *IRS* and the *IRD* strategies both provide incentives to increase scientific exchange; neither contains any stopping rules. From the perspective of the scientific community, exchange is always productive. Some kind of worthy science can be found in any country. At a minimum, unique geographical, biological, or archaeological sites that justify research can be found in any country. From the perspective of diplomacy, it always pays to increase ties among nations, especially when the ties are easily reversible and the diplomatic establishment pays few of the costs. Even when implementation falters – as it often does – and becomes a source of contention, the contention permits the additional negotiation, discussions, and explanations that are the routine staples of diplomacy. In any case, failure to implement at agreed levels of activity or failure to implement at all is not as serious as failures in capital assistance or trade agreements. Scientific exchange matters diplomatically, but not that much, and that is the source of its strength and its weakness as a diplomatic tool.

Failures to implement or to implement at agreed levels are highly common in the administration of scientific exchanges, because budget is hard to obtain. Although the actual claims on resources by the totality of all agreements are very small in absolute magnitude, budgetary authorities dislike agreements because of their open-ended nature. In principle, the only limit to the number of bilateral agreements is the number of pairs of nations, and scientists and diplomats can always pursue multilateral agreements. Claims for resources that have no upper bound are of great concern to budget authorities. In their rhetoric concerning international science, budgetary authorities always ask for "optimal" program levels. Although they know full well that the optimum is determined jointly by a scientific calculus and a political calculus, they have great difficulty taking these matters into account. The OMB and other cognizant agencies always have difficulty in handling budgetary claims that cut across their organizational structures.

Implementation of exchange agreements and the associated costs are not usually assigned to the diplomatic establishment. Raising funds for implementation becomes a matter of squeezing the domestic activities of functional agencies. When resource claims for scientific exchange arrive at central budgetary levels, they are a part of a domestic agency's budget and are judged in terms of relevance to the agency mission, not in terms of maintaining the currency of the indigenous U.S. enterprise or international political purposes. Since the OMB is organized according to functional groupings of agencies, it acts as if it had no rational means to judge the claims for the international science budget as a whole. The representations of the State Department concerning the value of the entire U.S. government effort carry little weight, because it is well known that international science has a relatively low priority in the State Department. The things that contrive to make scientific exchange valuable as a diplomatic tool also limit its claim to priority and budget.

The representatives of the operating agencies similarly carry little weight. If an agency justifies international exchange programs in terms of the *IRS* strategy, then the question is, why should invisible colleges and information markets fail internationally, since they work so well domestically? This is the international analogue of questions about domestic market failure when it comes to programs for innovation. Why are private levels of exchange not sufficient? While the barriers postulated in the *IRS* strategy may once have held true, it can be argued that modern communications do not stop at national borders, regardless of national preferences about controlling information flows. It is difficult to demonstrate convincingly that world scientific output will be greater in quality and quantity with a government-sponsored exchange program than without it.

If an agency justifies its international exchange programs as relevant to its domestic mission — and this is the way most have to be justified — then the presumption of effectiveness is against international science programs. Basic research done overseas, it is argued, will eventually be captured by domestic programs without any special efforts, for that is the nature of basic research.

If an agency justifies its international programs on diplomatic grounds, as serving either the president or his foreign policy, such reasons are not a warrant for agency proposals. Either the State Department or the president have to provide this authorization. Warrants provided by the State Department about programs in the R&D agencies are not weighted heavily, and issues involved in small-scale, routine scientific exchanges rarely rise to the presidential level. Diplomats will be unable to make persuasive arguments about the incremental value of this or that specific agreement and will, therefore, rarely be persuasive about the relevance of a given budget to their diplomatic concerns. The historical results are always budgets at or below critical minimum for scientific exchange programs, despite the fanfare and publicity that attend the signing of agreements.

Technology Transfer and the Developed Nations

In contrast with basic science, no one has suggested that some worldwide industrial research enterprise exists whose output should be maximized. However, economists have long argued that free trade in commodities and services would maximize world output, provided all nations permitted principles of comparative advantage to operate. These principles apply as well to trade in technological information as they do to trade in tangible goods and services. Differential holdings of such information are one source of comparative advantage. They mean that the goods and services produced by one country will be superior in quality or cost, enhancing competitiveness. Like most other goods and services, technological information itself can be traded in international markets for reciprocal information or foreign currency. Directly or indirectly, trade in technological information benefits, in the short run, those nations that hold the information. In the long run, all can be better off because information, once gained, can be used to increase output and productivity.

If technological advantage implies economic advantage, then the problem, from the perspective of nations that hold marketable information, is to try to hold on to it or to sell it on favorable terms while the advantage lasts. Some technology is always being transferred, since information is "congealed" in the goods and services traded internationally. In the long run, technological advantage will erode and comparative advantage may be reversed. Once asymmetries in information are reduced, many nations may have the human capital to produce high technology goods more cheaply than the original innovators. The long-run problem for technologically innovative countries is to reduce the value of their current holdings of technological information by creating even newer, more cost-effective technologies. While competitors may not be able to replicate entire technologies, trade provides many clues. At least on the civilian side, maintaining holdings of information is difficult. Some loss is always occurring; that is the nature of free trade. Until the late seventies and early eighties, U.S. decisionmakers were not particularly sensitive to losses of technological information on the civilian side of the economy (Graham 1978). Few administrations showed concern about the transfer of civilian technology abroad. They were all concerned about maintaining the traditional U.S. position on the benefits from free trade. Trying to regulate the flow of technical information on the civilian side of the economy would have been inconsistent with the U.S. free-trade position.

For the Eisenhower administration, trade was a necessary condition for U.S. economic strength. It was a source of demand to keep American factories going, and it provided goods and services that were scarce in the United States (CFEP 1954, 1957). Expansion of trade helped not only the United States but also friends and allies, and economically strong friends and allies were necessary for political stability. Removing barriers to trade, particularly barriers to private sector trade, was a main aim of Eisenhower's foreign economic policy.

The Kennedy administration maintained the traditional concern with ensuring free trade. It spent much political capital in promoting trade expansion, particularly with Western Europe (Sorenson 1965). For the Johnson administration, universal trade relations were an objective well worth seeking. Tariff reductions would increase the effectiveness of competition and raise the nation's real income by putting resources to their most valuable use (President's Task Force on Foreign Economic Policy 1964).

Promotion of high-technology exports was not a conscious strategy for achieving economic growth at home during any of these administrations. Such promotion did not have to be explicit. Free trade enabled all economies to export those commodities for which a comparative advantage existed; there did not have to be special efforts to export high-technology goods. If technological information was the source of U.S. comparative advantage, freer international markets would select those commodities embodying that information. Even when other countries gained the same information and began to compete successfully in markets where the United States once held a technological edge, the U.S. economy appeared to be able to generate sufficient tradable innovations to compensate for losses of old technology.

Economists argued that there might be a product cycle, with the United States having a comparative advantage in the early part of the cycle, in the initial production of innovations. Under product cycle theory, once an innovation became a standard product or was produced with conventional know-how, then other nations could achieve comparative advantage in its mass production. If product cycle theory were true, some U.S. goods would always be moving abroad for production, but the U.S. capacity for innovation would provide tradable new ones to fill in behind the old ones. Trade policy thus required correlative innovation policy. The formal connection between the two came in the late 1970s when first Nixon and then Carter became concerned about declining technological opportunities for the United States and increasing ones for competitors. The technology transfer strategy they used (denoted *TTD*) can be stated as follows:

TTD.1 *In the case of trade between developed nations, technological superiority implies economic competitiveness, other things being equal.*

Republican and Democratic administrations alike held to *TTD.1*. Industrial innovation led to increased productivity, which led to lower costs, which led to expanding international markets. However, other countries were always trying to reduce U.S. comparative advantage by encouraging innovation. The federal government could not remain indifferent to the U.S. rate of innovation and needs to augment incentives for innovation in U.S. industry (Nixon 1972; Carter 1979a).

TTD.2 *For the United States, comparative advantage in existing products comes from holding higher-quality technological information than other nations.*

TTD.3 *The United States gains comparative advantage only when it is first to innovate.*

> **TTD3.1** *U.S. capability to produce novel and usable technological information is declining.*

TTD.4 *Comparative advantage flows to other nations when (1) they are first to innovate, or (2) they imitate or follow innovating nations.*

TTD.5 *U.S. rivals have the ability to acquire whatever civilian technological information is produced in the U.S., and they can use this information to gain comparative advantage over U.S. exports.*

TTD.6 *U.S. capabilities for the acquisition of technological information from abroad are highly limited, nor can the United States acquire information from rivals sufficient to gain comparative advantage over the rivals' exports.*

TTD.7 *Policy implication: To maintain technological superiority, the United States should (1) use the technological information it holds to increase its innovation rate, and (2) increase its ability to acquire other nations' technological information.*

Logically, the *TTD* strategy could well include an eighth proposition. If loss of technological superiority implies the loss of international markets and consequent domestic unemployment, then it is possible to argue that the government ought to exert control over information flows abroad from the civilian side of the economy (Morgan 1983). This is already done in the case of information with possible military application. Some industrial leaders and government officials argue that losses of civilian technological information are at least as important as losses of military information. The *TTD* model could thus be extended to:

Possible TTD.8: *The government should regulate and control all flows of technological information abroad from either the defense or nondefense sectors of the economy.*

Proposing *TTD.8* entails a set of at least five supporting beliefs: (1) there exist cost-effective and appropriate means of regulation and control, (2) no great regulatory burden would be imposed on U.S. firms operating in international markets, (3) regulation of information flow to the developed countries would not hamper flows needed to assist developing countries, (4) technological information delivered to developing countries would not be subsequently transferred to rival developed countries, and (5) retaliatory regulation of information flows to the United States by its economic rivals and partners would cause only bearable damage to the U.S. economy.

So far, decisionmakers have resisted attempting to implement a *TTD.8* because of the complexities and uncertainties. However, the asymmetric notions that, (1) the United States must be an innovator and not an imitator to gain comparative advantage, and (2) other nations can easily create comparative advantage by being U.S. imitators, push decisionmakers and stakeholders toward regulation of information flows abroad. Since loss of comparative advantage is associated in the short run with loss of jobs, pressures for controls come from U.S. export and import-competing industries. Although there are some who gain from transfers (the owners of transferred technologies), and technology transfer may be accompanied by adjustment assistance from the U.S. government, the political and economic costs of transfer are usually seen as specific and high. The benefits are seen as diffuse and broad.

The historical U.S. position on free trade, including trade in technological information, is that aggregate benefits exceed aggregate costs. However, if we believe we face a lengthy structural innovation problem that cannot be solved and competitors who achieve comparative advantage by using U.S. technology for either innovation or imitation, it is easy to reverse the historic U.S. trade position. If a nation believes it has lost its powers to innovate, then it has to hold onto what it has. Thus, one can predict more efforts to protect U.S. goods from foreign competition and more attempts to regulate international transfer of technical information.

Technology Transfer and Economic Development

Perhaps the most poignant encounter between science and technology and economics comes in arguments and strategies for aiding the developing countries. The trade battles of the developed countries, among themselves and against the Soviet Union, are tainted by needs to gain economic or military advantage. But the drive for economic development, with technical and capital assistance from the industrialized countries, has the cooperative characteristics that are congenial to science and engineering. While economics might suggest capital deepening and human capital formation as ways to obtain development, the S&T community has long believed that technology transfer is at least a necessary, if not sufficient, condition for development. If so, the formation of indigenous S&T enterprises becomes necessary. Indigenous scientists and engineers can perceive the match or mismatch of prospective imported technologies with conditions in the receiving country. They help in selecting foreign technologies that are "appropriate," adapting them to local conditions. To be cost-effective, technology must usually be modified to reflect local factor proportions and conditions facing local industry. Given the ingenuity of local scientists and engineers, there are few technologies whose factor proportions cannot be modified productively. By building a research infrastructure, developing countries can find ways to develop themselves.

Since such an infrastructure has to be built, technical assistance from scientists and engineers in developed countries, particularly U.S. scientists and engineers, is necessary. Technical assistance has long been either a minor or major theme in U.S. development strategies, and a stream of government and nongovernment technical assistance agreements has been negotiated over the years. The purposes of these agreements are to help create indigenous scientific and technical enterprises and bring scientific habits of mind to development choices. Even though technical assistance programs have never received large-scale resources, they have been seen as high leverage and as strong influences on patterns of development. In fact, the scientific community has seen technical assistance as so critical to development, that it has long argued the function should be separated organizationally from other development assistance efforts. A number of administrations have tried to remove technical assistance from the overall U.S. aid bureaucracy and provide the function through a separate agency. But such attempts have always failed, because Congress has been concerned that there be centralized oversight of all assistance and because, from a budgetary perspective, technical assistance is one of many alternative instruments and cannot be given the absolute claim to resources that scientists always want for their endeavors.

The development strategy of the scientific community (denoted *SDS*) can be stated as follows:

SDS.1 *It is morally, economically, and politically sound for the United States to assist the developing nations in raising their levels of income and welfare.*

> **SDS1.1** *A world of developed nations is more stable, politically and economically, than a world with a mix of developed and developing nations.*

> **SDS1.2** *Even though the developing countries may become economic competitors, they will eventually provide the U.S. economy with a very large foreign market.*

SDS.2 *Rising levels of income and welfare imply increased political stability.*

SDS.1 and *2* are shared beliefs of decisionmakers and scientists; they connect economic aid to U.S. foreign policy objectives.

SDS.3 *The soundest kind of development occurs when a country takes Western (U.S.) technology and adapts it to local conditions.*

Economics alone cannot tell a country which imported technologies to choose and use, since prices and market signals are highly distorted in developing countries. These distortions bias technological choices toward those inappropriate for a developing nation, but the distortions can be discovered and removed by indigenous scientists and engineers.

SDS.4 *The acquisition of indigenous scientific and technological capabilities is a necessary condition for appropriate development.*

> **SDS4.1** *The best way to make rational decisions about employing Western technology in development is to have a scientific and technological community in place, which knows how prospective imported technologies will work.*

SDS4.2 *The knowledge and intellectual habits of an indigenous scientific and technological community permit modification of imported technology to meet local conditions.*

SDS.5 *Policy implication: The United States should strive to build indigenous scientific and technological capabilities in developing countries through exchanges of people and information. Technical assistance should be given at least equal priority with capital assistance in policies for development.*

How the Strategy Worked

Decisionmakers' faith in the value of technical assistance has fluctuated over time, depending upon budgets and overall political preferences. Belief in the power of technical assistance to do the development job is correlated with an administration's perceived need to conserve expenditures. Technical assistance efforts are also correlated with shifting theories and views about how to induce development and gain foreign policy influence and leverage. For some administrations, development is properly a matter of internal mobilization and self-help. If so, what is needed is external assistance that gives developing nations the capacity to help themselves. For other administrations, development takes large-scale capital assistance.

For the Eisenhower administration, technical assistance was the preferred way to promote development. Its purpose was to make a country more attractive to private investment, on the one hand, and, on the other, to increase its "absorptive" capacity. If a developing country created a friendly economic climate and necessary infrastructure, then the administration believed the private sector would grow rapidly and pull the country along into modernization.

Technical assistance from the United States created an infrastructure that the private sector could use, but it did not interfere with private decisions or distort them. The private sector was always a superior agent of development compared to government, because the decisions and operations of firms were based on economic criteria of efficiency and profitability. The governments of developing nations were not in a position to use efficiency criteria. Nationalism and the desire for self-sufficiency implied that capital projects the U.S. government would be asked to support would not be based on principles of increasing productivity or comparative advantage. The demand for development assistance was often skewed toward large, costly, and ineffective projects, because they were required symbols of progress (Dodge, undated). By changing the perceptions and incentives of the private sector, foreign and domestic technical assistance had a multiplier effect. Capital assistance had no such effect, because political considerations inevitably dominated considerations of productivity and comparative advantage.

In any case, the United States had a comparative advantage in know-how, and that was what the developing nations needed most. Since the export of know-how, rather than development capital, was appropriate for all parties, the United States did good and conserved scarce budgetary resources at the same time (Eisenhower 1955). The administration was helped along in this view by the Congress, which had admonished the president in 1953 and 1954 that assistance meant experts and know-how rather than large flows of commodities and equipment.

The Kennedy administration, as in other policy areas, was critical of Eisenhower's efforts in economic development. Despite the long concern of the outgoing administration in making development assistance effective and efficient, the incoming administration saw the existing programs as wasteful and overextended. That was so, because Eisenhower's programs were operated on the wrong premise. The development problem was not one of creating technical infrastructure that could be used by the private sector but of providing large-scale, long-term assistance for public projects. Only when developing countries knew that the United States would send them aid over a long time and on a large enough scale would they take the difficult political measures that development required. Assured capital assistance was necessary to induce countries to start building the social infrastructure in the short run.

President Kennedy was impatient with the limited scope and size of technical assistance programs. He was interested in aid as a way of supporting and advancing U.S. foreign policy, and unlike Eisenhower, he believed U.S. development assistance could influence the domestic economic behavior of other countries. What was crucial to Eisenhower — encouraging the private sector and limiting government assistance — was irrelevant for Kennedy. His administration believed that it did not matter whether steel mills in developing countries were run by the private or the public sector. What mattered was the output of steel. Incentives for public or private action over the long run were simply of second priority as long as concrete things got done in the short run. In any case, the private sector in most developing countries was weak and did not have the roads, harbors, and storage facilities that make private sector initiatives feasible. In terms of both doctrine and focus, the Kennedy administration turned from limited technical assistance programs to sustained, long-term support for development via loans and capital assistance.

So far as S&T was of concern, a Kennedy administration review concluded that the aid program had not made effective use of available

U.S. science and technology. It was felt that the development programs were not adequately connected to the academic world, which held relevant information. Eisenhower's aid agencies simply did not know enough to choose the right kind of development assistance programs. Consequently, the aid programs needed an internal R&D capability that would have closer ties with practicing scientists and engineers, especially those in universities (PSAC 1968).

The issue of sufficient knowledge was connected to the issue of organization. Because of the dualities inherent in aid — military versus economic aid, technical versus capital assistance — no organization had ever been able to make the aid programs function as a coherent whole. President Kennedy decided to unify all aid programs in a single agency, Agency for International Development (AID). This merger proved difficult for the cause of technical assistance, since technical assistance did not have strong representation in AID, nor did it have powerful champions in the White House or the OMB. Neither AID nor the president believed that technical assistance was a powerful contributor to development. Prevailing economic theory paid little attention to scientific and technical infrastructure, and AID was staffed by economists who had strong faith that capital assistance was the way to "take off." The economists had little knowledge of the potential of S&T as seen by the scientific and technical community.

To the scientific community, the requirements for successful technical assistance were antithetical to the requirements for capital assistance. Technical assistance had to be apolitical and long-run. Good political outcomes would result from letting the U.S. scientific and technical community build infrastructure over a long period of time without political and diplomatic intervention. Capital and technical assistance could go their own ways without damaging overall foreign policy. In fact, since the scientific community strongly believed infrastructure was necessary for development, the inevitable lack of attention to long-run technical assistance in the aid bureaucracy meant that the United States was inflicting damage to its own long-run foreign policy objectives.

The concern over administration of technical assistance continued into the Johnson administration, because development "gaps" were seen as widening. But development theory and practice continued to underplay the role of education and of science and technology. The SDS strategy holds that technical assistance permits developing nations to make their own choices among feasible technologies. Providing resources for eventual self-help was a general theme for aid in the Johnson administration, and this logically implied greater emphasis on infrastructure. Letting the developing countries make their own choices was morally proper and would result in correct choices, provided that the countries developed their own cadres of scientists and engineers.

Not only did they help choose appropriate technology, but their habits of mind and work, which were "modern," created a hospitable climate for new ideas (PSAC 1968). In the long run, the encouragement of new ideas — and new ways of doing things — was the essence of development. If the United States wanted development, it should encourage education, management, science, technology, and professional activities.

Pursuing development without an S&T infrastructure in place was self-defeating, because development was a process of adapting technology to local conditions. Without an indigenous infrastructure, a country could not know what choices were appropriate, since market signals were not a sound guide in developing countries. Governments usually were unable to set shadow prices that were economically sound because they lacked the knowledge. Thus, self-sustaining growth without an infrastructure was not possible, but the production of an infrastructure was a long-term process, not strongly linked to short-term capital assistance.

Thus, PSAC argued once more for a separate agency that would be designed and operated according to well-validated principles of science administration. PSAC preferred a national foundation for technical assistance that would operate independently of AID's capital assistance programs. The foundation's structure and operations were to be similar to those of the domestic NSF. Given an NSF-type structure and operation, the new foundation would be insulated from short-term political and economic considerations. Although economists believed that capital assistance could serve as an incentive for building the kind of infrastructure PSAC wanted, PSAC believed that the assurance of long-term technical assistance, delivered regardless of other considerations, would induce developing nations to build the required infrastructure.

Although AID responded to the pressure for more attention to technical assistance by setting up a technical assistance bureau within the agency, the issue of a separate agency carried over to the Nixon administration. Nixon, like preceding presidents, found the organization of development assistance difficult. He originally planned to disestablish AID and set up a development corporation and an international development institute. The institute would execute the technical assistance function (Neuriter 1971). This institute would strengthen infrastructure in developing countries and carry out research relevant to development; it would be managed by people who cared about technical assistance, not economists (David 1971d). Under Nixon's self-help doctrine, the institute would receive technical proposals from developing countries; it would not itself design projects for developing countries to execute. Once the proposals were ranked, the institute would then fund up to the marginal project permitted by its budget. But the budget, in turn, would be a function of the number of acceptable proposals the institute received. Although there was no formal budget constraint, resources would be conserved by concentrating on a few development areas, such as population control, food supply, and industrialization. The number of projects was also to be limited by using measures of self-help and "seriousness," for example, the amount of its own resources a country was willing to commit to a proposed technical assistance project.

Nixon's proposed reorganization of AID never took place, and a technical assistance institute was not formed. Congress proved resistant. The proposal was "put on ice," and the idea of a technical assistance agency lost its champions when Nixon disestablished the OST in 1973. The Ford science advisory operation, based in the NSF, did not have the time or resources to grapple with aid issues nor was it in a bureaucratic position to do so. In 1975 the Congress, with the consent of President Ford, restored a science arm to the Executive Office of the President. Given the scientists' view of development, the new Office of Science and Technology Policy quickly became another champion of an independent technical assistance institute or foundation. Using the *SDS* strategy, the president's science adviser argued anew that strengthening of technological capabilities would help developing nations to help themselves (Press 1979).

In 1979 President Carter used an executive order to try to establish his technical assistance institute (Institute for Scientific and Technical Cooperation). He said his objective was to create sufficient capability in the developing countries, which would then guide technological choice to satisfy "their own unique requirements" (Carter 1980). Although the proposed institute received legislative authorization, the Congress never gave it an appropriation. Congress feared that there would be conflict and duplication, rather than specialization between the institute and AID. New resources for an institute sent signals of "excessive" foreign assistance when the United States had difficulties at home. The administration apparently concluded that the institute could not be a viable presidential initiative, or it did not rank high enough in priority to expend the president's waning political capital. President Carter's second report to Congress on science, technology, and diplomacy contains no mention of the aborted institute nor any mention of a general technical assistance strategy (Carter 1981). Technology transfer is addressed, if at all, in the context of specific problems such as health rather than as an activity in its own right.

The Reagan administration's views on development have come full circle back to those of the Eisenhower administration. It feels that the best way to transfer technology to the developing countries is through foreign investment and trade. The most important assistance the United States could give the developing world was to get the U.S. economy going, since the U.S. economy, operating at full capacity, provides an immense market for imported goods and services. As the economy revived, foreign investments by U.S. firms would also become more attractive – provided developing nations maintained a favorable business climate. U.S. investments abroad carried modern technology with them (Reagan 1982).

Reagan solved the perennial problem of administering science and technology for development by a reorganization of AID rather than by the establishment of a separate institute. Reagan's AID set up a science and technology office that nominally cut across the functional problem areas where AID was working, such as agriculture, nutrition, energy, and the environment. AID's new Bureau for Science and Technology would provide technical support and research information to the operating branches of the agency, but the new bureau did not encompass all of AID's technical staff and was to be symbiotic with the technical staffs in other bureaus.

PSAC, in earlier administrations, had argued that just such an arrangement was disadvantageous, because it believed that technical assistance programs would not be insulated from politics and time pressures. Insulation could not be achieved if the technical assistance organization had to compete for resources with other organizations within AID. But AID solved this problem by making the National Academy of Sciences the provider of nominally innovative research and technical assistance services. The Academy would make grants for research and capacity building in areas where it had special expertise.

Summary and Observations

Whenever asymmetries exist in holdings of scientific and technical information, information can be traded for economic gain through private markets or given away by governments for political gain. Even nations willing to rely mainly on the outcome of market exchanges cannot remain entirely indifferent to the economic consequences of such transfers. Since transfers also provide signals about political preferences and intentions, they are a means of achieving political and diplomatic objectives. For the United States, the objectives include the economic and social transformation of other nations, and so the design of information transfer policies becomes especially complex. When information is held mainly by the private sector, trade-offs have to be struck between giving the private sector incentives to pass on its own information or having the government provide it.

Most U.S. administrations have struggled with these trade-offs since

President Truman's Point Four Program. Presidents have constantly tinkered with both trade policy and trade organization. Given the diffuse nature of the issues and conflicting objectives, presidents have frequently felt the need for ad hoc coordination. Thus, Eisenhower established a Cabinet Committee on Foreign Economic Policy; Kennedy abolished it, but reorganized the AID programs; Nixon established a Committee on International Economic Policy and tried to reorganize the structure Kennedy had set up; Carter tried an Export Council and reorganization. Reorganization and coordination attempts have been accompanied by a search for concepts and doctrines that would be consistent with higher-order political and economic doctrine and would reconcile or at least mediate conflicting objectives.

In the case of basic research information, the strategies used by scientists and politicians have both been unbounded. Comparative advantage in some field of science can be demonstrated for practically any nation, and some minimal political and diplomatic gain can always be found, even if it is only increased contact and communication. Although strategies differ, they are mutually reinforcing, since some benefits always accrue, and costs are always shifted away from diplomats. There is always incentive to sign more agreements. The proliferation of basic research agreements causes later difficulties in implementation, since a clear and persuasive rationale for a whole set of agreements cannot be constructed easily, and there is no bureaucracy charged with producing such a rationale. The result is low budgetary priority and underfunding.

International transfers of technological information between developed countries have traditionally been viewed as a matter for the private sector. Private trading in information directly and as embodied in goods and services was illustrated in the workings of comparative advantage. The United States exported some kinds of information and imported others. Outside of the military domain, there was no need for regulation. With perceived declines in innovativeness, both decision-makers and stakeholders have become concerned about U.S. information flows abroad. Exports of information are equated to exports of jobs. But there are not yet formal constraints on U.S. firms holding nonmilitary information that is attractive to other countries. Designs for new industrial policies logically entail a harder look at outflows of technological information to competitors and rivals and greater effort to capture information produced abroad.

Delivery of technological know-how, however, has always been a strand in U.S. government efforts to promote growth in developing countries. Although one can argue that developing countries need "low" technologies for growth, particularly in food and energy, the developing countries have not usually agreed with such a view. They have pressed the developed nations for general access to technological information on favorable terms. The United States, in particular, has found it necessary to argue that it was powerless to provide civilian technology on more favorable terms than the market provides, because the ownership of most technology resides with private firms. If the developing nations want more technology, the United States has said they should make themselves more attractive to private foreign investment.

To be appropriate, high or low technology cannot be transferred without change and adjustment. The scientific community has long argued that a main objective for U.S. development policy should be increasing indigenous research and training capacity. An increase in capacity would ensure that a country had sufficient knowledge to make correct choices for itself from the international menu of feasible, but not necessarily economic, technological possibilities. Because labor is the least scarce factor of production in developing countries, the correct possibilities were believed to be low-level, labor-intensive technologies. The indigenous infrastructure, because of the rationality derived from approaching things scientifically, would not be affected by political and symbolic requirements and demands or, at least, could fend them off. It would select technologies that matched the nation's resource endowments.

Because technological rationality and international politics were believed to be incompatible, the long-run efforts at building infrastructure were to be accomplished without regard to short-run political and diplomatic objectives. Whatever the latter might be, work on infrastructure would not be affected. Linkage of short- and long-run objectives would be self-defeating, although diplomats would always have incentives to make such linkages.

Judging Strategies for Science and Technology Policy

7

At this stage of the inquiry, I have explored the design and deployment of the strategies that lie at the core of U.S. science and technology policy. Although I have translated the often emotive, poetic language used in these strategies and have tried to state clearly their implicit factual and value content, I have refrained from overall judgments or "appreciations." Since these strategies are an amalgam of current facts, passionately held values, and predictions about the future, they are always difficult to evaluate. Now the time has come to provide some tests or rules for judging their quality. Such tests or rules are not unique, and alternative rules are always possible. However, different sets of rules should correlate with each other. My intent here is not to state many different possible sets of rules but to provide a few serviceable ones for practitioners of the S&T policy craft, decisionmakers, and the public.

There is no elegant method involved in providing rules for judging strategies. What one has to do is formulate a reasonable set of answerable questions that can be posed whenever confronting competing strategies. Formulation of such questions is ordinarily the province of the philosophy of practical reason and normative discourse. However, this literature has not been applied specifically to policy arguments (Taylor 1961; Raz 1975). On the other hand, not much has been done in mainstream policy analysis on distinguishing between convincing strategies or models and unconvincing ones, let alone "true" ones and "false" ones. For example, Hambrick suggests searching through policy arguments for ten kinds of statements that they should have to be complete (Hambrick 1974). But, in any actual debates and decisions, many of the ten will not be stated or will only be implied. Completeness, in any case, does not mean that propositions are true or false, or justified or not. Nor does a complete strategy imply high quality. My concern is with assessing the quality of alternative strategies and accounting for peculiarities that may arise, because a strategy concerns S&T policy.

Some Problems of Language

Before one can judge the quality of any strategy, he needs to know what it says. Strategies articulated for S&T policy are especially prone to language that is emotive and ambiguous. Their language has a touch of poetry, because it is connected to the language used in discussing high personal or social values — "truly inquiring minds," "properly educated citizens." It is a language designed to persuade, to touch the emotions as well as the intellect, thereby generating desired actions. So the first questions to ask whenever encountering such a strategy is:

Question 1. *What is the real subject of discussion and debate?*

One should always be aware that the nominal subject of discussion and debate is not necessarily the real one. Consider the following passage from PSAC concerning science education. Although written in 1958, its language and structure are highly typical of current arguments for more federal effort in science literacy:

> Science affects the life of every contemporary man every day. It conditions decisions that need to be made by his government on many matters, including national defense, foreign policy, and public health. It affects the decisions made by individuals on business problems, on selecting a community in which to live, on choosing an automobile, a record player, or perhaps even a dentifrice. If an individual is ignorant of science, he must guess what to do or believe what he is told. Even if he is told what to do by an expert, he has no way to check on this advice or even to understand it. This unhappy predicament is precisely that of most citizens of the United States today. Their fate in important matters and in trivial matters alike may be decided by their participation. And it will not be otherwise so long as they remain illiterate about science and technology. (PSAC 1958, 4)

What can such a passage mean? It seems to say that science and technology, in some unspecified way, so highly pervade daily life and decisions that citizens cannot understand their own personal decisions, let alone the policy decisions of the government that represents them, without special education in S&T. The passage clearly cannot be meant literally. In the first place, one is given little sense of how science and technology do their "conditioning" or where they do it. Because the current stock of scientific and technological information is used to make cars, record players, and even intercontinental ballistic missiles, it does not follow that one needs to have much technical knowledge of that stock and its characteristics to make sensible decisions about employing it, regulating it, or buying artifacts made with it. In the second place, there are large numbers of citizens, if not all citizens, making reasonable decisions every day without being in the predicament described. And when citizens make unreasonable or poor decisions, it is not at all clear that the cause is their scientific illiteracy. There are many other candidates as causes. Third, given that all citizens have limited time and resources, institutions and organizations are designed to cope with complex decisions, including scientific and technical decisions. It makes sense and is cost-effective to delegate some things and some decisions, and this is done every day. The policy problem then is designing effective institutions, not making all citizens scientifically literate, although literacy may be desirable for other reasons.

What may be meant is that, without some knowledge of science and technology, citizens cannot control, check, or guide those whom they have delegated to make the goods and services that use S&T information intensively or have chosen to make policy decisions with S&T content. What these agents can accomplish depends on the stock of S&T information that society has elected to provide in the past. What PSAC may be arguing is that citizens cannot exercise oversight of their agents without knowing something about the same stock of information. One can argue that the procedures used for controlling and checking those who use S&T information depend in some way on knowing the scientific and engineering principles involved, and that, therefore, the collective ignorance of these principles puts us citizens in a predicament. But this kind of argument confuses the domains of policymaking and scientific inquiry. We make policy all the time in areas where we personally have little technical expertise.

We use political and legal processes to elicit the information relevant to making policy. That information is about stakeholders; expected outcomes, costs, and benefits; equities and efficiency; and not scientific principles. We make economic policy all the time without having technical knowledge of macroeconomic theory or the empirical models used to predict the GNP. Even in the field of national defense, no great knowledge of scientific principles is required. In the case of strategic nuclear weapons, for example, the technology maps into a few performance characteristics — circular probable error, weapon radius, and reliability. Policy hinges on what one does with weapons of such and such characteristics. There is no reason to believe that the same approach in making S&T policy decisions or policy decisions "conditioned" by science and technology is not feasible. We know it is feasible because we do it.

One can, of course, hold that S&T policy decisions or policy decisions with S&T content are intrinsically harder to make than other kinds. Or, one can argue, that decisions would be better or more acceptable if one knew more technical substance. But policy decisions are hard enough because of their intrinsic nature, for example, conflicts of interest, competing values, or uncertainty, without infusing them with alleged deficiencies in the technical understanding of science. Decisions may certainly turn on the kind of systems performance S&T can provide, and we may have to make decisions with incomplete information about systems performance. But our decisions turn on expected performance, not physical principles. Physics will permit any number of reasonable performance characteristics, so we can decide what we want without a detailed knowledge of physics.

By a process of elimination, the meaning of the passage in question is reduced to maintaining that a knowledge of science and engineering principles is required to be an educated and cultivated citizen. This is certainly a statement we can discuss. Since we believe, along with Jefferson, that educated and cultivated citizens make a democracy work better, we want our educational system to prevent scientific and technical illiteracy. But we also want it to do many other things. If so, we can and should argue about resources and programs for S&T literacy, compared with other worthy educational activities. The case for reducing scientific illiteracy then rises or falls on our educational beliefs and strategies and not on any predicaments arising from citizens' lack of technical information.

To consider the problems of language further, let us look at two related passages, this time from the public interest strategy of technological innovation:

> America's emerging social values might well be termed "post-industrial" and are espoused by a growing number of more educated, politically influential citizens who are disenchanted with many existing institutions and priorities but, for the most part, still believe their objectives can be reached by restructuring business and government machinery through constitutional means. (Henderson 1978, 277)

> Vastly increased information flows may prove to be our best hope for irrigating our impacted social system and modifying its structure, casting some of them into oblivion while deflecting the course and refining the goals of others. Information is, of course, the basic currency of all economic and political decision making. The quality and quantity of information and the way it is structured, presented, and amplified control all of our resource allocation. (Henderson 1978, 287)

What can these passages mean? Unlike the first example, it is at least clear that this involves a policy argument. Terms like "restructuring business and government machinery" and "controlling the allocation of resources" signal choices we can make and actions bureaucracies can take. These are not terms used in scientific or engineering inquiry. Increased knowledge may be useful and needed, but it is knowledge relevant to economic and political decisionmaking. Together, the two passages seem to say that increased information flows are either a necessary or sufficient condition for obtaining social change. They might be necessary, since they are only "our best hope," not our best "certainty." But they might also be sufficient, because their content and structure are asserted to control all resource allocation.

Whether necessary or sufficient, it is unclear how the postindustrial values are to be installed via vastly increased information. How information does its work is unspecified, and whether information can do such work at all is left unquestioned. That vastly increased information might cause more conflict in the social system and less modification in its structure is not argued. But one can construct highly plausible counterarguments that this could well turn out to be the case.

If information is the basic currency for decisionmaking, the growing number of educated and politically influential citizens who have seen or acquired "postindustrial" values will presumably offer their views to decisionmakers. But what do decisionmakers do in exchange? Probably the answer is that they accept or are expected to accept the correctness of the values about which they are being informed. Alternatively, the gain to decisionmakers might be the avoidance of a class of citizens that does not believe its postindustrial objectives can be achieved by mere "restructuring" through constitutional means.

What these passages really say is that it is important that certain classes of citizen make their values known to decisionmakers, since there is some congruence between these values and those required to live reasonably in a postindustrial society. The postindustrial society has already arrived or will in the near future. Given the congruence of values with emerging economic and social structures, all citizens have to acquire the new values currently held by a few. Consequently, decisionmakers should give priority to policies and programs that will instill and promote these values. Such policies and programs would then be consistent with the requirements the postindustrial society will impose. Decisionmakers will make clearly superior public choices because the decisions will be validated by history.

Given a clear formulation of what is being said, one can evaluate the claim presented and investigate the empirical statements about the emergence of postindustrial society. Through surveys or other techniques, one can check on the stated degree of disenchantment of educated citizens. Furthermore, one can make ethical inquiries about the values of the disenchanted citizens and whether their values ought to be embodied into the resource allocations or weighted more heavily than those of "enchanted" citizens. In other words, one can begin to ask the questions and make the inquiries that are appropriate to discourse and decisions in any public policy matter.

Let us take a third example of ambiguous language in science policy-making, this one concerning the international aspects of science and technology:

> International exchange of scientific information is of growing importance. Increased specialization of science will make it more important than ever that scientists in this country keep continuously abreast of developments abroad. In addition, a flow of scientific information constitutes one facet of international accord which should be cultivated.
>
> The Government should take an active role in promoting the international flow of scientific information. (Bush [1945] 1980, 22)

What is Bush trying to say here? By the specialization of science he could mean that, given different endowments of scientific labor and capital, nations will pursue principles of scientific comparative advantage, with all nations specializing in the inquiries they do relatively best. Keeping abreast of scientific developments abroad could mean that one watches for trades of information that maximize the world's research output, since science, or at least basic research, is a world enterprise. More probably, he could mean that all scientific disciplines are becoming more and more specialized as they develop, by using narrower and narrower topics of inquiry or finer-grained methods of inquiry. Given that science is a world enterprise and that a large number, if not all, nations pursue research, advances in disciplines and subdisciplines can occur anywhere, geographically. This condition means that desirable information will be lost without government assistance.

Since all scientists share the same canons of reporting and exchange of information, it is difficult to see why these canons do not suffice to distribute information properly around the world. They seem to work well enough within nation-states. Presumably, some barrier exists, perhaps of language, or perhaps in the international operations of the "invisible colleges." If so, lags may exist that hamper the efficiency of the research enterprise. It is up to the government to reduce these international lags because of the self-evident character of the government interest discussed earlier.

Bush also believes that international flows cement international relations. If there were no lags in information flow, this characteristic would still justify government actions to increase international exchange. But how international exchange furthers international relations is not explained; there is a missing piece to the Bush statement. From the perspective of diplomacy, international scientific treaties and agreements may be seen as low-cost actions, rich in symbolic content and signals about intentions. Since they are low-cost, they can also be reversed whenever diplomacy requires, and the reversal may also be taken as a signal. Because they are so cheap and effective but limited in scope, nations may use them frequently, even in cases where an indigenous science enterprise is weak or nonexistent.

If a duality exists in the justification for government support of international scientific activity, then it is certainly possible that the reasons for any one set of exchanges or agreements may be obscure. Sometimes the scientific community will rely on international information barriers. Sometimes it will rely on the international accord that scientific exchange is said to bring. Finding and proving barriers to private international communications may be difficult, however, especially when alleged revolutions in communications technology significantly reduce the costs of transmission. If barriers are insufficient justification, then one switches to international harmony. As one slides between the two justifications for exchange, the ability to explain the entire range of exchange activity becomes difficult. Thus, the usual kitchen-sink approach to justifying scientific activity creates real-world muddles.

Having discerned two policy problems in Bush's claim, one can then determine whether communication barriers continue to exist and whether their effects should be considered significant. It may be that a sufficiency of exchange already exists with respect to progress in scientific disciplines. However, if the purpose of exchange is international relations, or both international relations and information exchange, then one should be able to design agreements and implementing mechanisms to reflect this.

In all three of these examples, the meaning was initially not clear. The search for a reasonable meaning eventually revealed problems that were more complex, or at least different, than one would think, if one only read the three passages and passed on without reflection. Unfortunately, one is very likely to do this, because S&T policy language is stylized, repetitive, and, ultimately, numbing. Of course, the language in strategies for S&T policy will always be more stylized than that in other policy areas. Broad assertions of the rights, entitlements, and deprivations of citizens are made in all policy domains, because they bolster the case being presented. But a citizen's right to unemployment benefits can be debated more precisely than a citizen's rights and obligations to have a scientifically literate state of mind. Serious examinations of entitlements to scientific literacy are difficult to mount. When decisions turn on predictions of disastrous consequences for the whole society sometime in the future, there is a strong temptation to avoid close encounters with claims and issues. Decisions then become a matter of letting another pressure group have some symbolic resources.

Language for S&T policy is not only stylized but weak in explanatory power. Causal connections are hard to specify with precision. One will commonly find assertions of connections between science and society which are not testable at all or, at most, for which tests would be very hard to design. One will continually encounter statements about the necessity or sufficiency of S&T in achieving desired social outcomes or avoiding harmful ones, but will rarely be told how science and technology do this work. The entire discussion of S&T as a thing that acts on other things, or as a "force" that interacts with other forces lends itself to very imprecise, general statements about causation. Such discussion raises doubts about how seriously to take S&T arguments. At the very high levels of abstraction common in science policy discourse, one cannot know how much causal power to attribute to S&T, compared to other "forces." Often, when one encounters other forces in an argument, they, too, will be suffused with S&T or indirectly caused by S&T, on some nth round of impact. But if S&T causes everything or is related to everything, it does not really cause anything.

Given the stylized and causally ambiguous language, advocates and decisionmakers alike will usually let science policy arguments flow around them without too much conscious attention or too many probing questions. None of the parties will be forced into presenting warrants or justifications for what they are saying, because everyone's attempts to convince are subject to the same limitations. Attempts to probe will bring retaliation; there is "stable deterrence," because all parties are equally weak and subject to attack. And so when various parties propose social contracts about what the S&T enterprise is to do or how it is to be regulated, it is in their immediate interest to use highly stylized, abstract language.

The difficulty is that when one speaks in a policy mode of discourse, one wants clarity, precision, and rigor. Actions count. They use up resources, time, and attention. In the case of S&T activity, one is making implicit decisions about the future and should want the best and clearest warrants and justifications for them. Without precision and attention to words, one will trip up, no matter the good intentions. S&T language always expresses noble intentions, yet it is a language whose messages are difficult to understand. It is highly abstract and imprecise about causation and contains large numbers of unsupported assertions about interaction with other domains. Although such conditions are not peculiar to S&T, one needs to apply *Question 1* consistently, carefully, and patiently if one wants to emerge from policy debate with correct warrants and actions.

Tests and Questions for Policy Inquiry

Given the capability of translating statements, assertions, and belief into language appropriate to policy discourse, a number of evaluation tools become available. The collective craft wisdom of actors and analysts in many policy domains as to good practice is also available and useful. There are many different tests or questions that can be applied to distinguish good, or perhaps well-grounded, policy analysis from that that is bad or ill-grounded. The tests or questions are highly correlated with each other and try to get at the same issues. For example, in most assessments or appreciations of policy analysis or inquiry, one wants to know whether uncertainty was treated. Uncertainty can be treated in different ways, relative to the kind of inquiry. Some studies may use sensitivity analysis, varying predicted environments in a qualitative way; others may use statistical models containing test statistics that bound uncertainty; still others may use personal subjective probabilities or hunches about the likelihood of predicted outcomes. But these are all different ways to ask about the treatment of uncertainty.

Evaluations and tests can be framed in terms of desired attributes, for example, whether or not an inquiry has validity, soundness, timeliness, relevance, and actionability. Put negatively, a test may concern whether or not an inquiry avoids a whole set of so-called pitfalls (Averch 1975; Majone and Quade 1980). Pitfalls can occur anywhere within a policy inquiry — at the beginning, say, in handling statistics — or at the end, in presenting results to decisionmakers. In another approach, Hambrick looks for propositional types that a good or, more precisely, a complete policy inquiry should have. For example, in the Hambrick scheme, it should have a "grounding proposition" that more or less convincingly establishes an empirical or conceptual claim (Hambrick 1974, 470).

Before proceeding with any assessment scheme, we have to know whether there is anything peculiar about S&T policy discourse that would prevent us from applying any of the kinds of tests commonly used in policy research and analysis. Suppose we ask whether predicted social calamities from some technological innovation have any justification. As noted earlier, the purpose of this calamity prediction is to force us to avoid it. If we take the desired actions, we may or may not avoid the calamity, but if we avoid it, we may not be able to attribute its nonappearance to our actions. If we did not avoid it, we cannot necessarily attribute the calamity to our lack of action. It might have occurred anyway, despite our best efforts. This paradox is true of policy inquiry in general, but we usually have some experience in attempting to resolve it. Policy inquiry is usually "marginal" and conservative in nature. It does not project conditions very far beyond what has been experienced.

The *sine qua non* of S&T policy inquiry is that the outcomes we are worried about involve major discontinuities from what we know and what we currently experience. S&T causes, or more precisely, the use of S&T information causes "revolutions," and we are not very good at inferring the consequences of revolutions. No matter how sophisticated they are, our tools are based on current experience. The near future is difficult enough to predict, but when faced with requests for action *now,* based on sixth-order impacts two or three generations from now, the analytic machinery begins to break down. While this situation is not unique to the S&T policy domain, it is less common in others, because they are not so concerned about the very distant future.

There are two ways to handle this peculiarity. If we are operating in an a priori, analytic mode, looking for reasonable strategies to implement, we can weigh the ones that preserve flexibility and allow adjustments over time more heavily than the other alternatives. We can make an option-preserving capability an important criterion in judging an alternative and can insist that alternatives be robust, were they to confront situations for which they were never designed. We can value those alternatives that avoid major, irreversible decisions and actions more highly than other alternatives. Thus, assessment schemes for S&T policy discourse will be more complex than those for ordinary policy discourse. What is important in the former is not only the standard weighing of benefits and costs, suitably monetized and discounted, but the decision characteristics of the system that is supposed to deliver the benefit-costs.

The other way to handle sparse and limited experience is to pick a preferred alternative, to select strategies that appear reasonable as far as is known, and to implement them. Then we adjust them as experience accumulates and knowledge grows. We may end up with programs that look like some preferred alternative suggested by a priori analysis, but they will have been designed by a process of small adjustments and accommodations. More likely, a process of adjustment and accommodation will result in policy alternatives that do not resemble any of those in an original a priori set. Unless the implementing organizations and administrators are totally insensitive, they will have done their work in history rather than before history and will know a good deal more about what works and what does not and whether or not predicted contingencies and calamities have occurred. Of course, the construction of policy via trial and error, feedback and learning, is difficult, both politically and bureaucratically. But in the face of major uncertainties and large-scale and irreversible decisions, learning organizations may be preferable to the present choice of a particular strategy pursued to the end by an inflexible bureaucracy. If so, this means we need to work hard on the design of our implementing organizations, trying to make them flexible, resilient, and capable of learning from experience.

A priori strategies are the most common form found in S&T policy discourse. When we find them, we should proceed, in as simple and practical a way as possible, to pose assessment questions. As an example, we can take some of the strategies considered earlier and see what kinds of answers we get. We will then try to decide whether the answers are reasonable, given the special conditions described above, and whether we learn anything by making such assessments.

Problems of Specification

The second set of questions concerns perceptions of current reality, the situations that lead to making policy prescriptions:

Question 2. *Does the problem exist in fact?*
Q.2.1 *Is the problem correctly specified?*
Q.2.2 *At what time did the problem commence?*
Q.2.3 *Will the problem persist?*

While such questions are germane to all policy analysis, they are especially salient for the analysis of S&T policy. Problems here are usually hard to see or do not even exist now, but there is a claim that they will exist in the future. For example, consider the problem of national underinvestment in research, particularly basic research. No one sees the nation underinvesting; there is nothing tangible to see or touch. The policy analysis of poverty can count the poor, and the policy analysis of education can examine achievement scores and find that they are decreasing. But the policy analysis of science does not measure degrees or units of underinvestment. The reason for considering underinvestment to be a problem is that various theoretical and empirical statements have been so arranged that they foster a belief that we are underinvesting. In other domains, a problem is the condition of something; in science and technology policy, a problem is the conclusion of an argument. While we cannot make the poor or uneducated go away, we can sometimes make S&T problems go away or appear differently, because the problem statements are incorrect, imprecise, or subject to revision by improved theory or new empirical findings.

In the case of underinvestment, the existence of the problem rests on a divergence between social rates of return and private ones, with private returns prospectively too low to justify research investments. Although this argument was used extensively in the sixties and seventies, further analysis of national R&D behavior suggests the distinct possibility of overinvestment in a number of sectors. The R&D investment problem is that too much is being invested in the wrong direction. There may not be a problem of too little volume, but of too much. Given information about technological breakthroughs via patents or the market, firms in rivalrous competition may rush to invent or to deploy their R&D in ways highly similar to successful firms. This means that we overinvest in some sectors and also reduce the variation in the R&D effort (Hirschleifer and Riley 1979; Nelson 1982).

Once we admit that the world can show cases of over- as well as underinvestment, the policy problem is not the simple one of compensating for some general underinvestment, but is one of sending public funds to the right areas. If we send funds to sectors with overinvestment, we are wasting resources and are, perhaps, making inefficiency worse. However, neither economics nor science policy provides unambiguous indicators about which case is which, and we often try to avoid using highly specific micropolicies in a market economy. Thus we need much better intelligence on what is happening over time and decisionmakers who can handle differences between sectors. Furthermore, since R&D is subject to uncertainty and our estimates may change, situations may tip from one condition to the other. This implies that there is a problem of stopping public funding as well as starting it. But there are no stopping rules now.

Given these situations, the simple rules for funding research that have been historically employed to cure underinvestment may no longer suffice. More complex rules may be required. However, government has a good deal of trouble administering complex decision rules of any kind. So there is a problem of interaction between adequate substantive prescriptions for action and the design of institutions to administer them.

Overall, our questions about specification should lead to a more refined statement of the problem we are trying to solve. In the case of research, we might make the following new specification:

For a given volume of research funds, how do we identify sectors where there is underinvestment? What will be the impact of government funding in the underinvested sectors, and how should we treat sectors where there is overinvestment? What kinds of government organizations and programs can we design that will be effective in a situation we have come to realize is more complex than we originally believed?

Action Questions

Since we are dealing with policy, a reasonable question to ask, once we have made a translation into policy language is:

Question 3. *What action, policy, or decision is being proposed?*
Q.3.1 *Is the action capable of being realized?*
Q.3.2 *Is there someone who can realize the action?*
Q.3.3 *Is the action appropriate for the proposed agent?*

Science policy argument is full of generalized appeals to action, often to society as a whole. Quite frequently, the action desired is for the government to do something, with the something left unspecified. S&T policy advice, being commonly a committee effort, is especially short on details and implementation. The federal government is supposed to take the general appeal to action and translate it into programs and procedures. But if it is not feasible to respond to the appeal, even in theory, then we need to reject its current form and recast it.

Consider the following statements that exemplify the public interest strategy of innovation analyzed in Chapter 3:

> From the public interest perspective, the rate of innovation is subservient to the question of the direction of innovation. We see the critical issue to be the direction of innovation in society. While there may or may not be a problem with the rate at which society is innovating, we do detect distinct problems with the social and economic significance of the present innovations. (Public Interest Subcommittee on Economic and Trade Policy 1979, 27)

> The Public Interest Subcommitte argues that public efforts to enhance or increase innovation in industry should be directly targeted to innovations that will move the society closer to the fulfillment of the goals set forth in the social/legal framework above. A "public" accounting of the effects of any such efforts or policy is necessary. . . . We need both an economic efficiency dimension to tell us how much difference a policy may make on the economy and an ethical dimension to tell us the way such increases in the economic efficiency variables change the quality of life and for whom the changes are occurring. (Advisory Subcommittee on Public Interest 1979, 289)

Here one can understand the nature of the problem: From a public interest perspective, higher economic and social values are not now considered in decisions to innovate. A market economy does not deliver enough innovations that are consistent with these values. The remedy to be taken is for government to direct or regulate the market economy to produce more good innovations and less bad ones, or innovations more consistent with higher social values and less consistent with lower ones.

Let us apply *Question 3*. First, we know that, in any complex economy, it is very difficult for the government to control macroeconomic variables and make them consistent with stated social goals of full employment and price stability, let alone control individual decisions to innovate. Even though we may give the federal government latitude to direct or regulate industry in order to get the kinds of innovation we want, it may not be possible to design microeconomic policies and incentives that deliver only the kinds of innovation wanted. Since we wish to maintain a market economy and private decisionmaking, we know different economic agents will be in different situations and react differently to general government actions and policies. From the perspective of these economic agents, it will pay some of them to act in ways contrary to what was intended with the policy action.

If we do not want to maintain a market economy, however, and wish to use some form of central planning, there is no evidence that this mechanism has the information required to identify good innovations or the power to achieve them, once known. We can argue that central planners have greater incentives than the market to find and deliver good innovations, but this is certainly arguable on empirical and theoretical grounds. Empirically, there are very few cases of successful central planning, but many failures, and the few successful ones tend eventually to use markets as their major mechanism of resource allocation.

Furthermore, since innovation sometimes occurs because of "technology push," that is, technology becomes "ripe" and makes innovations possible, the federal government is in no better position to know the direction of innovation than are agents in the market. When a technology becomes ripe, all interested parties can know. While the market provides some insurance against incorrect guesses about ripeness — someone else who will guess correctly usually exists — the federal government does not.

From the perspective of welfare economics, one of the reasons to use markets is that they ordinarily do not force producers and consumers to hold prescribed higher values. At least they do not have to express them in the marketplace, if they have them. Consumers and producers can take prices or leave them without worrying unduly about "goods" and "bads" embodied in outputs and inputs. There are many who believe this very property makes market mechanisms highly preferred vehicles of resource allocation. Innovation to achieve good social purposes may clash with the noncoercive properties of markets that we like so much. However, a clash of preferences may easily occur with central planning.

It is the objectives of the planners that count, and they may have objectives, such as rapid economic growth, that conflict with the output of "good" innovations.

For these reasons, it may not be possible for government to do the job the public interest model assigns to it. The government's influence may be highly marginal, because it controls neither demand pull nor technology push. Consequently, those who happen to be advocates of the public interest strategy may (1) want to reconsider the job they want done, (2) reconsider who should do it, or (3) work to educate their fellow citizens to hold higher values and to provide incentives for their realization. If everyone holds higher values, markets will respond accordingly. However, the installation of higher values is not a job for economic or technology policy, but for the educational system or other institutions.

Questions of Mechanism

A fourth set of questions concerns the connections claimed between the problem and the proposed actions. In S&T policy, the problem or crisis to be avoided usually occurs in the future. The actions designed today have to work across time and mesh in such a way that the problem or crisis is ameliorated or never takes place. For example, consider the problem of assuring a sufficient supply of computer scientists and engineers ten years from now, and assume that we know what "sufficient" means. Assume also that unaided labor markets will not provide sufficiency. The policy problem then is one of providing enough incentives some years before the expected shortage so that talented individuals first choose science and technology as a career and then, among all S&T disciplines, assuring that they choose computer science. That is the problem on the demand side.

On the supply side, we need sufficient computer scientists in the educational system now, in the short run, so that those who choose computer science careers will be adequately trained. This means some way has to be found to compensate for the lower salaries currently paid to computer scientists who remain in the educational system, or else those computer scientists currently in the industrial system need to receive incentives and encouragement from their employers to provide training to new entrants.

Meanwhile, as we try to meet these requirements with government programs, the market itself will be making adjustments. Scientists and engineers in fields related to computer science will switch to computer science. Industry will provide training or retooling for its current work force, and the jobs for which there is excess demand for computer scientists will be redesigned so as to reduce the requirements for an input that is scarce — highly trained computer scientists. Market signals will operate so as to eliminate or alleviate the problem. If government is to help with the problem, it must be able to act soon enough. Otherwise, it may end up adding to an already adequate supply that has been determined by market forces, thereby creating unemployment problems.

In this kind of situation, we have to ask a number of subtle questions about the means to be employed. A reasonable set of questions is:

Question 4. *Why do we believe the means proposed to solve the problem will be effective at the margin?*

The term *at the margin* implies that, relative to doing nothing special and letting the situation develop, we have some reason to believe that our means can have a significant incremental effect, allowing for the interactions between our means and the ongoing situation. But asking this question implies:

Q.4.1 *Is the scale of our proposed means large enough?*
Q.4.2 *If the scale is small, are there "multiplier" effects that can magnify our programmatic efforts?*
Q.4.3 *Is there political and budgetary support to maintain a program for sufficient time to have the expected effect?*
Q.4.4 *Can we act at the right time?*

Most S&T policy programs are limited in scale. There is no way the S&T area can command the resources of, say, the welfare or health areas. Merely making programs large enough to have any discernible practical effect will always be difficult. Although the bureaucracies that expect to run prospective programs will always say that they can do a good job with whatever resources they are provided and a better job with an optimal (always larger) level of resources, we need some reason to believe that the proposed programs are targeted at relieving critical bottlenecks or that they generate "leverage" or "multiplier" effects as market forces operate. If this is not the case, a program may have only symbolic or political value. Signals of concern by the government may induce private actors to solve the problem. But this is a different means than that with which we started, and we should now consider the effects of alternative government signals and how they will be received.

Scale is not the only aspect of effectiveness to worry about; continuity and timing will also be significant. Any program designed to solve an S&T problem will have to operate over relatively long times to be effective or even appear effective. In designing some policy, a priori, we have to believe that we will be permitted to operate it long enough for it to have the impacts it was designed to have. But S&T policy programs are neither glamorous enough nor do they have sufficiently powerful constituencies to guarantee continuity. As organizational and individual memories fade and markets and institutions continue to make their own adjustments, the reasons the program was started will be forgotten. There will be a demand for results or impacts now or in the immediate past. If, as careful S&T policy analysts and designers, we tried to match the design of our programs to have optimal impacts in the future, we are going to be short of results at the beginning, and it will not be long before we encounter demands for cancellation or redirection. The S&T enterprise is always undergoing one crisis or another, and we have limited means for distinguishing serious crises from minor ones. As new crises develop, there will be a demand to stop the programs designed to alleviate the past crises that we have become used to and that are now weighed less heavily.

In addition to declines in the perceived urgency of solving some past crisis, programs needing time to produce effects or even programs that we agree have been designed optimally, with respect to time, will encounter more and more resistance from budgetary authorities. Without any powerful constituency to protect the programs, budgetary authorities will demand a stop now even though they may well have acquiesced in an original intent to produce later results. The question, "What have you done today?," always has more power with budgetary authorities than does the question, "What will you be doing tomorrow?"

There is also an opposite side to the timing problem — we may act too late and continue too long. It takes a long time to design programs that bureaucracies believe will solve a problem. Finding reasonable substantive designs takes time, and there is always a process of bargaining and negotiation about control of new inputs. S&T policy is mainly concerned with inputs, and so fierce struggles are to be expected between contending S&T agencies, all of which will claim that they can allocate the inputs better than can other agencies. It takes time to adjudicate the claims. By the time bureaucracies, decisionmakers, and affected constituents agree on what is to be done, substantively and politically, the time when action was relevant may have passed. But design and political processes generate expectations and momentum. Once started, it is very difficult to stop, short of execution of some program, if not the one with optimal design.

If the program is effective and starts late, paradoxically, it may end up making the problem that we started to solve worse. Thus, federal programs started to alleviate shortages of scientific manpower in the 1960s contributed to excess supply in the 1970s. But, as was indicated in Chapter 4, such programs were difficult to reduce or terminate. Political and bureaucratic costs of termination can be very high on the sudden discovery that a well-intentioned program is contributing to a problem, rather than helping to solve it.

Questions of Adaptability and Flexibility

The fifth set of questions concerns the ability to change and adapt programs if it is discovered that they are not working as planned or when new information is acquired. If, in 1945, we saw a problem of providing general-purpose support for basic research, but, in 1985, we discover that the problem has been all along, or has become, the *direction* of basic research support, can we easily change the design and operations of the programs? If we discover that we have created an excess supply of computer scientists by our interventions in the market, can we stop the interventions? If current evidence suggests that we need more chemistry research and less physics research at the margin, can we switch marginal resources from one to the other easily? If current evidence suggests that a field or sector currently supported with government funds or programs is now adequately and appropriately supported by the private sector, can we stop the flow of funds or the programs?

The questions can be stated as follows:

Question 5. *How flexible are the proposed programs and institutional arrangements?*

   Q.5.1 *What provisions have been made to account for uncertainty of outcomes?*

   Q.5.2 *Can a program be redesigned or changed as a result of experience?*

   Q.5.3 *Is there sufficient stability in the design to avoid arbitrary and capricious changes?*

   Q.5.4 *Does the proposed program have a natural endpoint?*

The answer to these questions, for close to all current S&T programs, is: probably not. Strategies for S&T, as noted earlier, are terribly difficult to change. The original postwar strategies for the S&T enterprise have great weight intellectually. Change involves facing a network of claimants to resources who operate according to received doctrine and historical treatments. If physics has always received X percent of a total budget, it is seen as always entitled to X percent, whether the total budget is rising or falling and regardless of the scientific ripeness of competing fields. Changing these entitlements is a risky and unrewarding venture, whatever a decisionmaker's interest in improving the productivity of the S&T enterprise. Reform and renewal are difficult enough in enterprises for which there is much greater knowledge of inputs and outputs — witness all the attempts to reform the postal enterprise – let alone situations in which every claimant must be presumed to carry weight.

The answers to the five sets of questions provide some crude tests for the substantive quality of S&T policy argument. The answers test completeness and quality, relative to some widely held canons for reasonable policy analysis. However, since the programs will be working over time, a sixth set of questions should be considered explicitly in S&T arguments:

Question 6. *How will we know whether the program designs are working or will work?*
Q.6.1 *What indicators are to be used and why?*
Q.6.2 *What values of the indicators will trigger policy action?*
Q.6.3 *Does a set of indicators capture side effects?*

Within the S&T domain, there are no unambiguous indicators. We can always think of good reasons why an indicator that claimed to show a crisis or problem does not really illustrate the crisis or problem. In addition, it is possible to find a crisis by citing some indicator. For example, the decreasing filing of patents by U.S. firms in the United States and the increasing filing by foreign firms have been alleged to be indicators of the declining technological superiority of the United States, but, clearly, many other reasonable interpretations are possible. Firms' preferences for patenting, as opposed to other means of retaining property rights in inventions, may shift, and new technologies may shift away from the patentable kind. In fact, some marginal loss of "inventiveness" in the United States may be swamped by these other effects.

From an analytical perspective, we may be genuinely puzzled by the meaning of patent statistics. However, those who believe, a priori, that there now exists or will soon be a damaging loss of technological superiority will have no difficulty in citing patent statistics as indicators of the correctness of their belief. Raising all the sophisticated technical arguments about why patent statistics may not indicate any loss of superiority will have little persuasive power, since the perceived damage from even a small decline is very large. Trying to prove negatives where the policy argument involves some future outcome or state of affairs is not a productive kind of activity. However, citations of science and technology indicators always carry a bias toward action, even though the answers to some of the other questions might indicate that no action was appropriate, effective, or possible.

In this kind of situation, the best way to address the sixth set of questions is to find multiple indicators of the same phenomena with various indicators derived from different sources or collected at different levels of aggregation. For example, even though aggregate U.S. patent statistics by U.S. entities may be falling, one may well find specific industries where they have begun to rise or where technological change is occurring very rapidly, in fact, so rapidly that patents have little value. Properly designed surveys of industrial decisionmakers may show their preferences have shifted to trade secret modes of protection, in part because, by the time a patent is issued, it may be obsolete. If statistics and surveys both indicate declining inventiveness, greater credence should be placed in assertions about some crisis of inventiveness. Then one can proceed to employ the other question sets in addressing alternative programs. Consistent, highly correlated information provided by indicators of different types gives greater confidence that programs, once designed, are working as expected.

Testing Entire Strategies

Question sets *1* through *6* go to the substantive issues involved in evaluating S&T policy strategies and arguments. They address the completeness and the estimated quality of proposed actions and are questions we should ask a priori; they are analytic. In the real world, there will be very few times when the answers all come together to make an overwhelming case for policy action (Vickers 1965). In an imperfect world, S&T arguments and strategies will be imperfect. How then does one evaluate entire strategies, as opposed to evaluating particular parts? The six sets of questions in this chapter are directed at judging the adequacy of the parts. If we know all the parts give unsatisfactory answers, we are justified in rejecting the strategy. But what do we do when we face contending strategies that only satisfy some of the criteria? Having rejected various strategies on the basis of the questions, there will be some left that compete with each other. The six questions will not give unambiguous answers about the merits of remaining strategies. Their advocates will hold on to them with something approaching justified true belief, or belief as true as one is going to find in an uncertain world.

From a logical standpoint, one can proceed to an analysis of how an S&T strategy relates to some network of higher-order social and individual objectives (Taylor 1961). Some strategies may encompass more high-order objectives than others. In some cases an analysis of higher-order values and objectives will still leave one unable to choose. Different higher-order objectives and values may be realized with one strategy than with another, but there is not time to carry out an infinite regress of inquiry to even higher-order objectives, even if it was known that, at some point, it would be conclusive. One can either choose now or leave the analytic modes of assessment and go to the various social and political processes designed to handle such cases. One can try political compromise and persuasion and try to extract some minimum

program on which all parties can agree. For example, in the discussion
of technological innovation policy, nearly all strategies had a core statement that good innovation policy requires enhanced information flows
between stakeholders. One can then accept this recommendation and
pursue information programs as satisfying all camps. Alternatively, one
can employ an implicit or explicit voting procedure. There can be commissions, committees, boards, or panels to sift the evidence and the
assertions and come down on one side or another. The preferences of
these commissions or panels impose constraints on the choices, since
they will ordinarily be expressed publicly. The exact processes one uses
depend on the situation and its history.

   Group decision processes are exceedingly common in problems with
high S&T content. While the six questions above are not scientific or
technical questions, but questions relevant to a policy analysis domain,
getting the answers may depend on scientific or technical information.
The most recently validated scientific and technical information may
only be available in the invisible colleges and not in any formal information systems. So it makes sense to draw the information out via some
consensus process, and it makes sense to place scientists and engineers
on broader inquiries qua scientists. Such inquiries may be conditioned
on scientific or technical developments. There is, of course, the danger
of sliding from scientific and technical discourse into policy discourse
without being aware of it, but one should be able to guard against this
by watching the language and by careful rules of deliberation.

   Having exhausted analytic, a priori inquiry and consensus processes,
one may still face conflicting strategies. There may be some issues for
which current scientific information does not exist or will not exist in
time for a decision. There may be certain values that are irreconcilable,
no matter how hard stakeholders try. At some point, policy analysis will
reach a point of diminishing returns. All of the assessment work, if it
has met quality standards already discussed, has eliminated bad alternatives and left a choice to be made among good, if not perfect ones.
The expected costs of choosing wrongly will have been reduced. While a
decisionmaker may not be entirely comfortable with his decision, he
may at least believe that it has the best warrants possible. From an
assessment perspective, the final choice is a matter of indifference, since
logic and analysis have done as much as can be done productively. So
analytical silence is appropriate at this point.

Testing Advice

Although advice is common to many policy domains, it is a process that
has been relatively unexplored (Goldhamer 1977). Here advice is distinguished from the formally stated strategies discussed in earlier

chapters. Strategies provide a background for advice, and one may be able to distinguish an adviser's policy position from his previously known strategies. For example, one can get some clues about Henry Kissinger's advice as national security adviser and secretary of state by reading his published strategies. But, in giving advice, strategies need not be articulated. Advice consists of informal judgments or instructions delivered rapidly. A decisionmaker will usually have specialists on call, and they will interact with him on a continuous basis, providing their own views and their opinions of the views of others as issues come up. For example, the Executive Office of the President has the Council of Economic Advisers, a national security adviser, and a science adviser, as well as other advisers who do not carry that title.

Giving advice in any domain has common features. The special features of S&T advice are the concern here. Before considering rules for testing science and technology advice, let us ask what it is about. Views differ. In the view of the first formally designated science adviser, James R. Killian, the function of the science adviser was to place objective scientific facts before the president so that judgments and policies could be well informed and so that the president would not be embarrassed by policies and programs that could be seen as contradictory to information held in the scientific and technical community (Killian 1964). According to President Kennedy's science adviser, Jerome Wiesner, the president's S&T advisers should anticipate future problems, presumably driven by discoveries or events within the S&T enterprise (Wiesner 1980). In the view of President Carter's science adviser, Frank Press, science and technology are components of other problems or possibly solutions to other problems. In this case, the science adviser's mission is to focus the decisionmaker's attention on (1) the incremental role S&T might be playing in causing problems, and (2) the ways that S&T might be used to attack problems or opportunities (Press 1980).

If one takes the view of the first science adviser, advice is limited in scope. It provides assurances that a decisionmaker's judgments will not be flawed, because he did not know the scientific and technical facts of life. In Wiesner's view, the science adviser provides early warning for decisionmakers. He observes the flow of scientific and technical information and identifies future policy problems early. In other words, he does technology assessment without the formal analytic apparatus. President Carter's science adviser believed that S&T factors are latent in most policy problems, and the function of his advice is to reveal the latency and unmask the true nature of a problem. Here, advice warns the decisionmaker of the pitfalls of making decisions without knowing how science and technology relate to problems, or how they provide an opportunity to solve some problems.

Such distinctions are not trivial. Science and technology advice does not command much in the way of resources. Since resources are limited, every S&T advisory body has to decide where it will concentrate its resources. Its perceptions of its own function condition the claims it will make in the competition for decisionmakers' limited attention. For example, the need to interact with other parts of the White House staff is minimized, if one views the advisory job as delivering objective scientific facts and making them clear, compared to viewing the job as demonstrating, for instance, the interactions between technology and the economy. In the latter situation, science advisers have to confront other advisers, particularly economic advisers. In the former, one does not need input from other advisers. "Objective" scientific facts can stand alone without being related to "subjective" economic and political facts.

The definition of the advisory job also affects the kind of advice one can feel confident in giving. The rules for checking assertions of pure scientific and technical facts are reasonably well understood. If one wants a fast answer, one checks the truth by going to the producers of the information. The warrants for the facts are those appropriate for scientific findings. However, advice is rarely about facts, but about the consequences, interactions, and implications of facts and values. If the advice covers fact-value interactions, then there is a problem. The rules for testing advice about such interactions are not at all well defined.

One can hope that the advisers have wisdom and experience and rely on that. But there are many advisers, and all claim to have these attributes. One can try to keep track of the advice that has been given and see if it turns out to be good advice. But, as in the case of a priori analysis, many times decisions cannot wait. Furthermore, one cannot always attribute good outcomes to having taken good advice nor bad outcomes to bad advice. Unless an adviser is unusually sagacious, successful advice in one domain may not carry over to other domains. Most public policy problems involve a mixture of domains. Few advisers can span multiple domains and still give high-quality advice. For example, Henry Kissinger's grasp of economics was not as strong as his grasp of politics and the ways of bureaucracies. What is needed are some common sense rules for deciding about the merit of the advice as it is received. Let us take a piece of scientific advice that President Kennedy received and see what we can make of it. By trying to make sense of this advice and checking what we do in the process, some common sense rules may suggest themselves.

Consider the following advice on technological innovation, advice very similar in substance to the advice of today:

> We believe that we face a situation that not only poses a threat to our national welfare, but also offers an opportunity for imagina-

tive solution that could be one of the signal achievements of your administration. New and effective policies must be developed for so allocating and managing the country's finite technological resources as to achieve simultaneously our high priority objectives of economic prosperity, military strength, and space conquest.

. . . We are convinced that there is now also a need and a corresponding Federal responsibility, to stimulate development and use of civilian technology in industry so as to insure a strong free enterprise system and our ability to support the other high priority national needs.

. . . We believe that industry, using only its own means, cannot solve these problems, if for no other reason than government's increasing hold on technological resources . . . the vast majority of which, as we have noted, have decreasing immediate relevance to civilian technology and economic prosperity.

. . . We are in danger of losing some of our technological preeminence in commercial markets at just that time — four or five years hence — when the real impact of freer trade will begin to be felt. It is then that we will most need technological innovation if we are to sell at competitive prices.

. . . Governmental action of the kind we envision is already the practice in other industrialized countries of the West. It is not entirely new to us either; we pioneered in the technical collaboration of farms and government to build an agricultural system of unparalleled efficiency. (Hodges, Heller, and Wiesner 1962)

What should a decisionmaker think of this advice when he gets it? First of all, he ought to take a skeptical posture. The first thing to do is beware. The language is emotive with clear persuasive intent — "opportunity for imaginative solutions," "signal achievement of your administration," and so on. If the decisionmaker rejects the proferred opportunity, the implication is that he has rejected the imaginative solutions and signal achievements that any administration and president needs.

The second thing that can be done is to check the form of the advice. S&T policy arguments have a stylized form. By checking the form, one can know whether the advice is complete and at least internally consistent. In this advice, one finds causal connections between action in the S&T domain and strongly desired outcomes in other domains — economic prosperity, military strength, and space conquest. A bad outcome in one of these other domains will occur sometime in the future. To prevent it, we have to take action now in the S&T domain. The actions taken now are appropriate for the federal government, because other sectors cannot take them. This is because the market for civilian technology is working imperfectly. Closing the advice, the market works imperfectly, because the government has become a monopsonist for S&T inputs. Since the government is causing the imperfection, it is up to government to make corrections. There is more than ample precedent to take federal action, for such action is not too different from time-honored interventions that we know have worked.

The advice here almost serves as the canonical formulation of an S&T policy problem. Essentially, the advice boils down to (1) a predicted bad outcome in economics and foreign policy, (2) a solution through government action in the S&T domain, and (3) a warrant for the action, in this case, based cleverly on the government causing a market imperfection. If one matches the advice according to such properties, one can proceed to a dialogue with the advisers on their degree of belief — in effect, asking the same kinds of questions posed for analytic policy arguments.

Although we cannot test the overall truth or falsity of the advice, we can check the confidence of the advisers in it. How much are they willing to bet on what they are saying? The advisers clearly cannot claim that they possess knowledge of the situation in the sense of having justified true belief. Part of the case constructed here involves future events, and advisers cannot have justified true belief about events that have not occurred. But decisionmakers can ask their advisers to append to their advice some estimate of the uncertainties involved in what they are saying. Is the bad outcome highly likely to happen? Do they believe — are they willing to bet — that acting now strongly decreases the probability of the bad outcome they are predicting?

Knowing the advisers' degree of belief will not predict the future, and it does not guarantee correct action, but it should give the advisers pause, forcing reflection on the evidence and analysis behind the advice, if any. While analysis is neither necessary nor sufficient for good advice, in the advice cited here, the science adviser's Panel on Civilian Technology had spent months in deliberation and diagnosis. Those deliberations were the warrant for the advice given to President Kennedy. They, in turn, rested on a host of assumptions about government absorption of science and engineering skills and about the relations between technology, trade, and growth. There was little probing of these original assumptions and connections. The panel believed in a particular kind of strategy to achieve growth through technology and innovation. Forcing the advisers to justify their degrees of belief or to make them more precise would have forced a tougher examination of the shared background strategy and analysis that they believed warranted their advice.

The most critical part of advice is the claim of knowledge about some future outcome. S&T outcomes are usually stated in terms of harm or damage, for which the decisionmaker will be held responsible. That is the case in this example. Decisionmakers pay dearly for publicly perceived errors on their part, while their successes are far more ephemeral. Success is devalued rapidly, but bad outcomes are remembered far longer than good ones. In addition, public policy should, at a minimum, do more good than harm and, if possible, little harm at all. The assertion that current policy is doing harm to the future of scientific enterprise and, consequently, to related national enterprises is a powerful motivator for responsible decisionmakers. That is why such assertions appear so frequently in S&T strategies.

The epistemological status of predictions, forecasts, and assertions of future outcomes has been controversial. We need some common sense rules for believing the predictions that advisers make and acting on them. If the advisers had some strategy that explained the working of the S&T enterprise and its impacts on other enterprises, then their predictions of future events would rest on the quality of their strategy. A bad outcome — showing up as the value of a dependent variable — would be derived from current values of the independent variables, holding constant the variables representing decisionmakers' current behavior. Testing the predictions of a bad outcome then would be reduced to making the best tests possible of the model (Meehan 1968). There would, of course, be controversy over what tests might be relevant and decisive, but at least one could employ them and come to some judgment. But there is no such strategy, and we are unlikely to get one, for reasons discussed earlier.

Clearly, there is an informal, implicit causal strategy at work in the advice we are considering. The advisers have to make causal connections in their advice, for their advice would not be worth very much if they saw no way for the decisionmakers to make the desired positive changes. If this were the case, their advice would have to be confined to finding ways of limiting damage when the bad outcome did occur. Now a decisionmaker can certainly force his advisers to state their beliefs about causation and query them about the mechanics. Stating beliefs and their justifications is part of a dialogue decisionmakers should have with their advisers. Most of the advice is very crude with respect to the timing of predicted bad outcomes, the phasing in and phasing out of curative policy and actions, and the possibilities of adjustment as more information becomes available. The decisionmaker can certainly force clarity on the part of his advisers. Much advice is probably bad advice and should be ignored (March and Shapera 1982). Structural dialogue with advisers should make it easier to distinguish good advice from bad.

Having obtained whatever warrants possible for the advice and made the advice more sophisticated, it is then up to the decisionmaker to act or not act. Despite the best warrants for action that are attainable and the most prudent actions imaginable relative to the problem, he faces irreducible uncertainty. Action based on advice confronts the same situation as action based on formal analysis. A decisionmaker can try to hedge by taking small, reversible steps, while obtaining more information. He can try to reach his objective by crawling toward it rather than suddenly leaping at it. Such a conservative strategy can, of course, conflict with the underlying character of the S&T problems. These problems can conceivably, but not in the case here, be large-scale, systemic, discontinuous, and irreversible. In such a case, it takes large-scale action or much leverage to make any difference, and these are hard to get without general mobilization of available resources.

So far as advisers are concerned, after a series of critical dialogues, they have completed their role. The tests of their merit are (1) their willingness to state degrees of belief based on the most critical view of the evidence at hand, and (2) objective presentation of opposing views and the reasoning behind them. This is a hard test and no mean achievement, if accomplished.

Summary

I have now argued that the first job in S&T policy analysis is translating the language and the statements encountered into a language appropriate to policy discourse. I have also stressed sensitivity to the form of S&T policy arguments, since we have some notions of what a well-formed policy argument looks like. Most of the S&T arguments encountered will not be entirely well formed. Their strong linkage to higher values means that much will be assumed as self-evident. Important parts of S&T arguments will often be left implicit, but, like all models and arguments, S&T policy strategies require many supporting statements. Some are empirical, some concern values, and some concern connections between facts and values. I have argued that explicit presentation of all of these should be preferred when confronting analysis or advice. A strong critical, analytical tradition is not characteristic of policymaking in the S&T domain. Thus, it is important that decisionmakers compensate by continually asking questions about the analysis and advice they do receive.

Once translation and completion of a strategy or advice have been achieved, the various tools for assessing them can be put to work along with the craft knowledge of many practitioners. These tools are crude, but they are sufficient to distinguish reasonable alternatives from unreasonable ones. Their ability to identify better alternatives among sets of good ones is much weaker. But confronting a decisionmaker with a set of reasonable, well-analyzed alternatives is superior to the way S&T arguments and claims are put forward at present.

Summing Up: Toward Policy Analysis for Science and Technology Policy

8

The S&T enterprise itself is very different from what it was thirty years ago. Whole new fields and subfields have emerged. The technology available for research and inquiry has become far more powerful, permitting new and surprising connections between fields and disciplines. In contrast, policymaking for the enterprise has not changed very much, although the scale of resources is much larger. It remains informal, qualitative, and intuitive. The predominant form of policy argument and persuasion remains the proclamation now of some crisis that will lead to future disaster, either to the S&T enterprise itself or to social enterprises closely connected with it. That most of the predicted disasters do not occur and that society does manage to solve or live through genuine crises have never proved to be deterrents to new proclamations of crisis. The fact that many of the cures formally implemented have proven ineffective or marginal has never served as a deterrent to a stream of new solutions. So, today, the United States allegedly faces an innovation crisis, losses of comparative advantage, and failure to apply its technology to development of the Third World. Within the S&T enterprise, there is a crisis in engineering and computer science manpower, in instrumentation, and in precollege science, mathematics, and technical education.

There are undoubtedly individuals and groups whose intuition about such crises and their possible solutions are very good. If decisionmakers and the public could distinguish them from those with unreliable intuition, current practices might be tolerable. If they knew that the solutions offered had a reasonable probability of being effective, relative to problems worth attacking, then they would not have to pay much attention to the logical and empirical warrants for proposed policies. Their posture could easily be one of benign neglect. They would not have to worry about how to get reasonable public policy and how to know that they were getting it. But they cannot easily make such identifications,

173

and there is little assurance that the problems selected are the correct ones or that the proposed solutions will really work. A public posture of benign neglect is not clearly superior to one of thinking things through. The question all along has been how to identify and specify right thinking in a domain that is strongly resistant to logical and empirical clarity.

The last thirty years have seen significant advances in how public policy questions are approached. At its very best, policy research and analysis transforms the questions that initially concern decisionmakers and alters perceptions of what happens to be a significant question. If policy analysis is not powerful enough to distinguish between better alternatives, it at least eliminates worse alternatives. To be sure this minimum condition is met, analysts make strenuous efforts to guard against error. Much of the craft of policy analysis lies in knowing what not to do — how to avoid logical and practical pitfalls. The main canon of analysis is to eliminate, control, or at least discuss all the sources of significant error that are "thinkable." Consequently, the best practice in the craft requires analysis to be clear and explicit about critical assumptions and sensitivities. Furthermore, these critical assumptions have to be explained and repeated to decisionmakers until they are well understood. Proposed options for action are supposed to be tested or considered in a variety of off-design circumstances.

There are no such canons for the analysis of the S&T enterprise, or they have not been applied consistently. I have stated and demonstrated throughout this volume, this enterprise is intrinsically harder to analyze than many others. But there are some equally difficult areas of public choice where analysis has flourished, so in this last chapter I will discuss some of the barriers to extending analytic approaches to public policy for the S&T enterprise. I will argue that analytic traditions are related strongly to the language used and to the problems specified. It may be possible to approach the former by changing the latter.

Lack of Critical Tradition

For most public policy choices, there now exists a cadre of analysts whose business it is to examine skeptically claims and arguments made by interested actors and constituencies. While there is no professional code of conduct for these analysts — and there do exist many "hired guns," willing to tell decisionmakers whatever they want to hear — a critical and skeptical posture is the norm and is desired and encouraged. Policy analysts are paid to bite the hand that feeds them, to "speak truth to power," as Wildavsky puts it (Wildavsky, 1979).

No such cadre exists in S&T policy. Thus, reports, findings, claims, and proposals from strongly interested and probably biased parties are often taken to settle discussion and debate, not to begin them. For example, if science educators argue that all citizens must acquire science literacy, the argument is taken as self-evident, not as a signal to ask what it might mean, how it might be gotten, and what its relation might be to achieving other skills and values. Because the number of policy instruments available to make S&T policy is very small, criticism and skepticism are seen as directly negative influences on those instruments. Since decisionmakers can and do use criticism to cut budgets and treat science and technology unfavorably, criticism is often equated with disloyalty, as illustrating an intent to subvert the well-being of the enterprise and the high-level social values that it carries and transmits.

Nature of the Policy Problem

Even if there were a critical tradition, it would be difficult to apply. First, policy analysis works best when the user is a single decisionmaker with significant control over resources and instruments. The S&T enterprise contains multiple decisionmakers, each of whom, individually, has little control. Second, the tools of policy analysis work best when the objective is making existing markets, bureaucracies, or institutions more efficient or effective. They provide less guidance on markets, agencies, or institutions that need to be created to solve problems and little direction on how to create them.

Policy analysis involves a priori modeling, either verbal or mathematical. It asks about marginal improvements — those that can be made around the status quo — but it is not well suited to laying out reasonable paths of development when one moves far from historical experience. In such cases, the resolving power of available tools and models is discernibly weak. The degree of confidence one can have in, for example, a piece of futures research projecting trends in economic growth for the next one hundred years is less than that one can have in a linear programming model for an oil refinery, using technology that is a decade old. Faced with true ignorance on where science and technology is taking the nation, the preferred policy mode may have to be one of search and learn, of acquiring information as one goes, and adjusting actions sequentially. The policy problem in this case is designing public or private institutions that are "light on their feet," can carry out rapid reconnaissance, process information quickly and correctly, and take rapid action. But if this is the true nature of problems posed by S&T, conventional policy analysis may not reveal very much. For example, one might need to show decisionmakers how they should design for flexibility and not appear wasteful or how to maintain staff morale when facing inherently ambiguous situations. Conventional policy analysis has to be stretched a good deal to accommodate such issues.

Language, Logic, and Truth

The structure of policy debates and disputes over S&T involves inter-locking values, facts, and predictions. It is difficult to find any decisive tests of truth (or falsification) for competing strategies. Whatever the philosophy of science says about testing theories for truth or falsity is not highly applicable. Truth or falsity will be known some time in the future, but we are asked to act now to assure good outcomes or avoid bad ones. To be sure, we can say that current facts warrant some prediction over another, but current facts are highly ambiguous without supporting theory, and salient new ones can arise unexpectedly. For example, current facts about patenting, for some people, are precursors or leading indicators of a looming innovation crisis. For others, the same facts suggest a shift in tastes to other means of preserving rights in information or that innovation is proceeding so rapidly, patents have little value. It is even harder to define tests for competing values without, at some point, running into difficulties. For example, appeals to higher-order, background values bring their status into dispute. So, logically, we are either forced into an infinite regress of justifications, or we have to stop justifications at some point and impose some set of values in what, to the minority, will always appear to be an arbitrary and coercive fashion.

Some philosophers argue that the search for a priori tests of facts or values is hopeless and suggest that some form of open, uncoercive con-versation or dialogue between strategies would be helpful (McCarthy 1978; Collingridge 1980). If we could agree to hold our strategies provi-sionally and would be willing to shift when informed "conversation" reveals surprising and unpleasant implications of our own preferred strategies or alternatives superior to our own, then we could agree on a process that would select the best strategy human ingenuity can design. The alternative that finally emerges at the end of such an open process would be superior to those held at the beginning of the process. At least there would be much clearer notions of what was involved. But having such conversations is difficult, from the perspective of decisionmaking. The aim of conversations or dialogues over public policy is action, and action very frequently cannot be delayed. The time needed for the per-suasion and conversion of antagonists may be far longer than the time available for decision. The temptation and the necessity are then to make dialogues coercive and decisions arbitrary. An arbitrary decision in public policymaking will usually seem better than no decision.

One way around this situation is to make flexible, reversible decisions that remain sensitive to continuing dialogue and new information. But S&T decisions frequently involve discontinuous, irreversible outcomes. Once we go down a path, once we take a branch, it is highly unlikely we are going to be able to return to the status quo ante. Thus, we have to define problems and the ways to approach them so that we can return, or else we have to be reasonably confident that we can find alternative paths and branches just as good as those we have forever excluded. Instead of making once-and-for-all command decisions, we can try to learn more through experimentation and evaluation. Based on what we learn, we can improve the options we have and preserve the ability of choice.

Yet even if we are clever enough to do this, we would still face practical difficulties. Flexibility and reversibility do not come free. In the short run, they will seem to be waste, inefficiency, and organizational slack, tempting reductions in budget or staff in the name of efficiency. A long-run view that makes judgments on the basis of effectiveness over time is uncommon in most bureaucracies and their overseers, but especially so in scientific bureaucracies. To the latter, the long run is the length of a budget cycle. The S&T bureaucracies are so nakedly sensitive to downward budget fluctuations within that cycle that any desire for long-run strategic flexibility will usually be overcome by the very strong and immediate desire to preserve current budgets. Flexibility within smaller budgets will nearly always be considered inferior to rigidity within larger budgets.

Attitudes and Institutions

Making policy language and logic more precise requires analysts who are willing to take some risks, but they are in short supply. Most public policy analysts come from a social science background; S&T issues do not provide the kind of platform where sophisticated methods can be applied and careers can be made. Scientists and engineers do not value policy analysts very highly, since the latter do not usually have any substantive knowledge or hands-on experience in the "hard" sciences; the analysts lack standing. For these reasons, it is difficult to imagine good analysts trying hard to get into the nominal analysis and evaluation branches of the S&T agencies the way they try to get into the OMB or the Congressional Budget Office. The analysis and evaluation function is well accepted in these latter organizations, but the notion of analysis and evaluation in S&T agencies is strange and not wholly accepted. To many scientists, evaluation and analysis must always be qualitative and intuitive, a matter to be judged by those served, not analysts. Hard, tough evaluation and analysis, even if feasible, can only cause budgetary damage, insuring violation of the budget maximization objective that holds for most S&T agencies. And, to most of the S&T community, lower budgets imply harm to the enterprise. Analysis is supposed to support the enterprise, not criticize it.

Formal training in policy analysis is heavily biased toward economics, operations research, mathematics, and statistics. If these are applied to public problems and decisions, analysts claim that they can achieve surprising, useful, timely, and reproducible results. A field where the predominant mode of analysis has to be qualitative and which uses analogy and history to make its points is not likely to attract the best products of public policy schools or departments of economics or operations research. However, even technically well-trained scientists and engineers who are engaged in public policy debate rarely show much sensitivity to the canons of public policy analysis described here. Skilled and perceptive practicing scientists and engineers, it is argued, can make superior prescriptions for the enterprise, using their substantive and disciplinary knowledge, compared with analysts never exposed to hands-on, natural science inquiry. Policy prescriptions should meet whatever standards of policy inquiry that have been tried and work reasonably well, yet scientists and engineers making policy recommendations rarely refer to these standards.

Choice of Strategies

In the preceding chapters, I have traced the rise, fall, and some time transformation of alternative, competing strategies used in decisionmaking. Although they do not explain decisionmaking, they provide the public justifications and warrants for the decisions that are taken. Whatever bureaucratic or personal motivations lie behind decisionmaking, some kind of substantive strategy or image is needed in public. Most concerned actors and constituencies will be indifferent to the personal or organizational calculations of gain and loss that enter into decisions. These gains and losses may be the most important facets of a decision for those making them, but the question for the public is whether the decisions are consistent with some articulated, accessible strategy that is reasonably well justified.

The scope for analysis and criticism may be especially large for the S&T enterprise. Unlike the diplomatic enterprise, the private language and logic of S&T decisionmakers are not very different from their public language and logic. Just as Keynes observed that decisionmakers are often prisoners of long-dead economists and their strategies, S&T decisionmakers are prisoners of the less coherent strategies examined in earlier chapters. Strengthening the logical and empirical warrants of the public strategies ought to translate quickly into improved decisionmaking and should help in the emergence of a critical and analytical tradition for S&T policy. Where then do we stand with respect to the choice of strategies and the organizations required to implement them? Let us now review these.

Resource Allocation

The strategy currently used for setting the overall level of resources for R&D assumes that social underinvestment exists, relative to some unknown — and perhaps unknowable — social optimum. The closer one comes to basic research, the greater the underinvestment. Public policy is predicated upon injecting enough government resources into the S&T enterprise to make its total inputs and, consequently, its level of research activity approach what is socially desirable. But an underinvestment theory of research funding suggests that more resources will always be required than would be deployed by an unaided market. This holds, because market incentives, at least for basic research, are inherently weak and will remain so indefinitely.

The most sophisticated strategies of the R&D process currently suggest that the policy problem is less one of available resources than one of avoiding maldistribution of resources. There can be overinvestment in some sectors, that is, a "rush to invent," underinvestment in other sectors, that is, a reluctance to invent, and neither in yet others. Observations of the market do not provide unambiguous indicators about which conditions hold at which time. Consequently, the public policy problem is (1) to choose a portfolio of research programs and projects that track, with the best available knowledge, under- or overinvestment, and (2) to be able to change that portfolio as conditions change and more information is gained. But S&T bureaucracies do not have the intelligence systems, administrative systems, and incentives to address R&D as a portfolio problem. For them, the prime command remains aggregate budget maximization. Until now, the distribution of budgets has not concerned them except when they have been forced by political and economic decisionmakers. So there is a question of whether distribution questions are even "thinkable."

Where there is a case of underinvestment, I have argued that, once the level of resources enters a range or band of sufficiency, it will be difficult to discern differences in the quantity and quality of information output. I have also argued that the bands should not be too narrow or precise. Nevertheless, the budget procedures currently used by S&T bureaucracies rest far more on historical shares and constituent pressure than they do on the most primitive notions of the marginal productivity of research dollars in alternative uses. In part, this is why the bureaucracies are always demanding new resources; their ability to do anything new depends on receiving new inputs, since they are unable to reallocate the resources they have. Thus, a strategy suggesting that their objective be one of generating a reasonable portfolio of research activities might provide some counterweight against conventional, fixed-ratio means of allocation.

Technological Innovation

In the last thirty years there have been three major federal investigations of innovation and technology policy. Although much more is now known about the impacts of innovation on economic growth and international trade, decisionmakers are still short of policy tools to produce innovations. No consensus on innovation, technology, or industrial policy has formed, nor is one likely to do so. Everyone agrees that a favorable economic climate might be necessary, if not sufficient, but achieving that climate is a problem in macroeconomic policy, not S&T policy. With respect to the latter, there is a consensus that increasing information flows between universities and industry could at least do no harm and would, with some reasonable degree of probability, increase the rate of innovation. Beyond increased information flows, the grounds for government action covering industrial R&D are predicated on the value propositions of the strategies that have been discussed. Action is grounded, alternatively, on slow growth or loss of international markets, on market failure, or on true representations of the public interest. For adherents of the engineering strategy, government programs are feasible and desirable, because bureaucracies have more information than do private economic actors, who can only look at one market at a time. Supporters of the market strategy prefer very few, if any, government programs, because of the limited competence of bureaucracies and their inherent lack of detailed knowledge about supply and demand conditions in particular markets. Those who support a public interest strategy believe that, before there can be correct government programs, there has to be an improvement in the processes government uses in deciding on programs.

Where there are strongly conflicting values about an issue, and where there are conflicting specifications for a problem, policy prescriptions ought to be weak, not strong. Thus, calls for national industrial policies, revitalization policies, or innovation policies should be regarded skeptically. Given that value conflicts cannot be resolved and ignorance cannot be diminished in the short run, any government programs should be small-scale, experimental, and terminable. These are difficult design criteria to meet, since there will always be political and bureaucratic demands for expanding small or experimental programs to full coverage. For example, some programs supporting "generic" technology might be appropriate and effective, but the number of technologies proposed as generic will be very large, and the generic attribute will be hard to verify. Rather than trying to make such verifications, bureaucratic incentives will suggest using available resources thinly for all the technologies claimed to be generic, even if such a thin, wide distribution were known to be ineffective.

A strategy of keeping one's options open is not likely to appeal to those who believe an innovation crisis now exists or to those who believe that unaided markets, at least in the long run, cure any and all innovation problems. It certainly will not please those who believe they truly know higher social goods, since such a strategy does not constrain decisionmakers to the options believed to deliver such goods. However, if correct action is more likely with good strategic intelligence, then decisionmakers can and should wait until they know the conditions they actually face, provided they are shrewd enough to maintain flexibility.

Waiting for the future to reveal itself is uncommon in S&T policy because of potentially discontinuous, large-scale, irreversible effects, but there are analogies in other areas. The Federal Reserve System does not set the money supply for all time. As information comes in about economic conditions, it chooses the money supply it hopes will make economic performance consistent with the goals of policy. Although innovation policies would take longer to act than monetary policy, and information flows to decisionmakers might not be as good, the ability to take limited, tailored actions, while reserving the decision to continue, modify, or stop is desirable.

Good intelligence will probably reveal that there is no single innovation problem, but many small ones, and their roots are probably different. Market failures occur because of a variety of things. If problems differ from industry to industry, then policies probably should be different. Since policy appropriate for one sector may conceivably damage some other sector, it follows that bureaucracies ought to consider the interactions and externalities that policy will produce. However, tailored policies and their interactions imply that bureaucracies concerned with innovation cannot operate with a limited number of macroscale policy instruments. For example, one of the usual instruments of innovation policy is an add-on to general fiscal policy — tax credits for any incremental R&D. But in some sectors, this could generate a "rush to invent," which would not be socially productive, that is, the innovation would have been forthcoming without the credit. So policy instruments would have to be fine-grained and specific to particular industries and sectors.

Innovation policy then faces a dilemma. General, macroscale interventions are not sensitive to local market conditions and may thus turn out to be inefficient, ineffective, or worse. Tailoring policy to local conditions runs up administrative costs and increases ignorance over time. Bureaucrats in charge of administering policies tailored for local market conditions cannot know any more than the actors operating at that level. They probably will know less, because they cannot receive the daily information on prices and quantities that firms receive. And they cannot react as fast. However, microeconomic policies, by their nature, will be highly political, for they require targeting benefits to particular industries or classes of business. Those who do not receive benefits will claim they are just as worthy as those who do and will make their views known to political and budget authorities. Perceiving threats to their overall budget, the S&T bureaucracies will work hard to make their micropolicies equitable. Funds and programs will be spread to avoid claims of undue concentration and favoritism, no matter that spreading makes the micropolicies ineffective. Lack of effectiveness is harder to see and hear than lack of equity.

If tailored policies do work, there will be interactions between them. These will increase ignorance further, especially when policies are administered by different agencies. Problems of coordination, information flow, and incentives will mount up. Most bureaucracies are indifferent or hostile to what other bureaucracies do. They optimize on their own policies but suboptimize on government-wide policy. They usually feel strongly that the existence of other bureaucracies with overlapping missions gets in the way of reaching their own organizational optimum. This raises the question of central coordination of innovation policy, but, as was indicated in Chapter 3, a case can be made against the feasibility and worth of central coordination.

The way out of such dilemmas may be to refuse to seize them. Innovation may be most closely related to the general economic climate. The macroeconomics for improving the economic climate are at least partially known. At the microeconomic level, any policies and programs can be made small and experimental and have a termination date built in so that it cannot be changed except at great cost. Innovation policy at the microscale should be designed more to elicit information than to provide permanent frameworks. Some decisionmakers and policy analysts believe that the United States can, a priori, select prospectively innovative industries and sectors for special treatment by government. The special treatment makes prospects real. However, the historical inability of the United States to reach closure over innovation policy suggests otherwise; without closure, an agnostic policy posture seems necessary and appropriate.

Science Education
The consequences of poor science education are predicted to be so bad that the need for more effort and resources is taken as self-evident. If the United States does not want to lose critically important international markets and wants to continue making sound public decisions, then more science education for the public is said to be necessary. If the United States wants to have the most productive human capital working in research, more science education for the talented is necessary. The

puzzle then is why science education programs fare so badly in the competition for attention and resources. Why does it take perceptions of crisis, of galloping mediocrity, to generate more resources for what is said to be so transparently evident?

When decisionmakers and analysts encounter failures in realizing the self-evident, they should suspect poor problem specification and suboptimization. In the case of science education, the chain of causal reasoning may be wrong. Most advocates of science education make their public case on utility grounds, although privately they believe exposure to science is worthy in itself. Science education is said to be necessary for economic growth, productivity, and maintenance of comparative advantage. But one can observe that nations do grow and prosper without high levels of science education, by U.S. standards. Technology may reduce aggregate demand for high-level skills and knowledge or restrict it to only certain types of workers. If high technical skills are necessary for production but are costly, they will be economized.

High-technology goods and services on the output side do not necessarily imply that the human capital on the input side needs some deep knowledge of science or technology. One finds developing countries able to produce high-technology goods without great science literacy on the part of their labor force. Instead of education causing growth, growing and trading countries may earn enough so that education in the sciences becomes affordable. Economic growth and development and science literacy may eventually be determined simultaneously, and at some point they may interact strongly and directly. But then decisionmakers need better causal specifications than those offered recently by science educators.

Science education is also said to create literate citizens who can make good decisions, but a technically informed citizenry does not necessarily lead to sound or acceptable public decisions. While scientific and technical information bounds what is reasonable to consider in public policy debate, admissible policy options remain very large in number. Choosing among them is not a job for which one's knowledge of science or engineering principles helps very much. Instead of arguing about the economic or political utility of science education, one might better argue how science education creates the attributes desired from schooling: creativity, problemsolving ability, flexibility, tolerance, and so forth. An educational justification is needed to make science education competitive with other worthy claimants of time, attention, and resources.

Science education programs and resources are not ordinarily traded off against other resource claims. Scientists and science educators hold, on the one hand, that education has to stay close to current research in order to transmit valid information and prepare talented people to do science. On the other hand, they hold that knowledge of science and technology must be part of the general education of informed citizens. If the purpose of science education is the production of human capital, then a reasonable problem specification is: What trade-offs can be made in the ways scientific research is done? Is human capital a bottleneck? Can the technology of doing science be changed so that we can economize on scarce talent? If, however, science and engineering are part of general cognitive and social learning, one might use a specification such as: How much science education should be provided, relative to other educational activities that also contribute to cognition, socialization, and skill creation? One might be tempted to say, a great deal, if one knew that economic growth and ability to solve public problems really depended on extensive science education. That is why the utilitarian arguments about economic growth, international trade, and education have such power and are cited so frequently. But one might just as well argue that these things depend on educating more entrepreneurs and risk-takers. One might argue that the U.S. international economic situation depends on having a population that is knowledgeable in the many languages of U.S. trading partners. Thus, more resources for language instruction might be needed. To make informed public decisions, one needs to understand economics and the policy process; therefore, more resources are needed to make citizens better analysts for public policy. There is no limit to the skills that can be reasonably listed as having utilitarian properties and, therefore, no limit to the educational programs worthy of public resources. The science education community claims priority for science and mathematics instruction, but the warrant for such priority is not clear. What has to be done is to consider science education against other claimants. At the moment, the educational system has more worthy jobs to do than resources with which to do them.

Aid and Trade
The science and engineering community has long believed that the acquisition of science and technology infrastructure by developing countries is at least necessary for development. The belief that science and technology forces correct economic choices and changes values has made technical assistance attractive to the U.S. S&T community. To choose sensibly among the technologies available to them, developing countries need their own talent, talent that understands how technology mainly borrowed from developed countries can be adapted to home conditions. Such talent does not now exist, but American scientists and engineers can produce it by proper instruction of foreign students in U.S. universities and by research and teaching in developing countries.

Development is about the transformation of economic and social institutions, but markets and price systems cannot make correct evaluations of the projects and programs that are necessary. Selecting new technologies via markets depends on relative prices, and these are always full of distortions in developing countries. Choice via political processes is also distorted, because power and influence are not widely distributed. An indigenous S&T infrastructure carries knowledge from scientists and engineers that can be used to determine correct public choices. In the process of applying such knowledge, scientists and engineers spread values and attitudes that will assist in the development process. Their rational, causal approach to events and decisions displaces tradition and superstition.

Technical assistance, in the view of scientists and engineers, has to be separated from traditional large-scale capital assistance. The latter is subject to the ordinary calculus of national benefits and costs involved in foreign relations and diplomacy. To the scientific community, making technical assistance part of that calculus is self-defeating, since the growth of infrastructure must be steady, unconstrained by short-term fluctuations in diplomatic climate. A competent infrastructure can be achieved if technical assistance is left to the U.S. S&T community and if choices are made through some process that resembles the peer review of research proposals. Developing countries and their native scientists and engineers ought to submit technical assistance proposals, and some central technical agency ought to carry out "peer" review and then balance U.S. assistance flows to developing countries. Over the long run, such a process would lead to competent infrastructure in developing countries. Since the focus would be on purely technical factors, the temptation of both the United States and developing nations to pursue political and diplomatic objectives through technical assistance would be minimized. Their respective scientific and technical communities would be talking to each other in their common language without too many unproductive political overtones.

In general, decisionmakers have rejected this strategy. While technical assistance may reveal those sectors that can achieve growth and comparative advantage, developing countries are always short of capital to apply to them. However, capital flows between governments always raise significant political and economic questions; this will occur even when it is believed that long-run benefits will exceed short-run and long-run costs to the country providing the assistance. While the S&T community has always worked to shield technical assistance programs from competition with other aid programs, there is no reason to believe that the cold calculus of national interest should exclude technical assistance. Since technical assistance is one of a number of aid instruments, it should be compared with competing and complementary instruments. That comparison would no doubt reveal, at the margin, that some dollars allocated to technical assistance would be more productive than some dollars allocated to capital assistance.

Civilian technology transfers from the United States have been a matter for international markets to decide. Although it has always watched transfers of military technology carefully, the United States has traditionally held that markets will make correct decisions whenever free trade flourishes and the private sector is left alone. Declining productivity and the perceived crisis in the U.S. innovation rate have meant strong pressure to promote innovation and regulate civilian technology transfer. The underlying economic assumptions are, first, that the United States can only gain comparative advantage by being an innovator and not an imitator, although, historically, the United States has been a fairly competent imitator, and second, that foreign competitors can achieve comparative advantage through either innovation or imitation. Such assumptions about technology transfer have put the United States into a bind between its long-run, historical preference for free trade and the intense short-run pressures from stakeholders, who see jobs and profits going overseas.

At this time, the promotion and regulation of civilian technology transfer remains an unsettled problem. It is part of the larger issue of reindustrialization and revitalization of the economy. If this has to be achieved using technologies that U.S. firms buy and sell overseas, then regulation of civilian technology transfer is an option for consideration. However, trade in civilian technologies may assist in reindustrialization; consequently, the government should stay out of the way. Resolution turns on values — what one believes about the virtues and efficiency of markets in solving problems against the virtues and competence of government action. Given the differences between economic sectors and industries, the previous discussion of innovation policy suggests an agnostic posture.

Scientific and Technical Information (STI)
STI has dual properties. It is used within the science enterprise to create additional, improved STI. The improvements are measured by the internal criteria of science — increased validity, precision, generality, and explanatory power. Some STI is also used to produce goods and services and to set public policy. Past government policy was predicated on continued high costs of accessing STI. Consequently, there was need for government subsidy and extramarket coordination. Today, the technology necessary to deliver large quantities of STI to users cheaply is available. It is a technology that is steadily decreasing the need for

intermediaries. Access is far less of a problem today for technology and economics now permit individuals and organizations to acquire whatever information they believe is relevant to their needs at reasonable cost.

The unsolved STI problem is not one of quantity but of quality. Within the research enterprise, the quality of information is tested by its contributions in defining and extending disciplinary frontiers. There is a constant revaluation of old information, based on newly acquired information. Stocks of information that were considered low-quality yesterday may be quickly regraded upward as new information arrives and vice versa. The efficiency with which this takes place is a public policy concern. The research community ought to make its assessments of quality as rapidly as possible with the resources available, but there is no persuasive evidence that this process is currently too slow.

To increase quality, government can try to reduce international barriers to the flow of information so that networks of knowledge have maximal connectivity and density. It should probably be willing to bet some resources on fields and areas where research output is currently considered to be low-grade. The process of forming new connections means that some scientists (those who are not risk-averse) will always be operating in areas where there are great difficulties and great uncertainty. In those areas, there will be questions on whether even low-quality information connections can be produced. The phrase, "he or she thinks like a physicist, chemist, or economist," is usually considered a high professional accolade. But for long-run effectiveness, government should provide some incentives for physicists, chemists, and economists who do not think within the confines of their professions but who cross professional and disciplinary lines, who are able to link STI from diverse sources. Even though information flow may be graded as low-quality, the attempt to forge new connections between fields is meritorious and will frequently lead to high-quality information later.

The most difficult STI problem lies not within science and engineering proper and not even in the production of goods and services, but in the public policy area. Here the notion of quality of information is much broader than in science and engineering. Decisionmakers have to worry not only about validity, but also timeliness, programmatic relevance, and actionability. Information that is high-quality in some scientific sense may be of only fair quality with respect to decisionmaking. For public policy, decisionmakers and analysts may be in a position where they have to be content with second-best bodies of information. They may never be able to wait long enough to get the first-best information that is needed. And there will be some cases for which additional investments in STI will simply not reduce ignorance. Additional

STI, at any reasonable cost, may be too coarse to give the needed information, and the technologies of inquiry may never be powerful enough to reveal or test alternatives of genuine policy interest.

The real STI problem is upgrading its quality for decisionmaking, on the one hand, and learning to cope with inadequate quality, on the other. Methods for acquiring and structuring STI for public policy purposes have a number of different names — technology assessment, risk assessment, benefit-risk, benefit/cost analysis, policy analysis, systems analysis. While these are not sciences, they are rational, analytic procedures. At a minimum, they increase awareness of the complexities of decision; at best, they assist in eliminating bad alternatives from the choices confronting decisionmakers and the public. They provide orderings for the STI currently in stock and show gaps in that stock.

The other way to cope with uncertainty and ignorance is to design institutions that can act on the basis of new information, that is, learning institutions. Flexible and fast but dissolvable institutions need to be designed. To address this design problem, there is some literature on institutional success and a large body of literature on institutional failure and on bureaucratic pathologies. Through systematic analysis of lessons learned, decisionmakers and the public can gain clues on what has not worked in the past. To the extent that we believe that S&T problems can be distinguished from other public policy problems, it must be because the difficulties they pose do not occur around some status quo, but take us far from current experience and prevent us from returning to what we know.

In this kind of situation, the best that decisionmakers may accomplish is preserving options, since they have some knowledge of the policy predicaments that arise when no options are available. But option-preserving activity is not a very high calling for bureaucracies. The image of successful government administrators — partly created by policy analysis — is of men and women who make tough decisions and stick to them in the face of criticism. The incentives for this kind of behavior, with respect to S&T problems, deserve very close examination. The tough decisions that policy analysts admire so much, unexamined in the light of arriving information and criticism, are more likely to cause trouble than to be successful.

There is, however, an interaction between a priori rational approaches to decisionmaking and learning by doing. The former should be regarded as a way to get the latter. Any of the benefit/cost approaches force the organization of available STI and show which STI is critical to decisionmaking, where decisions would be different if there were more or different STI. This can lead to a cycle of learning by doing in which decisionmakers search out the incremental information that could lead to differences in behavior and outcome. But, given additional information, more benefit/cost analysis would become appropriate. Benefit/cost analysis used iteratively along with learning by doing would help create more informed dialogue over public policy and, perhaps, improved policy as well.

Politics, Strategies, and Budgets

When trying to shift the focus of S&T policy to new or more subtle problem specifications, one needs to account for the politics of bureaucracy and the incentives of science advisers and administrators. Politics and incentives interact in ways that make shifts in problem specifications hard to obtain, no matter their rational appeal. The politics of S&T bureaucracies resembles that of other bureaucracies, but it is focused on far fewer dimensions — mainly the level of budget and its rate of growth. Other bureaucracies can take pride in their efficiency or even their effectiveness in delivering goods and services to eligible clients. Even run-of-the-mill bureaucracies can succeed by claiming greater efficiency, but such success is small solace in S&T bureaucracies. In the main, their output is their input — dollars go in, they are redistributed according to standard operating procedures, and they come out on their way to members of the S&T community. Success means ever-increasing volumes of throughput.

The limited scope and interests of S&T bureaucracies mean that, in a decisionmaker's search for alternative or innovative approaches to problems, there will be subtle shifts in focus and in what decisionmakers call terms of reference. Decisionmakers may begin a search wanting imaginative and innovative approaches to a problem like innovation or education. The canons of public policy analysis imply that decisionmakers need the most systematic and wide-ranging examination of alternatives that can be produced within constraints of time and budget. However, because of the intense focus of the S&T bureaucracies on their own current and prospective budgets, any examination of alternatives will become a vehicle for raising budget and turf questions. Public policy questions are like "garbage cans," containers that bureaucracies use to collect their major concerns, especially their budget concerns (March and Olsen 1979). Thus, work on innovation policy becomes equivalent to work on revealing the latent technological opportunities that could be realized, if only more funds were made available. If energy policy is the problem, then more budget is clearly needed so that scientists and engineers can explore the technical feasibility of unconventional alternatives like windpower or ocean thermal power. If there is excess demand for critical minerals, then more research budget is clearly needed to find technically satisfactory alternatives. As a result of these bureaucratic imperatives, one does not very often see broad-gauged systems analysis of alternative strategies to deal with problems that have S&T content.

Assessments of alternative strategies necessarily involve the bureaucracies. They hold key information. Their staffs are usually involved in doing assessments, since decisionmakers, especially the high-level ones, are usually short of analytical staff and have to use staff from interested bureaus. This means bureau staffs assess alternatives affecting themselves and their own bureaus. Prudent decisionmakers will also involve the bureaucracies, because they will have to execute the decisionmakers' preferred alternatives. Without co-opting cognizant bureaucracies and gaining prior consent, alternatives preferred by decisionmakers will have difficulties in clearance and sign-off. Overly radical strategies pursued by decisionmakers, that is, those that depart too much from the dominant culture and outlook of the bureaucracies, will often not be implemented, no matter the paper arrangements.

The search for alternatives becomes focused on those that are acceptable to the cognizant bureaucracies. Strategies acceptable to S&T bureaucracies have to promise increased budgets. However, any strategy acceptable to the bureaucracy may have only a limited chance for success. In all likelihood, a decisionmaker's search for some new S&T strategy was caused by some programmatic or policy failure inside an S&T bureaucracy. For example, it may have been not funding enough innovative research or the right kinds of science education or not being sensitive enough to industry concerns. However, the ability to depart from failed strategies or partial failures will be limited. So, after a while, a once new and promising strategy will be called a failure, requiring yet another "new" look by science advisers and administrators.

Bureaucratic politics and incentives are reinforced by the relations between the S&T community and the science advisers and administrators. Most of the latter come from the community, and after a short time, they will be going back — they hope, of course, to better jobs than they left. On the outside, their success as decisionmakers will be measured by the increases in budget or in the acceleration of growth rates in the budgets they administered directly or for which they had oversight responsibility. They will definitely not be judged on the efficiency their organizations attained or on the number of S&T programs they terminated, no matter how ineffective these may have been. Nor will they be considered successful if they involved themselves seriously in providing decisionmakers with a well-balanced, systems outlook. From the perspective of the S&T community, federal S&T administrators are its representatives, in government on loan, to assure that no harm is done to its interests. There is nothing unusual in such a situation — certainly businessmen or farmers view administrators and advisers in the departments of Commerce or Agriculture as their representatives — but because research and education contain higher-order social values, the S&T community believes that it is different in kind from dairy farmers or automobile manufacturers and that it deserves kind treatment and attention.

Although science advisers and administrators frequently say that they are not the representatives of the community but serve the president or other officials for whom they work, they cannot avoid speaking on behalf of the interests of the S&T community. They cannot avoid continually making a case for more budget in good times or bad without losing reputation and support from their short-run constituents inside the government and, more importantly for their future, from their long-run constituents in the research universities and other institutions connected with science and technology. Thus, science advisers and administrators will not have strong incentives to want to address public policy questions as a whole. One can be reasonably certain that an R&D tail will wag any policy dog placed in the care of science advisers and administrators.

There are a few things that can be done. At the beginning of a search for alternatives, decisionmakers ought to insist that any analysis they charter has to be comprehensive and systematic. For example, three times and in very diverse administrations, the United States has tried to define an innovation policy. Three times White House operatives farmed the work out to resident science advisers and S&T agencies. Three times they did their work without significant formal interaction with economics and budget officials, although the Kennedy administration was a partial exception. The common intellectual and budgetary fate of these examples should not be seen as random but rather as inevitable, given the personal and organizational stakes and incentives.

Forcing early and continuous awareness of the political and economic content of S&T inquiry would help some. In the short run, terms of reference can be worked out with all the competing and deciding bureaucracies in the same room. Most S&T policy inquiry does not begin with clearly decidable questions in mind; rather, it begins with a "woolly" specification of some general problem about which decisionmakers are curious or about which they have been persuaded to be curious. S&T advisers and administrators are usually the ones who begin such inquiry behind the scenes by writing the triggering memoranda for it. Shifts in questions of interest to the decisionmakers to those of interest to the S&T bureaucracies are the inevitable result. Decisionmakers can force themselves to think harder about what they want or how they would decide differently if they had different information, or they can instruct their analysts and advisers to force them to do so. The natural injection of agency, constituency, and personal self-interest can be controlled to some extent by decent design and reasonable command and control throughout a policy inquiry. Over the long run, there may be some chance to create a needed cadre of S&T analysts who are willing and able to bite the hands that feed them. But even given all this, I still need to ask one last question. Would the careful structuring of alternatives and the systematic comparison of performance make any real difference to the practice of S&T policy, and how can we know that it would? In short, would applying the policy analysis craft really help in making S&T policy?

Does Analysis Make a Difference?

Throughout this book, I have taken some pains to translate into policy language the strategies, statements, and claims that have been consistently important to actors in the S&T domain. I strongly believe it is important to make such translations.

Once translations into policy language have been made, it should be feasible to carry out "normal" policy analyses for the S&T domain. However, a cultural problem remains. Cold-blooded, quantitative policy analysis or systems analysis has never been characteristic. Since everyone's strategies were so soft and vulnerable to criticism, "stable deterrence" grew up; thus, true intellectual competition was neither possible nor desired. Quantitative or rigorous qualitative styles of policy analysis did not prosper, because they were truly difficult to carry off well, but also because they have to be clear, consistent, and revealing to be of much use. Their clarity makes them available to critics and adversaries. The objects of criticism — science, technology, universities, industrial laboratories, bureaucracies whose business is providing for S&T — embodied so many higher-order social values that tough criticism, even when possible, was never welcome. The extreme sensitivity of S&T agencies to downward fluctuations in their budgets reinforces this posture. Advocacy and protection become the bottom line.

There is also a cultural problem concerning policy analysis. Those who forged analytical and quantitative styles of policy analysis and debate never were particularly interested in S&T policy. Policy analysis has its roots primarily in economics and operations research. Its core vision contains single decisionmakers, maximizing expected utility, profits, or social welfare, with analysts at their side, helping them to choose "rationally." S&T policy is ill-formed with respect to this vision, with only partially identified decisionmakers and without specific, well-defined objective functions; it is not easily amenable to methods, approaches, and attitudes developed by economics and operations research.

Before I or anyone can gauge the feasibility and utility of analytic approaches to S&T policy, we all have to understand the almost conceptual latent strategies used by decisionmakers and other actors. These determine the feasibility of introducing modern policy analysis approaches as well as hospitality toward them. Specification of strategies in as complete a form as possible is a necessary step, as is the translation of their language into policy and decision language. Thus, I have spent a long time clearing away intellectual underbrush.

Once this was done, I tried to see how the strategies worked out in actual historical debate and decisions. Debate over S&T policy is, at root, debate over the input and deployment of resources, mainly federal resources. Over time, I can observe a series of resource flows, a series of budgets for the R&D bureaucracies. Triumph or tragedy is registered in those budgets, from the perspective of bureaucracies and decisionmakers. However, without access to their strategies, we on the outside cannot make sense of these budgets. We cannot know how well we are providing for the S&T enterprise, and we cannot know whether the S&T bureaucracies will have some future social triumph or tragedy.

Although the author of this volume was trained as an economist and has practiced systems and policy analysis, the deliberately cold-blooded, hard-hearted, critical analysis and inquiry used here should not be interpreted as any lack of concern for the well-being of the S&T enterprise. Quite the contrary — the main aim is to improve the well-being of S&T policy. To do this job, I believe a now-missing critical tradition is needed, and this tradition can best be learned by trying to use it.

Bibliography

1. Published Works

Adkinson, B. W. (1978) *Two Centuries of Federal Information.* Stroudsburg, Pa.: Dowden, Hutchinson, and Ross.

A. D. Little Corporation. (1975) *Passing the Threshold into the Information Age.* Boston: A. D. Little Corp.

Advisory Committee on Industrial Innovation. (1979) *Final Report.* Washington, D.C.: Department of Commerce.

Advisory Subcommittee on Public Interest. (1979) "Policy Paper." In Advisory Committee on Industrial Innovation, *Final Report.* Washington, D.C.: Department of Commerce.

Allen, T. J. (1977) *Managing the Flow of Technology: Technology Transfer and the Dissemination of Technological Information within the R&D Organization.* Cambridge, Mass.: MIT Press.

Ames, M. E. (1978) *Outcome Uncertain.* Washington, D.C.: Communications Press.

Arditti, R., Brennan, P., and Cavrak, S., eds. (1980) *Science and Liberations.* Boston: South End Press.

Armstrong, J. E. (1980) *Strategies for Conducting Technology Assessments.* Boulder, Colo.: Westview Press.

Arrow, K. J. (1971) *Essays in the Theory of Risk Taking.* Chicago: Markham.

Averch, H. A. (1975) "Notes on Improving Research Utility." *Inquiry* 13:231-34.

Baehn, P. R., and Wittrock, B. (1981) *Policy Analysis and Policy Innovation.* Beverly Hills, Calif.: Sage Publications.

Barfield, C. (1972) "Science Report/White House Views Intense Technology Hunt as Useful Exercise Though Few Projects Emerge." *National Journal* 4(6 May):756-65.

Baumol, W. J., and Oates, W. (1975) *Theory of Environmental Policy.* Englewood Cliffs, N.J.: Prentice-Hall.

Beranek, W., and Ranis, G. (1982) *Science, Technology, and Economic Development.* New York: Praeger Publishers.

Boffey, P. (1975) *The Brain Bank of America.* New York: McGraw-Hill.

Brooks, H. (1964) "The Scientific Adviser." In *Scientists and National Policy-Making,* ed. R. Gilpin and C. Wright. New York: Columbia University Press.

———. (1968a) "The Future Growth of Academic Research: Criteria and Need." In *Science Policy and the University,* ed. H. Orlans. Washington, D.C.: Brookings Institution.

———. (1968b) *The Government of Science.* Cambridge, Mass.: MIT Press.

———. (1978) "The Problem of Research Priorities." *Daedalus* 107: 171–90.

Brooks, H., and Bowers, R. (1970) "The Assessment of Technology." *Scientific American* 222:13–21.

Burger, E. J. (1980) *Science at the White House.* Baltimore: Johns Hopkins University Press.

Bush, V. [1945] (1980) *Science: The Endless Frontier.* Washington, D.C.: Office of Scientific Research and Development (1945); Washington, D.C.: NSF(1980).

Caldwell, L. (1970) *Environment: A Challenge for the 1980's.* New York: National History Press.

Carley, M. (1980) *Rational Techniques in Policy Analysis.* London: Heineman.

Carter, J. (1979a) *President's Message on Industrial Innovation.* Washington, D.C.: White House.

———. (1979b) *Fact Sheet: The President's Industrial Innovation Initiatives.* Washington, D.C.: White House.

———. (1980) "Science, Technology, and Diplomacy: A Report of the President to the Congress." In Department of State, *Science, Technology, and American Diplomacy.* Washington, D.C.: GPO.

———. (1981) "Science, Technology, and Diplomacy: A Report of the President to the Congress." In Department of State, *Science, Technology, and American Diplomacy.* Washington, D.C.: GPO.

Collingridge, D. (1980) *The Social Control of Technology.* New York: St. Martin's Press.

———. (1982) *Critical Decision Making.* New York: St. Martin's Press.

Committee on Public Engineering and Policy. (1972) *Perspectives on Benefit/Risk Decisionmaking.* Washington, D.C.: National Academy of Engineering.

Commoner, B. (1971) *The Closing Circle.* New York: Knopf.

Cooper, C. M., and Clark, J. A. (1982) *Employment, Economics, and Technology.* New York: St. Martin's Press.

CRS [Congressional Reference Service]. (1975) *The National Science Foundation and Pre-College Science Education.* Washington, D.C.: GPO.

———. (1976a) *Science and Technology in the Department of State.* Washington, D.C.: GPO.

———. (1976b) *Science, Technology, and Diplomacy in the Age of Interdependence.* Washington, D.C.: GPO.

———. (1978) *Scientific and Technical Information (STI) Activities: Issues and Opportunities.* Washington, D.C.: GPO.

Cumin, T. E., and Greenberg, S. D. (1969) *The Presidential Advisory System.* New York: Harper & Row.

David, E. (1972) "Statement, House Committee on Science and Astronautics." In *Science, Technology, and the Economy.* Washington, D.C.: GPO.

Denison, E. F. (1962) *The Sources of Economic Growth in the U.S. and the Alternatives before Us.* New York: Committee for Economic Development.

———. (1967) *Why Growth Rates Differ.* Washington, D.C.: Brookings Institution.

———. (1974) *Accounting for United States Economic Growth, 1948–1969.* Washington, D.C.: Brookings Institution.

———. (1979) "Explanations of Declining Productivity Growth, II." *Survey of Current Business* 59(August 1979):1–24.

ECS [Education Commission of the States]. (1983) "Draft Statement, Task Force on Economic Growth." 18 May, Mimeo.

Edwards, G. C., III, and Sharkansky, I. (1978) *The Policy Predicament.* San Francisco: W. H. Freeman.

Ehninger, D., and Brockriede, W. (1978) *Decision by Debate.* New York: Harper & Row.

Elster, J. (1983) *Explaining Technical Change.* New York: Cambridge University Press.

Fellner, W. (1971) "The Progress Generating Sector's Claim to High Priority." In NSF, *Review of the Relationship between Research and Development and Economic Growth and Productivity.* Washington, D.C.: NSF.

Fischer, F. (1980) *Politics, Values, and Public Policy.* Boulder, Colo.: Westview Press.

Fisher, A. C., and Peterson, F. M. (1976) "The Environment in Economics: A Survey." *Journal of Economic Literature.* 14:1–33.

Folk, H. (1972) "The Role of Technology Assessment." In *Technology and Man's Future,* ed. A. H. Teich. New York: St. Martin's Press.

Freeman, C. (1982) *The Economics of Industrial Innovation.* Cambridge, Mass.: MIT Press.

Gelpe, M. R., and Tarlock, A. D. (1974) "Uses of Scientific Information in Environmental Decisionmaking." *Southern California Law Review* 48:371–427.

Gerstenfeld, A. (1979) *Innovation: A Study of Technology Policy.* Washington, D.C.: University Press of America.

Giarini, V., and Lauberge, H. (1978) *The Diminishing Returns of Technology.* New York: Pergamon Press.

Gilpin, R. (1979) "Technology and the National Economy." In House Committee on Science and Technology, *National Science and Technology Policy Issues.* Washington, D.C.: GPO.

Golden, W. T. (1980) *Science Advice to the President.* New York: Pergamon Press.

Goldhamer, H. (1977) *The Adviser.* New York: Elsevier.

Goodwin, C. D. (1981) *Energy Policy in Perspective, Today's Problems, Yesterday's Solutions.* Washington, D.C.: Brookings Institution.

Graham, E. D. (1978) "Technological Innovation and the Dynamics of U.S. Trade." In *Technological Innovation for a Dynamic Economy,* ed. C. Hill and J. Utterback. New York: Pergamon Press.

Graham, E. F. (1979) "Technological Innovation, the Technology Gap, and U.S. Welfare." *Public Policy* 27:185–201.

Greenberg, D. S. (1967) *The Politics of Pure Science.* New York: New American Library.

Greenberger, M. (1972) *Making Technological Information More Useful: The Management of a Vital National Resource.* Washington, D.C.: NSF.

Griliches, Z. (1958) "Research Costs and Social Returns: Hybrid Corn and Related Innovations." *Journal of Political Economy* 66:419–31.

_____. (1981) "Issues in Assessing the Contribution of Research and Development to Productivity Growth." *Bell Journal of Economics* 12:92–115.

Habermas, J. (1973) *Legitimation Crisis.* Boston: Beacon Press.

Hambrick, R. S., Jr. (1974) "A Guide for the Analysis of Policy Arguments." *Policy Science* 5:469–78.

Heertje, A. (1973) *Economics and Technical Change.* New York: John Wiley & Sons.

Henderson, H. (1978) *Creating Alternative Futures.* New York: Perigree Books.

Hilman, D. (1981) "Decisionmaking with Modern Information and Communications Technology: Opportunities and Constraints." In NSF, *Five Year Outlook,* 2:421–28. Washington, D.C.: GPO.

Hirschleifer, J., and Riley, J. G. (1979) "The Analytics of Uncertainty and Information — An Expository Survey." *Journal of Economic Literature* 17:1375–1421.

House, P. W. (1982) *The Art of Public Policy Analysis.* Beverly Hills, Calif.: Sage Publications.

House Committee on Science and Astronautics. (1964) *Government and Science.* 88th Cong., 1st sess., 15 Oct.–20 Nov., 1963. Washington, D.C.: GPO.

————. (1966) *The National Science Foundation: Its Present and Future.* 89th Cong., 2nd sess. Washington, D.C.: GPO.

House Subcommittee on Appropriations, HUD-Space. (1972) *Science Appropriations for 1972.* Washington, D.C.: GPO.

Jequier, N. (1976) *Appropriate Technology: Problems and Promises.* Paris: OECD.

Johnson, B. A., and Chang, D. (1977) *U.S. Technology Policy.* Washington, D.C.: Department of Commerce.

Johnston, R., and Gumett, P. (1979) *Directing Technology.* New York: St. Martin's Press.

Jones, T. E. (1980) *Options for the Future.* New York: Praeger Publishers.

Kamien, M. I., and Schwartz, N. L. (1982) *Market Structure and Innovation.* New York: Cambridge University Press.

Katz, J. E. (1978) *Presidential Politics and Science Policy.* New York: Praeger Publishers.

Kennedy, J. F. (1963) *Public Papers of the President.* Washington, D.C.: GPO.

Keyworth, G. (1981) "Statement," House Committee on Science and Technology. 10 Dec., Mimeo.

Killian, J. R., Jr. (1964) "Science and Foreign Policy." In *The Dimensions of Diplomacy,* ed. E. A. J. Johnson. Baltimore: Johns Hopkins University Press.

————. (1977) *Sputnik, Scientists, and Eisenhower.* Cambridge, Mass.: MIT Press.

Kissinger, H. (1974) "Detente with the Soviet Union: The Reality of Competition and the Imperatives of Cooperation." In *Department of State Bulletin* 71:510. Washington, D.C.: State Department.

————. (1979) *White House Years.* Boston: Little, Brown.

Kistiakowsky, G. (1976) *A Scientist in the White House.* Cambridge, Mass.: Harvard University Press.

Knight, K. E., Kozmetsky, G., and Boca, H. R. (1976) *Industry View of the Role of the Federal Government in Industrial Innovation.* Austin, Tex.: Graduate School of Business, University of Texas.

Kranzberg, M. (1980) "Communication of Scientific and Technical Information: Implications for Federal Politics and Research." In NSF, *Five Year Outlook,* 2:509–20. Washington, D.C.: GPO.

Kuhn, W. (1971) *Post-Industrial Prophets.* New York: Weybright and Talley.

Lomask, M. (1976) *A Minor Miracle: An Informal History of the National Science Foundation.* Washington, D.C.: NSF.

Lunstedt, S. G., and Colglazier, W. W. (1982) *Managing Innovation.* New York: Pergamon Press.

Majone, G., and Quade, E. S. (1980) *Pitfalls of Analysis.* New York: John Wiley & Sons.

Mansfield, E. (1972) "Contributions of R&D to Economic Growth in the United States." *Science* 175:487–94.

Mansfield, E., Rapaport, J., Romeo, A., Villani, E., Wagner, S., and Husic, F. (1977) *The Production and Application of New Industrial Technology.* New York: W. W. Norton.

March, J. G., and Olsen, J. P. (1979) *Ambiguity and Choice in Organizations.* 2nd ed. Oslo: Universitetsforlaget.

March, J., and Shapera, Z. (1982) "Behavioral Decision Theory and Organizational Decision Theory." In *Decisionmaking: An Interdisciplinary Inquiry,* ed. G. R. Ungson and D. N. Braunstein, 92–115. Boston: Kent.

Marris, R., and Mueller, D. (1980) "The Corporation, Competition, and the Invisible Hand." *Journal of Economic Literature* 18:32–63.

McCarthy, T. (1978) *The Critical Theory of Jürgen Habermas.* Cambridge, Mass.: MIT Press.

Meehan, E. J. (1968) *Explanation in Social Science.* Homewood, Ill.: Dorsey Press.

Meltsner, A., and Bellavita, C. (1983) *The Policy Organization.* Beverly Hills, Calif.: Sage Publications.

Mensch, G. O. (1979) *Stalemate in Technology.* Cambridge, Mass.: Ballinger.

Mishan, E. J. (1982) *Cost-Benefit Analysis,* 3rd ed. Boston: Allen & Unwin.

Morgan, D. (1983) "High Tech: Leaving Home." *Washington Post.* 1–6 May.

Morrison, E. (1974) *From Know-How to Nowhere.* New York: Basic Books.

NAE [National Academy of Engineering]. (1972) *Public Engineering Policy.* Washington, D.C.: NAE.

NAS [National Academy of Science]. (1969a) *Scientific and Technical Communication (SATCOM).* Washington, D.C.: NAS.

———. (1969b) *Technology: Processes of Assessment and Choice.* Washington, D.C.: NAS.

———. (1974) *Science and Technology in Presidential Policymaking.* Washington, D.C.: NAS.

National Commission on Excellence in Education. (1983) *A Nation at Risk: The Imperative for Educational Reform.* Washington, D.C.: U.S. Department of Education.

National Science Board Commission on Precollege Education in Mathematics, Science, and Technology. (1983) *Educating Americans for the 21st Century.* Washington, D.C.: NSF.

NCLIS [National Commission on Libraries and Information Science]. (1975) *Toward a National Program for Library and Information Services: Goals for Action.* Washington, D.C.: GPO.

Nelkin, D. (1971) *The Politics of Housing Innovation.* Ithaca, N.Y.: Cornell University Press.

———. (1977) *Science Textbook Controversies and the Politics of Equal Time.* Cambridge, Mass.: MIT Press.

———. (1980) "Science and Technology Policy and the Democratic Process." In *Five Year Outlook, II.* Washington, D.C.: NSF.

Nelson, R. R. (1977) *The Moon and the Ghetto.* New York: W. W. Norton.

———. (1981) "Research in Productivity Growth and Productivity Differences." *Journal of Economic Literature* 19:1029-64.

———. (1982) "Public Policy and Technical Progress: A Cross Industry Analysis." In *Government and Technical Progress,* ed. R. R. Nelson, 1-9. New York: Pergamon Press.

Nixon, R. M. (1969) *Public Papers of the President,* Washington, D.C.: GPO.

———. (1972) "Science and Technology Message to the Congress." *Public Papers of the President,* 16 March. Washington, D.C.: GPO.

NRC [National Research Council]. (1979) *Impact of Regulation on Industrial Innovation.* Washington, D.C.: NRC/NAS.

NSB [National Science Board]. (1983) *Science Indicators, 1982.* Washington, D.C.: NSF.

NSF (1971) *Review of the Relationship between Research and Development and Economic Growth and Productivity.* Washington, D.C.: NSF.

———. (1974) *Annual Report, FY 1973.* Washington, D.C.: GPO.

———. (1977a) *Colloquium on Research and Development and Economic Growth and Productivity.* Washington, D.C.: NSF.

———. (1977b) *Models and Programs in Science Education,* Program Report. Washington, D.C.: NSF.

———. (1980) *Five Year Outlook.* Washington, D.C.: GPO.

———. (1981) *Five Year Outlook.* Washington, D.C.: GPO.

NSF and DOE [Department of Education]. (1980) *Science and Engineering Education for the 1980's and Beyond.* Washington, D.C.: GPO.

NSF Task Force on Information Science. (1977c) *Report on Science Information Activities.* Washington, D.C.: NSF.

OMB. (1978) *Special Analysis P: Research and Development.* Washington, D.C.: OMB.

OSTP [Office of Science and Technology Policy]. (1982) *Annual Science and Technology Report to the Congress: 1981.* Washington, D.C.: GPO.

_____. (1983) *Annual Science and Technology Report to the Congress: 1982.* Washington, D.C.: GPO.

OTA [Office of Technology Assessment]. (1980) *Government Involvement in the Innovation Process.* Washington, D.C.: GPO.

Pierce, W. S. (1981) *Bureaucratic Failure and Public Expenditure.* New York: Academic Press.

Polanyi, M. (1968) "The Republic of Science." *Minerva* 1:54–73.

Porter, A., and Rossini, F. A. (1977) "Evaluation Designs for Technology Assessment and Forecasts." *Technological Forecasting and Social Change* 10:369–80.

Porter, A., Rossini, F. A., Carpenter, S. R., and Roper, A. T. (1980) *A Guidebook for Technology Assessment and Impact Analysis.* New York: North Holland.

Press, F. (1979) "Statement, House Committee on Science and Technology." In *National Science and Technology Policy Issues, 1979.* Washington, D.C.: GPO.

_____. (1980) "Foreword: Advising Presidents on Science and Technology." In *Science Advice to the President,* ed. W. T. Golden, 7–8. New York: Pergamon Press.

PSAC [President's Science Advisory Committee]. (1958) *Improving the Availability of Scientific and Technical Information in the United States.* Washington, D.C.: White House.

_____. (1959) *Education for the Age of Science.* Washington, D.C.: White House.

_____. (1960) *Scientific Progress, the Universities, and the Federal Government.* Washington, D.C.: GPO.

_____. (1962) *Meeting Manpower Needs in Science and Technology.* Washington, D.C.: GPO.

_____. (1963) *Science, Government, and Information.* Washington, D.C.: White House.

PSAC, Environmental Pollution Panel. (1965) *Restoring the Quality of Our Environment.* Washington, D.C.: White House.

PSRB [President's Scientific Research Board]. (1947) *Science and Public Policy,* 5 volumes. Washington, D.C.: GPO.

Public Interest Subcommittee on Economic and Trade Policy. (1979) "Comment on Industry Report on Economic and Trade Policy." In Advisory Committee on Industrial Innovation, *Final Report,* 27–36. Washington, D.C.: Department of Commerce.

Public Interest Subcommittee on Environmental, Health, and Safety Regulations. (1979) "Comment." In Advisory Committee on Industrial Innovation, *Final Report,* 85–92. Washington, D.C.: Department of Commerce.

Rabinowitch, E., and Rabinowitch, V. (1975) *Views of Science and Technology and Development.* New York: Pergamon Press.

Ranis, G. (1980) "Appropriate Technology and the Development Process." In *Appropriate Technology and Social Values — A Critical Approach,* ed. F. A. Long and A. Oleson. Cambridge, Mass.: Ballinger.

Raz, J. (1975) *Practical Reason and Norms.* London: Hutchinson.

Reagan, R. (1982) "Letter of Transmittal." In Department of State, *Science, Technology, and American Diplomacy, 1982.* Washington, D.C.: GPO.

Rescher, N. (1978) *Scientific Progress.* Oxford: Blackwell.

Rieke, R., and Sellars, M. (1975) *Argumentation and the Decision-making Process.* New York: John Wiley & Sons.

Rosenberg, N. (1972) *Technology and American Economic Growth.* New York: Harper & Row.

———. (1976a) *Perspectives on Technology.* Cambridge, Mass.: Cambridge University Press.

———. (1976b) "Thinking about Technology Policy for the Coming Decade." In Joint Economic Committee, *U.S. Economic Growth for 1976 to 1986: Prospects and Pattern.* Washington, D.C.: GPO.

———. (1982) *Inside the Black Box.* New York: Cambridge University Press.

Rothwell, R., and Zegfeld, W. (1981) *Industrial Innovation and Public Policy: Preparing for the 1980's.* Westport, Conn.: Greenwood Press.

Rowe, W. (1977) *An Anatomy of Risk.* New York: John Wiley & Sons.

Rybcznski, W. (1980) *Paper Heroes: A Review of Appropriate Technology.* Garden City, N.Y.: Anchor Press.

Sagafi-neyad, T., Monon, R. W., and Perlmutter, H. V. (1981) *Controlling International Technology Transfer.* New York: Pergamon Press.

Sahal, D., ed. (1980) *Research, Development, and Technological Innovation.* Lexington, Mass.: Lexington Books.

Sato, R., and Suzawa, G. S. (1983) *Research and Productivity.* Boston: Auburn House.

Schelling, T. C. (1983) *Incentives for Environmental Protection.* Cambridge, Mass.: MIT Press.

Schon, D. (1981) "The National Climate for Technological Innovation. In *Science, Technology, and National Policy,* ed. T. J. Kuehn and A. L. Porter. Ithaca, N.Y.: Cornell University Press.

Science Curriculum Implementation Review Group. (1975) *National Science Foundation Curriculum Development.* Washington, D.C.: GPO.

Shils, E., ed. (1968) *Criteria for Scientific Development: Public Policy and National Goals.* Cambridge, Mass.: MIT Press.

Sieberg, H. (1981) *Economics of the Environment.* Lexington, Mass.: Lexington Books.

Solow, R. (1957) "Technical Change and the Aggregate Production Function." *Review of Economics and Statistics* 39:312–20.

Sorenson, T. (1965) *Kennedy.* New York: Harper & Row.

Spulver, N., and Horowitz, I. (1976) *Quantitative Economic Policy and Planning.* New York: W. W. Norton.

Staats, E., and Carey, W. (1973) "Fiscal and Management Dilemmas in Science Administration." In *Public Science Policy and Administration,* ed. A. H. Rosenthal. Albuquerque: University of New Mexico Press.

Stanley, M. (1978) *The Technological Conscience.* New York: Free Press.

Stokey, E., and Zeckhauser, R. (1978) *A Primer for Policy Analysis.* New York: W. W. Norton.

Stoneman, P. (1983) *The Economic Analysis of Technical Change.* New York: Oxford University Press.

Task Force on Information Science. (1977) *Report on Science Information Activities.* Washington, D.C.: NSF.

Taylor, P. W. (1961) *Normative Discourse.* Englewood Cliffs, N.J.: Prentice-Hall.

Teich, A. H., ed. (1972) *Technology and Man's Future.* New York: St. Martin's Press.

Tisdell, C. A. (1981) *Science and Technology Policy: Priorities of Government.* New York: Chapman and Hall.

Tocqueville, Alexis de. [1835] (1945) *Democracy in America.* New York: Vintage Books.

Twentieth Century Fund. (1983) *Making the Grade: Report of the Twentieth Century Task Force on Federal Elementary and Secondary Education Policy.* New York: Twentieth Century Fund.

Ungson, G. R., and Braunstein, D. N., eds. (1982) *Decisionmaking.* Boston: Kent.

Vickers, G. (1965) *The Art of Judgment.* New York: Basic Books.

Wachter, M. L., and Wachter, S. M. (1981) *Toward a New Industrial Policy.* Philadelphia: University of Pennsylvania Press.

Wall Street Journal. (1983) "A is for Atom: Nuclear War Turns into Hot Topic in Many Classrooms." 24 May, pp. 1, 10.

Weinberg, A. M. (1968–69) "Scientific Choice and the Scientific Muckrakers." *Minerva* 7:52–63.

Wiesner, J. B. (1964) "Statement." *Hearings before the Select Committee on Government Research of the House of Representatives.* 88th Cong., 2nd sess., 257–58. Washington, D.C.: GPO.

———. (1980) "Science and Technology: Government and Politics." In *Science Advice to the President,* ed. W. T. Golden. 33–40. New York: Pergamon Press.

Wildavsky, A. (1979) *Speaking Truth to Power.* Boston: Little, Brown.

Williamson, O. E. (1975) *Markets and Hierarchies: Analysis and Antitrust Implications.* New York: Free Press.
Winner, L. (1977) *Autonomous Technology.* Cambridge, Mass.: MIT Press.
Wolanin, T. R. (1975) *Presidential Advisory Commissions: Truman to Nixon.* Madison, Wis.: University of Wisconsin Press.
Wolf, C., Jr. (1979) "A Theory of Non-Market Failures." *Public Interest* 55:114–33.

2. Documents
Dwight D. Eisenhower Library

Cabinet Secretariat. (1958) Improving the Publication and Dissemination of Scientific Information in the United States, Draft. 6 Oct. Ann Whitman File, Cabinet series, Box 12.
CFEP [Council on Foreign Economic Policy]. (1954) Recent History of Economic Assistance. Dodge series, Box 2.
_____. (1957) Documented Statements of U.S. Foreign Economic Assistance. Policy papers series, Box 3.
Dodge, J. (1953) Memorandum on Research and Development. 9 June. Official Files, White House Central Files, Box 743.
_____. (Undated) Problems of Economic Progress in Underdeveloped Areas. Dodge papers, Box 1.
Eisenhower, D. D. (1955) Foreign Economic Policy Message to the Congress. 10 Jan. Council on Foreign Economic Policy, Box 3.
Flemming, A. (1954) The Development of Scientists and Engineers. 23 Dec. Washington, D.C.: Office of Defense Mobilization. Ann Whitman File, Cabinet series, Box 5.
Hughes, R. (1956) Memorandum: Hughes to DDE. 30 March. Official Files, White House Central Files, Box 743.
Killian, J. R., Jr. (1958) "Maintaining the Technological Strength of the United States." Address, Women's National Press Club. 7 Jan. Office of Special Assistant for Science and Technology, Box 14.
Kistiakowsky, G. (1960) Notes on Meeting with the President. 9 May. Office of the Special Assistant for Science and Technology, Box 12.
_____. (1976) Oral History Transcript. 17 Nov.
Minnich, A. (1956) Conference with the President on Coordination of Basic Research. 10 March. Official Files, White House Central Files, Box 743.
PSAC [President's Science Advisory Committee]. (1958) Draft Report of Research Panel. 17 June. Office of Special Assistant for Science and Technology, Box 5.
_____. (1959) Digest of Report of Panel on Science and Engineering Education. Ann Whitman File, Cabinet series, Box 13.

_____. (1960a) Presentation to the Cabinet. 7 Oct. Office of the Special Assistant for Science and Technology, Box 5.

_____. (1960b) Notes on Meeting with the President. 12 July. PSAC File, Box 3.

Waterman, A. (1956) Informal Memorandum for Conference with the President. 23 April. Official Files, White House Central Files, Box 743.

Weinberg, A. (1960) Memorandum to G. Kistiakowsky, 1 Nov. Office of the Special Assistant for Science and Technology, Box 5.

Gerald R. Ford Library

Cannon, J. (1975) Memorandum to D. Rumsfeld. 3 March. Schleede papers, Box 38.

Ford, G. (1975) Remarks, Meeting of Cabinet Officers and Heads of Regulatory Agencies. 10 July. Cannon papers, Box 29.

_____. (1976) Science and Technology Policy Message to the Congress. 23 March. Schleede papers, Box 40.

Loweth, H. (1976) Draft Letter for Congressman Thornton to P. MacAvoy. 21 June. Papers of the Council of Economic Advisers, Box 104.

OMB (1976) Working Memorandum. 21 June. Papers of the Council of Economic Advisers, Box 104.

Simmons, H. (1975) Memorandum to J. Cannon: Presidential Science Advice. 18 March, Schleede papers, Box 32.

Stever, G. (1974) Memorandum to RMN. 11 Dec. Schleede papers, Box 10.

Lyndon Baines Johnson Library

COSATI [Committee on Scientific and Technical Information]. (1966) Task Force Report on National Systems for Scientific Literature. Task Force reports, Box 17.

Gordon, K. (1969) Oral History Transcript.

Hodges, L. B., Heller, W., and Wiesner, J. B. (1962) *Technology and Economic Prosperity: Report to the President*. Gordon papers, Box 26.

Hornig, D. (1964) Memorandum to LBJ. 19 Dec. In OST (1968) Administrative History, II, Documentary Supplement H.

_____. (1965) Memorandum to LBJ. 29 Sept. In OST (1968) Administrative History II, Documentary Supplement H.

_____. (1967a) Memorandum to LBJ. 7 June. In OST (1968) Administrative History, II, Documentary Supplement H.

_____. (1967b) Memorandum to D. Cater. 20 June. White House Central Files, OST, Box 122.

_____. (1967c) Memorandum to J. Califano, 13 Sept. In OST (1968) Administrative History, II, Documentary Supplement K.

_____. (1967d) Memorandum to LBJ. 19 Sept. In OST (1968) Administrative History, II, Documentary Supplement H.

_____. (1968) Letter to R. Weaver. 17 Sept. In OST (1968) Administrative History, II, Documentary Supplement K.

Johnson, L. B. (1965) Memorandum to Department Heads. 13 Sept. In OST (1968) Administrative History, II, Documentary Supplement H.

OST [Office of Science and Technology]. (1964) "Argument to Support a Minimal Annual Increase of 15% in Federal Support of Academic Research." 28 Nov. In OST (1968) Administrative History, II, Supplement H.

_____. (1968) Administrative History of OST in the Administration of Lyndon Baines Johnson. I, II.

PSAC [President's Science Advisory Committee]. (1968) International Technical Cooperation and Assistance Panel, 28 Feb. In OST (1968) Administrative History, II, Reference Documents N, Science and Foreign Affairs.

Pierce, J. R. (1965) Letter to D. Hornig. 14 June. In OST (1968) Administrative History, II, Supplement K.

President's Task Force on Foreign Economic Policy. (1964) Report. Outside Task Forces, Box 1.

Schultze, C. (1965a) Memorandum to LBJ. 22 Nov. BOB File, White House Central Files, Box 51.

_____. (1965b) Memorandum to LBJ. 17 Dec. BOB File, White House Central Files, Box 51.

_____. (1965c) Memorandum to LBJ. 23 Dec. BOB File, White House Central Files, Box 51.

_____. (1965d) Memorandum to LBJ. 7 Jan. BOB File, White House Central Files, Box 51.

Zwick, C. (1966) Memorandum to J. Califano: Report of the Task Force on Economic Growth. 30 Nov. Task Force Reports, Box 16.

John F. Kennedy Library

Bell, D. (1961) Memorandum to JFK. 8 March. President's Office Files, Box 71.

_____. (1964) Oral History Interview Transcript.

Cabinet Committee on Economic Growth. (1962) Programs to Promote Economic Growth in the 1963 Administration Programs, 12/12/62–12/31/62. President's Office Files, Box 75A.

CEA [Council of Economic Advisers]. (1962) "Economic Growth and Government Policy." 1 Dec. Gordon papers, Box 26.

_____. (1964) Oral History Interview Transcript.

Gordon, K. (1962) Letter to L. Hodges. 23 Aug. Gordon papers, Box 26.

Heller, W. (1961) Memorandum to JFK. 14 July. President's Office Files, Box 73.

Kennedy, J. F. (1962) Letter to J. Bernard. 9 March. White House Central Files, Box 896.

PSAC [President's Science Advisory Committee]. (1961) Draft Briefing Paper for President Kennedy. 15 Nov. President's Office Files, Box 86.

Wiesner, J. B. (1962) Memorandum to JFK. November. Box 86A.

Wiesner, J. B. (1963) Letter to Congressman G. Miller. 27 March. White House Central Files, Box 896.

Wiesner, J. B., Kistiakowsky, G., and Brooks, H. (1960) Draft Briefing Papers for President Kennedy. 15 Nov. PSAC, Box 86.

National Archives

(Box numbers in Record Group 359, the records of the Office of Science and Technology, are subject to revision and consolidation. The box numbers given here reflect those current in 1981–82.)

David, E. (1970a) Memorandum to G. Schultz. 23 Dec. Record Group 359, Box 996.

_____. (1970b) Letter to Max Frankel. 4 Dec. Record Group 359, Box 996.

_____ (1971a) Letter to W. McElroy. 9 March. Record Group 359, Box 1072.

_____. (1971b) Letter to J. Ferrano. 29 March. Record Group 359, Box 1060.

_____. (1971c) Letter to J. R. Fahey. 14 June. Record Group 359, Box 1072.

_____. (1971d) Letter to H. Vagtborg. 21 June. Record Group 359, Box 1051.

DuBridge, L. (1970) Memorandum to RMN. 18 Aug. Record Group 359, Box 996.

Handler, P. (1971) Letter to J. Baldeschweiler. 5 Jan. Record Group 359, Box 1056.

Humphrey, L. (1971) Letter to RMN. 9 Sept. Record Group 359, Box 1072.

McElroy, W. (1971) Letter to E. David. 2 March. Record Group 359, Box 1072.

Neuriter, N. (1971) Memorandum to E. David. 15 Dec. Record Group 359, Box 1051.

PSAC [President's Science Advisory Committee]. (1961) Research and

Development in the New Development Assistance Programs. 12 May. Record Group 359, Box 95.

Weinberger, C. (1970) Memorandum to L. DuBridge. 19 Aug. Record Group 359, Box 996.

———. (1971) Memorandum to E. David. 2 Aug. Record Group 359, Box 1076.

Index

exclusion principle, 35; and growth accounting, 38–39; and human capital, 61; planning and budgeting systems for, 25; as portfolio problem, 179; quality of inputs for, 40; and rush to invent, 37; statistical estimation of impacts on, 39–40; and supply undepletability, 35

SATCOM report: and research consolidations, 111; and STI recommendations, 104–5

Science education: alternative problem specifications for, 184; budgets for, 73; decisionmakers' strategy for, 87; and democracy, 72; and economic growth, 183; externalities and federal support for, 77; maintaining existing research universities, 82; and manpower markets, 73, 83; needs assessments for, 87; precollege, 86; and quality of manpower, 83; and reform movements, 87, 92, 96, 97; and Soviet Union, 94; and strategy of scientific community, 74–76. *See also* Scientific manpower

Science literacy: information for the public, 90; and market failure, 90–91; and personal choice, 91; and political participation, 90; and public decisions, 91–92; role in policy debates, 95; and technological competitiveness, 94; and technological decisions, 91–92

Scientific manpower: forecasting, 73, 82, 85; market adjustments for, 83; quality of, 79; and unemployment, 83; and universities, 76; and young scientists, 75, 82

Soviet Union: basic research capabilities of, 14–15: and science education, 94; scientific exchange agreements with, 128–30

S&T enterprise: and applications of policy analysis, 175; decisions at national level, xii, 3; functions of, 1; structure of, 3

Stever, G., 27

STI: archival and historical functions, 109; and basic research, 107; and benefit/cost analysis, 121–22,

188; and Crawford report, 103, 106; external market defined, 110; flows between industry and S&T community, 98; and gatekeepers, 111; and government support, 123; and Greenberger report, 106–7; incentives to cross disciplinary boundaries, 187; industrial policy, 111; industrial uses, 112; and information science, 107; and innovation, 112; internal market defined, 99–100; international flows of, 105; and invisible colleges, 108; and market failure, 109; policy for internal market, 108; quality of information, 109, 123, 187; research consolidations of, 106, 111; role of NSF, 103; role of universities, 111; and SATCOM report, 112; scientists' information dissemination strategy, 101–2; and social regulation, 114–15; and social science, 114; and STS program, 112; use by nonscientists, 106; use in policymaking, 99, 106, 110; and Weinberg report, 103, 106

Strategies: completeness of, 54; continuity and timing of, 161–62; corrigibility of, 162; defined, xi, 1; definition of core, 59; and discontinuities in social experience, 155; and entitlements, 163; expectations and momentum of, 162; flexibility of, 162; higher-order values, 159, 165; language problems of, 147–54; learning by doing, 155–56; leverage of, 161; micro- vs. macropolicies for, 157, 159; preserving options for, 155, 181; specification problems of, 156; tailored programs for, 181; testing proposed actions for, 158; tests for validity of, 2, 165–66; timing of results of, 160–62; total evaluations of, 165; use of multiple indicators for, 164

STS (State Technical Services Program): design, 59; and STI, 112. *See also* CITP

Technical assistance: conflict with capital assistance, 140, 185; organization of, 140–43; role of private